A THEOLOGY of WORLD RELIGIONS

A THEOLOGY of WORLD RELIGIONS

Interpreting God,
Self, and World
in Semitic, Indian,
and Chinese Thought

PAUL VARO MARTINSON

AUGSBURG Publishing House • Minneapolis

A THEOLOGY OF WORLD RELIGIONS
Interpreting God, Self, and World in Semitic, Indian, and Chinese Thought

Library of Congress Cataloging-in-Publication Data

Martinson, Paul Varo, 1934–
  A THEOLOGY OF WORLD RELIGIONS.

  Bibliography: p.
  Includes index.
  1. Religions.   2. Christianity and other religions.
I. Title.
BL80.2.M295   1987   291.2   86-28772
ISBN 0-8066-2253-9

Manufactured in the U.S.A.   APH 10-6295

1   2   3   4   5   6   7   8   9   0   1   2   3   4   5   6   7   8   9

To my father,
with whom I would have enjoyed
conversing on these things

CONTENTS

PREFACE

Several intentions animate this study. One is to do some basic descriptive work on several religious traditions that may be helpful to the reader interested in religious traditions other than the Christian. However, this is not a typical introduction to other faiths; it attempts instead to fill out selected aspects of several faith traditions, aspects that have a particular theological relevance. In this respect it goes well beyond what one can expect from introductory texts.

There is also a theological agenda which fundamentally shapes this study. Some years ago Joachim Wach, historian of religions, called attention to the need to bring the historical study of the world's religions and theology into closer conversation. Joseph Kitagawa, for one, has taken special notice of this. Tillich made the same appeal from the side of theology. Much has happened since that double appeal. One can hardly do theology now without in some way taking faiths other than one's own into account. We are contextually obliged; we are also theologically obliged. In this study we seek to be responsive to this twofold obligation.

Various tendencies have developed over the years to meet this challenge. One tendency is to treat preliminary methodological matters dealing with the way people of Christian faith relate to people and traditions of other faiths. Another tendency is to explore the theological possibilities of engaging the Christian faith with another specific faith. Yet another tendency is to incorporate insights from the study of other religious traditions into the substantive theological discussion in which

11

one is involved. The attempt here is related to, but different from, these. I wish to begin the task of having several traditions speak across lines to one another simultaneously, as a kind of interwoven theological discourse. Theologically responsive categories that will advance the discussion will be sought.

Our third intention is to speak theologically from a Christian perspective. There is no attempt here to rise above the fray or to stand on neutral ground. To do so would be self-deceptive. We are in the midst of the play itself. The reader will notice that the study begins by picking up three distinct traditions in a descriptive way and, as the discussion progresses and the interweave proceeds, the Christian perspective comes more and more to the fore. This is intentional. Surely a Buddhist or a Confucian, were they to proceed in such a way, might discern some rather different categories and interrelations and move in very different directions. Such studies would be of immense help to us all.

Many limitations have had to be applied to this study. Two of these are particularly worth mentioning. First, the focus has been upon the norming streams within the traditions dealt with. The whole question of the folk religious tradition, its relation to the norming traditions, and the issues and questions this raises both for the study of religions and for theology has been set aside. The proportions of this study simply did not make this inclusion possible.

Second, it was determined from the beginning that the discussion would limit itself to those traditions that have had a serious impact upon the Chinese world. For one thing, that helped to give a sharper focus to the conversation; for another, it helped to provide a meaning for the limit. The limit is meaningful, because the Western, the Indian, and the Chinese religious traditions have all had extended interaction within the Chinese context. One cannot say the same for the Indian context. Even in the West neither the Indian nor the Chinese traditions have had the same degree of impact that the Indian and Western have had upon China. This limit, however, does not make the present book a study of Chinese religions, or of religion in China. The meeting of these traditions in China has become the point of reference to explore and exegete the theological issues that they implicitly, as well as explicitly, raise for each other.

The chapters have been ordered in what seemed to be a natural flow. Our opening concerns are of anthropological matters. Then comes the question of God or transcendence, and then God's interaction with the world. The ordering, we might say, is self, God, and world. We conclude with a more programmatic statement on how the Christian defines his or her own identity and its interaction with other faith claims.

Thanks are due to many persons and institutions. An enormous debt of gratitude is due to my colleagues at Luther Northwestern Theological Seminary. From them I have learned much in every way. Their theological insights and perspectives, the debates within the faculty, and the occasional sharing of papers have all had their influence in shaping my own thoughts, often unbeknownst to them. Special thanks go to the Systematics Department, whose members have permitted a non-systematician to sit in among them. The frequently intense conversations on many matters have left their mark on me. Since there is often as much disagreement as agreement among them, this shaping has come from several directions concurrently. I must also thank students for having patiently borne with me as my thoughts have been, and still are, in the process of formulation. Their reactions to this or that way of putting things have been helpful to me. I want to thank Carl Braaten and Wi-jo Kang for being willing to read the complete manuscript and for giving both encouragement and critical suggestions. A long-term debt is owed to Joseph Kitagawa, under whose tutelage I first began to think critically and constructively about divergent religious Ways. While I would not want to tar him with the brush of this study, I do want to express appreciation for that long-term debt. Both he and Kosuke Koyama had a look at the completed manuscript. I am grateful for their encouragement.

This study has been some years in preparation. It began in 1980–1981, a sabbatical year spent in China, Hong Kong, and Taiwan which was made possible by the generous sabbatical policy of Luther Northwestern and the generous support of the Aid Association for Lutherans in awarding the Fredrik A. Schiotz Fellowship. It has since been worked on, mostly during snatches of the summer months when teaching duties were not pressing.

Ida Marie and the children, Anna Marie and Peter, knew I was preoccupied with something, and endured the preoccupation. No doubt their encouragement that I complete the task was in part a hope that I would not always be so preoccupied. They perhaps do not fully realize that the life we lived together made it possible for me to experience a sense of wholeness and to persist in the preoccupation. A special thanks goes to my wife, Ida Marie, for letting me share in a six-month study in Taiwan on the religious response of the Chinese family to the crisis of childhood cancer. The data of that study does not enter in here, but a living sense of the folk tradition helped clarify what directions to move in dealing with the norming Chinese religious traditions.

Finally, it is fitting, perhaps, that the manuscript goes to the press as we depart for another sabbatical. Something is completed; there is more to be done.

1

BEING IN
THE WORLD

A. Prelude

Matter and mystery—between them we live. Being between, we come to this study, therefore, with a question. What question?

We humans are poised somewhere between matter and mystery. Sure that we are in some way identified with matter, we are less sure of the whence and whither of self and world. Somehow we belong to matter, and value that belonging, but in that belonging there seem to be untold questions. Does matter reveal possible answers? Might it rather obscure them? Or are we simply matter with no questions beyond matter to be asked, no answers beyond matter to be sought?[1]

To question is to quest; and to quest is to be in search of a value; and in this search are disclosed our cares and preferrings, our loves and hates. History is the story of our quest rightly to value human being in the world, a being poised between matter and mystery.

The outer perimeters in this quest seem to be set forth in a representative way by Marx and the Buddha: for one, matter appears to be without mystery; for the other, mystery is without matter. As we shall see, this stark formulation will need to be modified somewhat, but for other traditions that we shall explore, such as the Confucian, there is a far more explicit preference for some kind of "between" in which matter and mystery belong constructively to each other. This is surely the case also for the Christian faith. For these, neither is without the other, for mystery is not apart from matter, nor is matter apart from mystery. In the final analysis this becomes a question of how I, an individual, am to value self and world, and what place "God" might have, if any, in this valuing.[2]

Regardless of the answer formed—Buddhist, Muslim, Marxist, Christian, or Confucian—one thing is surely beyond dispute: each cares about the answer given; each in its own way cares about this individual, and its place in the world of matter, or mystery, or both. Max Scheler puts the issue well:

> I find myself in an immeasurably vast world of sensible and spiritual objects which set my heart and passions in constant motion. I know that the objects I can recognize through perception and thought, as well as all that I will, choose, do, perform, and accomplish, depend on the play of this movement of my heart. It follows that any sort of rightness or falseness and perversity in my life and activity are determined by whether there is an objectively correct order of these stirrings of my love and hate, my inclination and disinclination, my many-sided interest in the things of this world. It depends further on whether I can impress this *ordo amoris* on my inner moral tenor.[3]

Scheler goes on to observe that in coming to know "an individual, a historical era, a family, a people, a nation, or any other socio-historical group," it will be known most profoundly when "I have discerned the system of its concrete value-assessments"; at the root of these assessments is first and foremost "the *order of love and hate*." This system directs the way in which the subject, whether individual or group, sees his or her world, and his or her deeds.

These words pose for us a task that includes both description and evaluation. To get to know the other, as well as the self, in this "vast world of sensible and spiritual objects," it is required that one know the order of one's own and the other's loves and hates. But the orders of valuing are many, and this necessarily raises the question of the rightness in my own ordering, as well as that of the other. Does any order of valuing and care have a better intrinsic fit with the way things really are than do others? Are the "stirrings of my love and hate" truly fitting?

In this chapter we shall pose some of the issues that are at stake in the quest for this order. We shall begin by taking two representative boundary traditions, Buddhism and Marxism, and attempt to clarify in what way they value human being in the world. Both begin with the empirical data of human life, subject the way this data is appropriated and valued to an intense critique, and in the process of the critique reorder their own valuings which they deem to fit with the way things really are. In this process they display very different anthropological commitments. This difference—in which one points towards mystery, the other towards matter—will help us to raise basic questions about the quest rightly to value human being in the world and give us directions for the subsequent study.

B. Buddhist Anthropology: The Absolute Difference

Both the Buddha and Marx begin their critiques in the encounter with actual life. With the Buddha we are dependent upon tradition which was originally oral and only later transcribed. According to this tradition, the young prince Siddhartha ("he whose aim will be accomplished") of the Gautama family, of the Sakya tribe, destined for kingship, had a series of shattering encounters that led him in his early manhood to forsake the path of earthly enjoyment and power in exchange for the life of a hermit in quest of true value. This quest led to his discovery—enlightenment—after which he took up the life of a wandering beggar in the company of his disciples, preaching the truth he had discovered.

What, then, was the nature of this encounter, what the critique, and how did it relate to the eventual disclosure of the truth?

The encounters

The encounters as described were four: with a decrepit old man, an agonizing sick man, the corpse of a dead man, and the blissful visage of a holy man. The first three, old age, sickness, and death, provided the shock (according to tradition the naive young Siddhartha had been isolated from all such negative encounters), while the last suggested a way of deliverance from this shock.

The story is simple, and told and retold daily throughout much of Asia. The story is simply told so that even a child can understand its plain meaning. Yet, for all its simplicity, upon it rests the entire elaborate Buddhist critique.

Leaving wife, infant son, and expected throne, young Gautama mulled over these matters for several years in hermetic isolation and amidst yogic austerities, but all to no avail.[4] Nonetheless, having finally forsaken the way of extreme self-deprivation, and nourished by fresh milk, his meditations did finally culminate in the momentous discovery of his marvelous night of enlightenment.[5] The tradition crystalizes this discovery in the teaching on the Four Noble Truths: the truths of sorrow, its arising, its cessation, and the way to its cessation.

These four truths put in a systematic way what has become, and perhaps originally was, the basic Buddhist experience. Gautama resolved to seek enlightenment because he felt in the deepest way possible that human life, whatever joys there might be, brought in its wake the untold tribulations of old age, sickness, and death. Sentient existence seems to be bound up with a process of ceaseless liking and disliking and, because one's likings are never able to be fully satisfied, while dislikes are already dissatisfaction, human life is experienced as sorrow, a nonsatisfactory existence. This process, moreover, is embedded in an iron-clad rule of cause and effect, of *karma*. If only this karmic rule that governs existence can be taken advantage of and the process of liking and disliking overcome, liberation is possible and suffering will be superseded by the attainment of absolute tranquility.

An entire philosophy of religion, worthy of our attention, is contained in this fourfold claim. Above all, this claim concerns liberation. Such a claim presupposes, first, a description of the world as it is; second, a clarification of the need and possibility of liberation; and, third, a presentation of the way or method of securing this liberation. Thus, there needs to be a specification of the present human circumstance, of the final consequence, and the pathway or action that leads to the latter.

The fourfold claim fills these out. The first two specify the objective and subjective circumstance, and in doing so develop a cosmology (first truth) and an epistemology (second truth); the third truth specifies the goal or consequence to be attained and is the heart of the Buddhist

claim to truth and the basis for its Buddhology; the fourth specifies
the means or way of passage from present circumstance to final consequence and fills out the intermediate ethical as well as religious
(ritual, belief) categories.[6] Thus, this fourfold claim articulates a cosmology— i.e., a description of the present world; an epistemology—
i.e., a theory of consciousness; an eschatology—i.e., a description of
final reality, which is in content a Buddhology; and a religious ethic—
i.e., a prescription for behavior and belief that mediates between present circumstance and final consequence.

Two wisdoms

The first two truths purport to give a description of present reality.
In understanding what they in fact say, they must be seen together. At
least three things need to be attended to: (1) What is the ordinary way
of knowing and experiencing the world, according to the second truth?
(2) What does the world really look like when taken on its own terms
as it appears to us, according to the first truth? (3) Whence derives the
value judgment that existence is sorrow, ultimately nonsatisfactory?

Siddhartha's encounter with actual life led him to a description of
the ordinary way of knowing and experiencing the world. Conventional
wisdom, which describes our ordinary way of knowing and experiencing, is based on sense experience. Our various senses respond to
stimuli so that we experience sight, hearing, taste, smell, and touch.
We take that as real which we experience through these several senses.
Combined with this sense experience of an actual external world is the
inward sensation of a psychic center which experiences, organizes, and
responds to these externally derived sensations. With this is present to
us, then, the notion of a self with a world, a subject possessing, or
wanting to possess, an object.

This description of conventional wisdom seems fairly accurate phe-
nomenologically. Some Buddhist systems expand this basic insight into
elaborate descriptive psychologies of human consciousness, which in
many ways seem hard to improve upon.[7] In any case, whether put into
simple or complex terms, this descriptive psychology points its finger
at the psychic center, which experiences, organizes, and responds to
sensations, as the source of the human problematic, of the human

grasping of a world for a self. The second truth states it simply and directly: "Thirsting is the origination of sorrow."

The first truth, in contrast to the above, purports to be based on an objective, unbiased, description of phenomenal reality. It takes it to be self-evident that existence is characterized above all by change and instability; it is a realm of radical becoming. Who would want to deny it? When all is said and done, the sometimes elaborate Buddhist analyses of existence come down to two basic points: all existents are impermanent (*anicca*) and insubstantial (*anatta*).

Impermanence is the distinctive mark of this world and all within it when viewed in its temporal character. Temporally, then, the world is change, a continual succession of arising and cessation, an endless parade of events. Further, this world and all within it are insubstantial when viewed from a spatial or relational perspective. Every arising can be referred back to prior conditions, and these conditions to yet further conditions. All existents are therefore the composite of multiple conditions which conjoin at a given moment. These ideas are schematized in the following formula:

> When this is, that is;
> this arising, that arises;
> when this is not, that is not;
> this ceasing, that ceases.[8]

The consequence of this doctrine is that every fact and event, though an appearance, a phenomenon, lacks a definable nucleus, is empty of a self-possessed identity, is insubstantial. Together, the marks of the impermanent and the insubstantial suggest that the world is an endlessly shifting collage of events which can neither be stopped, since change is permanent, nor held on to, since there is no graspable core.

Taken separately, these are not entirely unusual ideas. As for change, some ancient Greeks saw reality this way, as did Taoists and others in ancient China. As for reality being conditioned, a composite of elements or forces in association, the Greeks had atomists and the Chinese had their fivefold elemental movements (*wu-hsing*). Even the combination of these two was not unique, as the Confucian *Book of Changes* tries to divine guidance for life from kaleidoscopic change, and the

Taoist philosophers spoke of nonbeing in continual transformation. Modern science seems clearly to push in the direction of such cosmologies, and Whitehead's ideas, which celebrate transcience in process, give it a metaphysical support.

All existents are indelibly marked by impermanence, and are inherently insubstantial, that is, without a self. These assertions seem to be quite convincing. But so also does the descriptive psychology. But it is here that the problem begins to show: the cosmology and epistemology are simply not congruous with each other. The cosmology underlying the first truth and the psychology of the second both purport to describe reality as it is experienced—but they are in conflict. Conventional wisdom assumes a more or less stable world and an abiding self, so that we have a world in which subject and object subsist together. However, if in fact all is impermanent and insubstantial, then how can there be a psychic center, and how might it go about its business of grasping a world for itself? In fact, it can not. If it can, then the cosmology must be changed. A choice for one or the other must be made.[9]

The Buddha chose the cosmology and rejected the epistemology. Because of their incongruence, that is, the incongruence of reality as it is internally constituted with the consciousness of it that a psychic center insists upon, all reality is experienced as inherently nonsatisfactory, as sorrow. The imagined self likes itself, and tries to grasp the imagined world, sorting it out in terms of its self-grounded likes and dislikes. But this grasping is ultimately elusive, for the insubstantial and ever-changing world is unimaginable and ungraspable in its own being. This persistent failure is experienced as a deep existential pain, as an unstoppable suffering. Nothing endures, indeed there is nothing to endure, yet we make every desperate attempt to cling to life and stave off death. Our subjective awareness (the second truth) is out of tune with objective reality which is insubstantial and impermanent (the first truth); therefore it bears the indelible mark of sorrow (*dukkha*) as well.

Human being in the world is therefore evaluated as *dukkha*, inherent restlessness, being ill at ease, sorrow. A closer look at the Buddhist anthropology involved in this assessment will show more clearly the basis upon which it is made and its relevance for understanding the Buddhist order of valuing human being in the world.

A *tri-level view of human being*

In Buddhism the individual can be viewed from at least three distinct but related points of view: we shall refer to these as the substantialist, the analytic, and the absolutist views. The substantialist view considers the individual in a conventional way as already described. It is a kind of simpleminded approach to the world. There is a self, an abiding psychic center, and this self appropriates a world that is external to it. The analytic view is rather more sophisticated, and considers the individual from a logical, intellectual point of view. It simply elaborates on the doctrines of impermanence and insubstantiality. From this point of view it makes no sense to posit a self—where would you locate it in ceaseless change? The absolutist view becomes far more esoteric. Self and world are apprehended in nondual, perhaps we can say mystical, categories. It points to reality as ineffable, and only to be known through mystic intuition.

The term *individual* means nondivisible. This is the precise opposite of the Buddhist analytic anthropology, for that which is taken to be individual is in fact analyzed into its constituents. The point of departure for this analysis is the empirical, corporeal existence of the individual.

The basic categories in this Buddhist analysis are two, *nama* (literally, "name") and *rupa* (literally, "form"). *Nama* refers in a collective way to the psychological or mental aspects of the individual while *rupa* is a collective term for the physical aspects. The individual is, therefore, the product of a conjoining of mental and physical aspects.

This twofold aspect of the individual is given a more detailed analysis in the theory of the five aggregates (*pancaskhandha*). According to this theory, the material aspect is constituted by four primary elements, the traditional elements of Indian cosmology: earth (*pathavi*) or solidity, water (*apo*) or viscosity, fire (*tejo*) or thermal energy, and air (*vayo*) or movement. The mental factor is broken down into four subcategories, and these in turn into numerous, even smaller units. The first mental function is sensation (*vedana*), which is comprised of the five physical sense organs with mind (*manas*) as a sixth. Perceptions (*sanna*) are the second. These, too, are six in number, being six faculties that correspond to and receive impressions from the six sense organs. There are 50 mental activities (*samskhara*) which together constitute the third category. This represents the mind in its active, conative aspect and covers a wide range of meanings. Finally, there is consciousness (*vijnana*), which is a passive awareness devoid of activity. It images what is presented to it, much as a mirror reflects whatever is brought in front of it. The six sense organs are its base, and mediate to it the multiplicity of phenomena.

Two or three things need to be stressed about this analysis. First, the duality of mental/physical is not a dualism, for the two belong to each other in an integral manner. There is no matter apart from the psychical, and no mind apart from matter, the arising of each contingent upon the arising of the other. Second, in this analysis primacy is given to mind. At the same time it is recognized that the mind is notorious for its instability and flightiness—it is often likened to a monkey. Just try for a moment to grab hold of the mind and bring its restlessness to cease. Were one to search for the greater stability, the preference would then be for matter rather than mind:

> It would be better for an untaught ordinary man to treat as self (*atta*) this body, which is constructed upon the four great primaries of matter (*maha-bhuta*), than mind. Why? Because the body can last one year, two years. . . even a hundred years; but what is called "mind" and "thinking" and "consciousness" arises and ceases differently through night and day.[10]

But, of course, Buddhist enlightenment does not seek for that sort of stability.

Finally, the individual as a moment that arises with the conjoining of these several factors, is essentially impermanent and insubstantial. As insubstantial there is no organizing center that is other than the conjoining action of the elements at this moment. The individual is not an abiding self, a something more than the composite, unstable whole, which is always liable to being resolved into its constituent parts.

This analytic anthropology, or, we might say, this cosmology of the human, mediates between the substantialist and absolutist views. On the one hand, it provides the basis for the Buddhist critique of the ordinary way of viewing human being in the world and, on the other, makes a different synthesis, an absolutist one, almost necessary.

The substantialist anthropology grows out of a confusion about the nature of the individual as a corporeal entity. In this corporeal unity or embodiment of psychosomatic factors the mental factors are reactive to the physical. Thus arises the possibility of a subject/object division. Furthermore, there seems to be a sense of unity, and thus arises the notion of a self. The falseness of this synthetic act that posits a self and sets it over against a world is put in these words:

> When one says "I", what one does is that one refers to all the *khandhas* [constituting elements] combined or to any one of them, and deludes oneself that that was "I". Just as one cannot say that the fragrance of the lotus belonged to the petals, the colour or the pollen, so one could not say that the *rupa* was "I" or the *vedana* was "I" or any other of the *khandhas* was "I". There is nowhere to be found in the *khandhas* "I am".[11]

It is this positing of an "I am" that gives rise to thirst and the restless desire for self-continuity and self-fulfillment.

This is combined in a substantialist anthropology with certain pan-Indian assumptions. These concern the doctrines of *samsara*—existence as an unending cycle of rebirths through the several realms of existence (lower world, animal kingdom, spirit sphere, human sphere, realm of gods)[12]—and *karma*.

This latter is of particular importance for understanding the ultimate fortunes of a self that grounds its identity in a sense of "I am" and that thirsts for personal continuance. *Karma* is a specific quality that inheres in all mental activity. Thought, desire, will, striving, the conative mind (*samskhara*, above, p. 23), puts into motion a force within things, this force being *karma*. *Karma* means action, and in Buddhist cosmology refers specifically to the energies set into motion by mental activity. This energy brings about effects. On the one hand, this energy is of a moral nature. Good thoughts, good actions bring about good, i.e., pleasant, results, and evil actions evil results. At the same time it is an impersonal cosmic energy that, regardless of whether good or bad results, perpetuates delusion, the continual re-becoming of a sense of self as originally and falsely posited. Thirst, which is the consequence of the ignorant positing of a self, reinforces in turn that false sense of self-identity, generating a process of endless re-becoming through the innumerable realms of existence, and cycles the self from past, through the present and on into the indefinite future. Endless becoming of this sort is endless sorrow, perpetuating the incongruence between thought and reality we have already described. Thus it is that existence is *dukkha* (first truth) and that the origination of *dukkha* lies in thirst or desiring (second truth).

In contrast to this substantialist anthropology, the absolutist view presupposes precisely the cosmology as described in the analytic anthropology. There is unending impermanence; consequently there is nothing permanent that remains or subsists through the succession of temporal events. Furthermore, there is constant relativity. Every unity is in fact a plurality. Should a single item in this plurality be examined, it too would be shown to be constituted by further pluralities. As a consequence, there is no identity with an individual self possible, only an identity with the totality, which proves to be unending impermanence and constant relativity. To be without-self is the discovery that what appears in an event is nothing else than an eventful manifestation of the totality. Negatively, with no self posited, there is no sense of "I am" to cling to, and, without a sense of "I am," there is no arising of thirst for the continuance of either the "I am" or the event. This is the dissolution of *dukkha*. Positively, there is an identification with the totality of reality, an experience that is ineffable, indescribable, and available only to the enlightened individual. The interior aspect of this enlightenment is experienced as absolute bliss, tranquility, joy.

The third truth, concerning the cessation of *dukkha*, simply states that with the cessation of desiring, and therefore of a false positing of a self, *dukkha* ceases. This cessation is Nirvana, and in the later interpretations is the without-self of the absolutist anthropology. With the cessation of *dukkha*, there is only tranquility, a realized and perfect identity of essence and existence. This three-tiered anthropology can perhaps be summarized in a diagram.

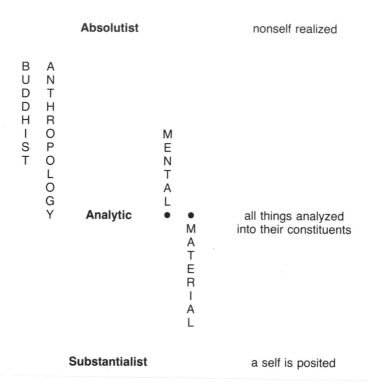

NIRVANA

(tranquility)

Absolutist nonself realized

B A
U N
D T
D H
H R
I O   M
S P   E
T O   N
L   T
O   A
G   L
Y **Analytic** • • all things analyzed
M into their constituents
A
T
E
R
I
A
L

Substantialist a self is posited

DUKKHA

(dis-ease)

All three of these anthropologies have their appropriate contribution to make to Buddhist faith and practice. The analytic view purports to be a description of phenomena as empirically experienced. Experience of the impermanent and contingent character of existence leads to ever more elaborate logical and philosophical critiques of substantialist theories in Buddhist history. The absolutist anthropology is most fully developed in the various forms of Mahayana thought and becomes the ultimate norming category for much of Buddhism. Even the substantialist anthropology, though judged to be finally false, has its place in the development of ethics in a Buddhist order of valuing. Indeed, without a positive use of this common sense anthropology much of that which is deemed most characteristic of Buddhist practice and piety would simply have to be set aside.

A way

Buddhism as a historical religion is, above all, a pathway, a pathway that leads from the ignorance of present circumstance (first and second truths) to the enlightenment of final consequence (third truth). To talk of Buddhism as a historical movement is to talk of this pathway, the fourth truth.

The fourth truth is the noble eightfold path: right understanding (*samma-ditthi*), right thought (*samma-sankappa*), right speech (*samma-vaca*), right action (*samma-kammanta*), right livelihood (*samma-ajiva*), right effort (*samma-vayama*), right mindfulness (*samma-sati*), and right concentration (*samma-samadhi*).[13] These eight, in fact, combine into three larger categories which identify the three principal modalities of Buddhist piety and practice upon this pathway. These three modalities are moral action (*sila, lü*), which includes items three, four, and five; meditation (*samadhi, ting*), which includes items six, seven and eight; and wisdom (*prajna, hui*), which includes the first two items. All Buddhism is an elaboration of one or more of these modes, which are properly pursued in concurrent fashion, differences arising from the variety of emphases. So-called southern or Theravada Buddhism is primarily an extension of moral action as an act of reclusion and which includes the others as aspects of the discipline; Ch'an or Zen is primarily an extension of meditation, as is also the *yogacara* or "consciousness only" school; and the elaborate systems of the *prajna* and Madhyamika school are elaborations primarily of wisdom. The Pure Land schools, dominant in East Asia, are perhaps best seen as a folk form of moral action, a devotional piety, inspired by insights growing out of the wisdom schools as well as the "psycho-mythology"[14] of the meditation schools. Details of this Way will draw our attention later.

Whatever the path or mode of operation, the goal is one—Nirvana, the consequence of the without-self experience. In the end the Buddhist pathway completes itself in an intuition of nondual reality that does not lend itself to rational discourse. Put into different words, the analytic anthropology occasions an intuitive insight. Having ridden the bark of Buddhism, one has now safely passed from the hither shore of material existence (naively assumed to be all solid and substance) to the thither shore of Nirvana, the experience of reality in its truly ineffable character.

C. Marxist Anthropology: The Dialectic Difference

Marx, too, begins his critique by engagement with actual life. To be sure, there is no stylized tradition of a fourfold encounter to lend a similar definiteness. Unlike young Gautama, Marx did not seem particularly distressed by human finitude and frailty,[15] being assured rather of the as-yet-untapped potential of human creative possibilities. Rather than preoccupation with certain deep psychological-ontological issues he was preoccupied with certain evident social-moral issues, in particular, the way existing human socioeconomic organization frustrated the realization of the full human capacity. As a young man Marx became intensely aware of a vast gulf between human ideals and their earthly realization. Yet, throughout his life he resisted a utopian approach; such an approach posits an ideal out there to which real life is to be made to conform. Marx made every effort to be realistic and, on the basis of discerning the way things are in the present, to come to some sense of the way things will be in the future. The "ought" must be derived from the "is," not the other way around. Eventually his theoretical reformulation of this problematic was to focus with a fierce practical intensity upon the plight of the laborer in the rising industrial society of his day and to argue the absolutely necessary historical consequence towards which the laborer's plight was leading.

Marx becomes a Marxist

Marx's thought as it developed from his youth into his maturity, if taken piecemeal with one phase contrasted with another, will appear discontinuous, but when taken as a whole it will show a definite coherence.[16] It is clear that his thought from the very beginning was grounded in a *moral passion*.[17] So energized, he proceeded by way of the *criticism* of the world as he experienced it in terms of its religion, politics, and economics. This critique *disclosed* the real world to be a definite kind of historical process that was moving towards an irreversible destiny. Equipped with this knowledge he was therewith enabled to make *programmatic*[18] suggestions as to how this process might be encouraged along its way towards completion. The moral passion in Marx, hidden to be sure in his presumption to be descriptive only, serves the same motivating function that the existential dismay, quickened by the fourfold encounter, did for Gautama.

To speak of a moral passion in Marx that preceded his developed thinking is by no means to suggest that he gives us an ethical system, though one must still be amused by Lenin's assertion that Marxism "contains no shred of ethics from beginning to end."[19] What meets us rather than any articulated ethical system is simply a description of the world (cosmology) which includes our necessary response within and to it (epistemology); nonetheless, it is evident that a subterranean, unstated moral commitment guides the hand that describes. If there is an ethics, it is that which is implicit in the description.[20] In his early acquaintance with Marx, Engels seems to capture the ethos of this raging, enigmatic prophet in a humorous caricature:

> But who advances here full of impetuosity? It is a dark form from Trier, an unleashed monster, with self-assured step he hammers the ground with his heels and raises his arms in full fury to heaven as though he wished to seize the celestial vault and lower it to earth. In rage he continually deals with his redoubtable fist, as if a thousand devils were gripping his hair.[21]

One might perhaps think of Luther, the Israelite prophet,[22] and the irrepressible Prometheus all wrapped into one.

The moral passion that kindles Marx's philosophical-revolutionary project was solidly in place by the time his thoughts were sufficiently clarified for that project to get on its way.[23] To be sure, moral passion is a profoundly personal movement of the heart, and its real history is buried in Marx's autobiography. Yet, there are ample public traces of the inward journey. Moreover, one can hardly doubt that the thick Jewish heritage of both parents in the family (with many rabbis on both sides); the enlightenment-type faith of his father (who had converted to Lutheranism for practical reasons), which was directed to an abstract God of morality; the profound influence in the Rhineland of French revolutionary ideas, with their commitment to individual freedom and social justice; the economic crisis of the Mosel Valley where he grew up; the economic pressures elicited by early industrialization and population growth; and the passion for poetry and aesthetics of his "fatherly friend," von Westphalen, with the rich romantic overtones there present—that all these influenced the teenage Marx considerably. Lofty ideals, though immature and hardly thought out, already crop up in his youthful high school essays, as this passage of purple prose, one among several, suggests:

> When we have chosen the vocation in which we can contribute most to humanity, burdens cannot bend us because they are only sacrifices for all. Then we experience no meagre, limited, egotistic joy, but our happiness belongs to millions, our deeds live on quietly but eternally effective, and glowing tears of noble men will fall on our ashes.[24]

Upon leaving home for university, however, his passions took a somewhat less noble, largely aesthetic turn, doubtless partly fired by the passion he felt for Jenny, his "fatherly friend's" daughter and his future wife, and accompanied by a fair amount of carousing and roughhousing. He drowned himself in writing flowery poetry, most of it lost, which if nothing else showed an inward attraction to the romantic ideal of full and free self-expression. This, however, was shortly subdued in his conversion to Hegelian patterns of thought, and forced upon him the question of how the idea relates to the real. In his doctoral thesis he found an affinity with the "moral" materialism of Epicurus, whose notion of the unpredictable "swerve" gets away from the mechanistic atomism of Democritus and leaves room for the autonomy of the human spirit and the play of "free individual self-consciousness."[25] Moreover, in this same dissertation he argues the practical value of philosophy:

> It is a psychological law that the theoretical mind, once liberated in itself, turns into practical energy, and, leaving the empire of Amenthes as *will*, turns itself against the reality of the world existing without it.[26]

No doubt his intimacy with the Young Hegelian radicals helped him to move in this critical direction and find his bearings in a philosophy that has "its heart. . . set on creating a world." It certainly gave a focus to his thinking, absent in 1837 when first overcome by Hegel. That had led to his self-confessed "confused state of my storm-tossed soul,"[27] eventuating in what might be described as a nervous breakdown.[28] As he turned to the real world he finally found the proper locus within which to articulate the stirrings of his heart and mind.

He turned to journalism with a vengeance after failing to obtain a teaching job. Here his moral commitment was for the first time articulated in unambiguous terms derived from Kant and enlightenment thought generally. Like Kant he affirmed the autonomy and universality of the ethical. In his writings against the press censorship of the Prussian state he chastised the "Christian legislator" for his inability to "recognize morality as an independent sphere sanctified in itself."

> Following the Instruction, censorship will have to repudiate such intellectual heroes of morality as Kant, Fichte, Spinoza for being irreligious and threatening discipline, morals and outward loyalty. All of these moralists proceed from principled opposition between morality and religion, because *morality*, they claim, is based on the *autonomy*, and *religion* on the *heteronomy* of the human spirit.[29]

This autonomy is given a more specific content when he writes that a free press is "the essence of freedom" as also "the essence of man consists. . . in freedom."[30]

We have seen, then, the self-sacrificing idealism of a high school youth yield to the romantic enamored of love and art, only to be overcome by the philosophical idealism of a graduate student who seeks through ideas to change the world, finally coming to the agitating journalist who begins to put this critique into practice in the name of reason and autonomy.

Needless to say, Marx is not yet a Marxist. Nonetheless, the themes of the humanism that shall henceforth influence his entire life's work are all now present, though in unorganized and non-Marxist fashion. Kolakowski identifies three basic motifs that pervade Marx's mature humanism: the romantic, the Faustian, and the rationalist-determinist.[31]

As a romantic, Marx deplored the absence of "organic" ties among human beings, whose relations had become impersonal and institutionalized, most notably through the abstract tyranny of money. Thus he viciously opposed the liberal notion of freedom as contained in the Declaration of the Rights of Man which was a mere privacy of noninterference rather than a voluntary unity of individuals. This unity, however, was to appear in his vision of the future. His Promethean strain cleared the way, for the human would destroy all that obstructs the passage from the inhuman present to the humanized future of unlimited human creativity. "The Promethean idea which recurs constantly in Marx's work is that of faith in man's unlimited powers as self-creator, contempt for tradition and worship of the past, history as man's self-realization through labour, and the belief that the man of tomorrow will derive his 'poetry' from the future."[32] But even this Prometheanism had its limits. Influenced by the enlightenment, Marx sought to define the reason within things as a law within things. He sought to discern the laws of social life much as a scientist describes the laws of nature. Thus, as in nature, so in society: all that takes place is necessary, and history is an inexorable process that leads to an inevitable future. Incongruent though these motifs—organic unity, creative freedom, historical determination—might seem to be, they are embedded in the warp and woof of Marx's attempted synthesis.

These humanist motifs, not fully formulated at the beginning, lead Marx into his life-long task of criticism. Already in his doctoral dissertation Marx had come to the view that "the *practice* of philosophy is itself *theoretical*. It's the *critique* that measures the individual existence by the essence, the particular reality by the Idea."[33] Whereas he was later not to speak in this way (i.e., critique the actual world with abstract ideals), it does make clear that it was time for philosophy to begin to do something about the way the world is.

In a letter to Ruge concerning a projected journal Marx outlines a program of criticism of sorts. As practical philosophy critiques the world, it must not do so dogmatically, anticipating the future design of things by presenting finished answers, but rather "try to discover the new world from a critique of the old one." And this must be a "ruthless criticism of all that exists," both in the sense that it does not balk at its own results nor hesitate to struggle with the powers that be.

Moreover, since "first, religion, and then politics are the objects which constitute the main interest of present Germany," they are the first things in the old world to be critiqued. "As *religion* is the index to the theoretical struggles of mankind, so the *political state* is the index to its practical ones."[34]

The sequence of religion, politics, and economics roughly indicates the chronological order in the attention Marx directed to these themes; more importantly, this chronology reflects the logical order. In the religious critique Marx assumes the success of Feuerbach. Feuerbach had reversed the subject predicate terms of Hegel's thought, which made the human world the predicate of Spirit or Idea, and instead argued that the human was the subject and God merely its predicate. Moreover, God was not real, being merely a figment of the human imagination, which imagination projected onto a sphere of supposed absolute being all of its own human potentialities. God was simply what human beings wished to be. "The fantasy, the dream, and postulate of Christianity," he wrote, is "the sovereignty of man—but of man as an alien being, separate from actual man."[35] But this kind of projection was no harmless matter, for by projecting human possibilities onto an imaginary being humans were to that degree robbed of their own power to act on their own capabilities. To remove the false idea of God is to restore human beings to themselves. As Marx writes, "The criticism of religion ends with the doctrine that *for man the supreme being is man.*"[36]

However, Marx was not satisfied with Feuerbach. For Marx it was not sufficient to posit God as a psychological projection; much rather, the very need psychologically to project a God arose out of the prior debasement of people in their social existence. As he writes, with dramatic flair, "The foundation of irreligious criticism is: *man makes religion*, religion does not make man. Religion is indeed the self-consciousness and self-esteem of man who has either not yet won through to himself or has already lost himself again." Feuerbach might have written such. "But *man* is not an abstract being squatting outside the world," as Feuerbach seems to think. "Man is *the world of man*, state, society." He then draws the conclusion of a socialized projection: "This state and this society produce religion, which is an *inverted consciousness of the world*, because they are an *inverted world*." On

33

these grounds he explores the pathos of human existence which finds it necessary to posit God: "*Religious* suffering is at one and the same time the *expression* of real suffering and a protest against real suffering. Religion is the sigh of the oppressed creature, the heart of a heartless world and the soul of soulless conditions. It is the *opium* of the people." Thus, the necessary corollary of exposing the idea of God as a "protest" of the oppressed against suffering and a "demand for their *real* happiness" is the "categorical imperative" to overthrow all conditions "that require illusions." And so he concludes: "The criticism of heaven turns into the criticism of earth, the *criticism of religion* into the *criticism of law,* and the *criticism of theology* into the *criticism of politics*."

With this, he turned to politics. These words, in fact, were written in his "A Contribution to the Critique of Hegel's Philosophy of Right: Introduction," which was put to writing after the "Contribution" itself.[37]

In the political critique Marx applied the same lesson learned from Feuerbach. It is not ideas (subject) that make the real world as it is (predicate) but the real world, or rather the real actor in the world, the human (subject), who produces ideas (e.g., God) or institutions (e.g., the state). No more than God are institutions to have dominion or exert coercive power over the self-determining human subject. What the critique of religion had gained for the human must not now be lost to the state.

With this premise Marx takes a look at Hegel's state. Briefly, Hegel viewed human society in terms of three interlocking spheres: the family, based on relations of love; civil society as the arena of business and daily life, wherein the self-interest of individuals prevailed; and the state, which served the common interests of humanity as a universal community. Marx attended to the last two, absorbing the family into civil society, and pressed the issue of a fundamental contradiction between the sphere of private life, civil society, based on conflicting self-interests and the sphere of public life, the state, existing for the sake of common and universal human interest. Hegel noted various secondary institutions that mediated between the contrasting spheres. Corporations, or political pressure groups representing specific special interests of civil society influenced the state, while the bureaucracy mediated to civil society the response of the state to this pressure. Marx rejects this attempt at mediation which, he says, gives no solution but merely masks the contradiction, making it possible for the most powerfully represented private interests to gain ascendance and through the state lord it over the rest of society. The root of the matter was that any solution based on the philosophical assumption of egoism—that each individual is a monad with his or her own interests that necessarily enter into conflict with the interests of other monads which requires the working out of some kind of accommodation—was bound to failure, necessarily giving primacy to some interests over others and turning the state into a mechanism of coercion on behalf of these interests, keeping in submission the mass of conflicting individuals.

In line with this, Marx draws a sharp distinction between political rights and natural rights. The right to vote is the quintessential political right. Democracy brings about a political emancipation—as in the French, English, and North American revolutions—but in doing so simply sharpens the contradiction between the state, in which all are presumably equal, and civil society, where private interests prevail and sharp economic inequities persist unabated. Moreover, political emancipation of this kind presupposes the so-called natural rights, the rights of life, liberty, equality, and the like. But these rights are egoistic and antisocial. Liberty, for instance, is "the right to do and perform everything which does not harm others. . . [and] is not based on the association of man with man but rather on the separation of man from man."[38] So also with private property and the rest.

> Therefore not one of the so-called rights of man goes beyond egoistic man, man as a member of civil society, namely an individual withdrawn into himself, his private interest and his private desires, and separated from the community. In the rights of man it is not man who appears as a species-being; on the contrary, society appears as an external framework to the individuals, as a limitation of their original independence. The only bond which holds them together is natural necessity, need and private interest, the conservation of their property and their egoistic persons.[39]

Thus, modern political society splits the human into two irreconcilable beings—the individual propelled by needs and dominated by self-interests and the abstract community (the state) coercing cooperation from without. As a consequence, understanding the human person as an individual who lives in view of society is lost and we are left only with the individual who lives in view of his or her own interests. The egoism of the individual runs into conflict with the coercive balancing of interests in the state.

In agreement with the premise already stated, that the individual is his or her own subject, self-determining, it is clear that the basis of the contradiction must arise from within the real world of sensuous, acting human beings, from within civil society, and not from the abstract world of the political state, once removed as it is from direct, sensuous activity. This means that the dynamics of egoism as they exist in civil society, the actual world, need analysis.[40] This leads Marx directly into the economic sphere, and from this point on he turns to a lifelong critique of economics:

> The first work which I undertook to dispel the doubts assailing me was a critical re-examination of the Hegelian philosophy of law. . . . My inquiry led me to the conclusion that neither legal relations nor political forces could be comprehended, whether by themselves or on the basis of a so-called general development of the human mind, but that on the contrary they originate in the material conditions of life, the totality of which Hegel, following the example of the English and French thinkers of the eighteenth century, embraces within the term "civil society"; that the anatomy of this civil society, however, has to be sought in political economy.[41]

Why this is so is elsewhere made clear:

> Already here we see how this civil society is the true source and theatre of all history. . . . Civil society embraces the whole material intercourse of individuals within a definite stage of the development of productive forces. . . . The social organization evolving directly out of production and commerce, which in all ages forms the basis of the State and of the rest of the idealistic superstructure, has. . . always been designated by the same name.[42]

Marx has been forced by the logic of his own analysis to a materialist conception of history, culture, and society. He had long determined, however, to follow his "ruthless criticism" wherever it led him. It had now led him into the factory and marketplace. Here he was to spend the rest of his life, eventually to produce only part of an envisioned magnum opus that would critique the economic foundations of human society, and therefore of human existence itself.[43]

Having arrived at this point we ask ourselves, "To what end, this elaborate critique?" Marx began with a rich mixture of humanistic assumptions, and by degrees bored through the obfuscations cast up by religious illusions, penetrated the depersonalizing strata of political organization until he reached the bedrock of economic activity. But, for Marx, economics had no intrinsic interest. He frequently complained of the tedium these endless economic analyses caused, and how he would like to get at matters of more intrinsic interest—philosophical, ethical, aesthetic. The answer, of course, is that this economic analysis was needed to expose the way in which human beings had been robbed of the conditions for realizing their own selfhood, and yet to show that this was only one stage on the way to full and universal self-actualization. The true subject of history—and of economics, for that matter—is the human individual. "Man" is still the highest being for "man," even if present economic activity seems to contradict that.

Marx's turn to economics, then, was for the purpose of understanding the history of alienation. The economic analysis was needed to disclose at what point the human species was in its development. The analysis presupposed, therefore, some knowledge of human derivation as well as human destiny. We turn, then, to his underlying anthropology.

A dynamic human nature

It is often said that for Marx there is no human nature as such, but only changing human nature. Indeed, Marx himself says that "the whole of history is nothing but a continual transformation of human nature."[44] To argue that point would seem to make Marx into an idealist, an almost unthinkable act. Marx, of course, makes many pronouncements on what it is to be human, often with language that is forceful, if not intemperate. If we can manage to reduce the decibel level somewhat we will find a rather complex, but coherent, view of human nature in Marx. While Marx did not systematize his remarks in this regard, there is, in fact, a constructive anthropology implicit throughout.

Human nature is constituted by three interlocking aspects: the already given, the changing, and the teleologically given natures. To be sure, Marx views human nature as changing; however, this logically presupposes that something in fact does undergo change; moreover, unless the change is to be willy-nilly, it must move in some direction. Marx does in fact account for all three tenses: present (changing), past (already given), and future (teleologically given).[45]

The already given characteristics are at least fourfold. The fundamental given is that the individual constitutes himself or herself in productive activity. The human individual acts upon external nature and manipulates it this way and that.

This characteristic includes several other constituents.[46] The individual is drawn into productive activity, Marx would maintain, by his or her intrinsic needs. These at least include the need for food, simply to live, and the need for sex, to become perpetuating. This need structure in human nature, the second given, is not closed, as with animals— only so many given needs and no others—but open. Need satisfied can lead to new needs, bringing about an indefinite multiplication. As these physical needs already indicate, the individual is a part of nature. The third characteristic, then, is that the individual is both a part of physical nature—having a body—yet distinct from nature—possessed of consciousness. To be sure, there is a prehistory to body and mind, both of which derive from nature; but when Marx speaks of the individual, even if "dehumanized," he presupposes these already-given and enduring features. Consciousness in particular distinguishes the human from the animal. As he says: "what distinguishes the worst architect from the best of bees is this, that the architect raises his structure in imagination before he erects it in reality." But every individual as producer is inherently an architect *ab initio,* even before the resulting product, for "at the end of every labour-process, we get a result that already existed in the imagination of the labourer at its commencement."[47] Creative imagination is, therefore, an already given, together with one's physical body, and is an irreducible constitutent of what it is to be human.[48] Finally, these already givens—productive activity, need, body-mind continuum—are completed by the human bipolarity of individual and social. The producer, as one having needs, is necessarily an individual, whether conscious of "individuality" in a modern sense or not, yet precisely at the same time is existent with respect to others, regardless of whether that relation is experienced as communion or alienation.

These already givens[49] are all but explicit when he writes in this vein:

> Labour is. . . a process in which both man and Nature participate, and in which man of his own accord starts, regulates, and controls the material re-actions between himself and Nature. He opposes himself to Nature as one of her own forces, setting in motion arms and legs, head and hands, the natural forces of his body, in order to appropriate Nature's productions in a form adapted to his own wants. By thus acting on the external world and changing it, he at the same time changes his own nature. He develops his slumbering powers and compels them to act in obedience to his sway.[50]

"He develops his slumbering powers. . . ." The second aspect of human nature is, then, that it is a changing nature. In contrast to those elements that are already given, we might speak of these as the "newly given." Whereas the already given elements are universally enduring human characteristics through all changes, the newly given are not so ontologically stable, some perhaps enduring (language, for instance),[51] but others appearing and disappearing, the sense of "having" (private possession, for instance).

Two assumptions underlie the doctrine that human nature is changing. The first concerns the nature of productive activity itself. In productive activity the individual externalizes himself or herself in a world of ever-changing objects. These objects, in turn, become fresh materials for the individual to act upon. In this way productive activity continually brings change to both the environment and the self. The second concerns the already given social character of the individual. While all productive activity is always in view of one's relations with others (whether that relation is positive or negative), the specific content of that relation is forever a shifting one, as with unstable designs in a kaleidoscope. This is the meaning of that famous phrase taken from the 6th of the 11 "Theses on Feuerbach": "But the human essence is no abstraction inherent in each single individual. In its reality it is the ensemble of the social relations."[52]

This is entirely consonant with all that has been said so far. As a producer, the individual brings about new conditions of existence, new technologies, new transformations of nature, that open up new possibilities in material culture. At the same time, these new conditions interact with the individual, a possessor of needs, perhaps satisfying some, but creating new ones as well—new culinary tastes, love of sublime art, so bringing transformations not only of a physical but also of a mental or psychological kind. Since, finally, the individual always constitutes himself or herself in relation to others, each act, each need, each thought, each resultant object, brings a new configuration to the social matrix. Thus, at each level—environment, self, society—novelty is introduced. The ever-changing social configurations, which include the subordinate terms of environment and self, define the individual.

Such is Marx's view of the human individual in terms of his or her already given as well as newly given natures. The first is more or less ontologically stable, and if looked at in isolation is inert, formal, sterile, filled with the barest minimum of content (e.g., need for food and sex, consciousness). It can only be perceived, i.e., looked back upon, from the standpoint of the individual in his or her newly given nature. This is to view the individual dynamically, only in and through *praxis*, through what humanity makes of itself by means of productive activity. It is no different from any other growth process: "and as everything natural must *come into being,* so man also has his process of origin in *history.*"[53] However, even this is not enough, for the human nature so viewed is still alienated, estranged, dehumanized nature. Truly human nature comes into view only through the higher and final given in this hierarchy of natures, that which is teleologically given.

This includes only two items, but it is for the sake of these two items that the entire Marxist critique was set into motion. These two items, or qualities, are freedom and community. *Freedom* means absolutely self-determining in such a way that neither nature nor other persons place any external constraints upon the acting individual. *Community* is a spontaneous association of humans in which the free activity of one is the enrichment of all. This simply says that individuality is only socially realized, or, which is the same, that one's social being is fulfilled in realizing one's individuality. In short, it is perfect mutuality.

These are teleologically given, not empirically actual—at least not yet. Whenever Marx viewed human nature he did so by first putting on these teleological spectacles.[54] As a consequence, all of human history up to the present, measured by this telos, became for him a history of alienation, merely a prehistory, the age of the prehuman.

It is this teleological, anticipatory perspective that made what would otherwise have been a mere hierarchy of natures into a historical process. The resultant "social ontology," as it is aptly termed and described by Gould, developed through three social stages: the precapitalist economic formations, in which the already given nature predominates amidst relations of mutual personal dependence (family, clan, tribe); capitalism, in which human nature as change increasingly predominates in relations of personal independence and abstract society (civil society, state); and the communal society of the future, in which the teleological nature predominates in relations of "free social individuality."[55] This social ontology, Gould points out, combines the realism of Aristotle (the ontologically real individual) with the dialectics of Hegel as well as, we might add, the socialist impulses of his day.

Freedom as teleologically given is integrally related with the newly given and already given aspects of human nature. In a sense, freedom presupposes itself, and there is without doubt a certain circularity in Marx's thought here.[56] How could one who lives in the constantly changing present have an intimation of the final end unless there were already some anticipation of that end? This is a gap in Marx's social ontology.

Freedom is already present in the beginning, in the already given nature, at its very foundation: human being as constituted in productive activity. We have already seen how that includes the idea of imagination. Through imagination, a form of consciousness, human needs, wants, and desires are not only consciously appropriated as such but transformed from needs into purposes. This process of self-transcendence is then carried further through productive activity (work) that creates objects that satisfy needs. This leads to new needs, to the positing of new purposes, to the engaging in further productive activity in an endless process of self-transcendence. This process of self-transcendence is concrete, always leading to new objects. At the heart of this self-transcending process of objectification is the self as agent.

The freedom of human agency, at this point, is twofold. It is first a freedom *from,* not in the sense that there are no external hindrances, but in the sense that one is free from conditions which prevent the positing of purposes and overcoming of obstacles. At the same time, it is a freedom *to,* in the sense that the individual is free to achieve a full self-realization through projecting possibilities and acting on them.

Nonetheless, this process is not all sweetness and light. Marx speaks continually of domination, oppression, dehumanization, and alienation as things which rob and destroy one's freedom. Obviously, present freedom under its manifold limitations and merely partial fulfillments, when compared with the teleologically given freedom, appears as a virtual slavery.

Mutuality as teleologically given is also integrally related to the two prior givens of human nature. In human nature as already given, mutuality obtains as a possibility in the formal sense that other-directedness is a constitutive quality of human being in the world, that is, the individual is necessarily social. This is so, if for no other reason, by virtue of the bare fact of propagation, which involves a "relation between man and woman, parents and children, the *family*."[57] In human nature as newly given, this social quality of the individual finds articulation in a bewildering variety of social forms, appropriate to the conditions of production. Amid all these social relationships—and "by social we understand the cooperation of several individuals, no matter under what conditions, in what manner and to what end"[58]—mutuality exists as a human possibility, even where absent in fact. As the teleologically given human nature, it is the final form that social relations will take, the form in which possibility becomes fact, and the self-actualization of one becomes the self-actualization of all.

As one reads back into present life from these teleological givens of freedom and mutuality, a severe discrepancy appears. Freedom and mutuality act together as an implied norm. The essential criterion for freedom is, negatively, that no conditions pertain which prevent the positing of purposes and acts and, positively, conditions that permit full self-actualization. The essential criterion for mutuality is social enhancement, that is, that the positing of individual purposes and aims enhance the purposes and aims of society, and that self-actualization of the individual enhance the full self-actualization of all. Measured by these criteria, present life appears as miserably limiting.

In capitalist society, for example, the apparent freedom of the capitalist to posit purposes and acts presupposes the severe restriction of the laborer to do the same. This is because the means of production—the necessary condition to posit such purposes and acts—are under the control of the capitalist. If purposes and acts cannot be posited, then the self cannot be actualized. At the same time the conditions for mutual enhancement are absent. If at the level of production freedom is restricted, at the level of exchange social relations are distorted. Rather than the product of one's action becoming an occasion for free enjoyment it becomes a commodity for exchange, available to the highest bidder or the one with sufficient money. Mutuality is there inverted into social relations which take on the appearance of equality but which are dominated by the medium of exchange—money—and abstract social equality becomes concrete inequality.

While the catalog is far from complete, the point is clear, that within present society, whether capitalist or precapitalist, the conditions for freedom and mutuality do not obtain. If freedom is to be mutual, there must be concrete equality in the positing of purposes and acts, and if mutuality is to be free, there must be free access to the means of production. Hitherto, history has been a history of unfreedoms and social conflict. If freedom and mutuality are that which ought to be, then history has been and is experienced as a succession of the suffering of wrongful dominations, of injustice, the dialectic of alienation.

D. Interlude

We began this study by saying that history is the story of our quest rightly to value human being in the world, a being poised between matter and mystery. Both Gautama and Marx show themselves to be direct participants in this quest. In this quest, the fundamental question for both is how the individual, a corporeal, psychosomatic unity, is to be reconciled with self and with the world. For the Buddha this reconciliation is gained intuitively, and is an already-present reality (transcendent though it be) which needs only a subjective realization. The realization is won when the distinction between self and world is forgone on the grounds that there is no subsisting self nor a permanent, subsisting world. For Marx this reconciliation is to be gained in the future as the outcome of human creative activity. By productive action nature will have been humanized—developed to sustain human needs and shaped to serve human intentions—and human relations will be characterized by absolute spontaneity and mutuality of purpose.

These answers, obviously, are quite different. In one, the self is dissolved, so to speak, eliminating the distinction of subject and object so that the problem of reconciliation ceases to be a relevant one; for the other, the self is to be fully actualized in a world of many subjects and numberless objects.

The Buddhist solution begins with what is given in experience, but emphatically rejects all commonsense conclusions about a real, subsisting self and a real, subsisting world. It also rejects any metaphysical doctrine of an eternal, unchanging soul or self, as well as any annihilationist doctrines. Rejecting these, the only way left open for later Buddhist elaborations of the culminating Buddhist insight is to speak of reality as ultimately ineffable and nondual. The result is a rich variety of subsequent Buddhist mysticisms, and accompanying ontologies.

The Marxist solution also begins with what is given in experience. In contrast to Buddhism, it insistently adheres to a real world of nature and a real human individual which enter into real, concrete relations. It emphatically resists every attempt to set aside the concrete, commonsense experience of self and world. Because of this, all subsequent developments in Marxism, whether philosophical or political, have had to build upon a materialist core.

With the Buddha and Marx, we too must begin with our concrete experience of a world. But whose footsteps ought we to follow? Is the self nonexistent or existent? Does it matter? How are we to take this world? Does that matter? Surely it does, and the story our lives write will have its consequence for a future valuing of human being in the world. Both the Buddha and Marx cared about something. Did they care rightly? Can—ought—we appropriate something of their divergent cares?

I think we can share some of their concerns, and the issues raised by the diverging Buddhist and Marxist cares deserve our exploration throughout the rest of this study. Indeed, though the cares are shaped so differently, the primary issues at stake in fact cluster at certain points. There are at least five points that especially deserve our attention.

First, both begin empirically with that which is given in experience. Most immediately this means they begin with the individual as a bodily, physical-mental unity. Second, both discern an identifiable wrong within existence as given to us. Third, each discloses a distinctive care that is grounded in a pathos that at the same time as it brings awareness of this wrong seeks to liberate from it. Fourth, both place great stress upon human agency, recognizing no external agency to which human agency is finally subject. At the same time, however, both do recognize other, subordinate determinations. Fifth, both posit a final and attainable reconciliation of self and world. These issues—corporeality, wrong, pathos, agency, reconciliation—will in one way or another preoccupy us throughout the succeeding pages.

E. Confucian Anthropology: The Slight Difference

Some three centuries before Christ, Mencius said, "that wherein humans differ from the birds and beasts is slight." As with all animals, observes Hsün-tzu, it is "the nature of humans that when they are hungry they will desire satisfaction, when they are cold they will desire warmth, and when they are weary they will desire rest." Unlike animals, however, humans have an innate capacity for social and moral behavior. This slight difference, this moral capacity, is the tiny doorway that opens out onto the vast vista of what human being in the world is all about.[59]

Three epistemologies

In the previous pages we have seen two very different ways of viewing human being in the world. The Confucian view differs substantially from both the Buddhist and Marxist. As with them, Confucius too begins with our ordinary experience in this world.

T'ang Chün-yi, a contemporary Confucian thinker, identifies three formal phases that fit what he takes to be a Confucian knowledge of the world. The first phase in his epistemology is a kind of pure awareness. This awareness simply grasps nature as a totality in its presented immediacy without reflection. In this prereflective phase, a self is simply not noticed[60] and therefore no selfish interest in a self or a world occurs. The world is intuited through "pure feeling," "pure emotive penetration."[61] The second phase arises from the continuing activity of human consciousness which begins to "open up" this totality and its contents, giving rise to the discrimination of self and world. However, it is not an amoral, merely intellectual subject/object discrimination that arises. It is much more like a sense of guest and host, and includes in it a sense of relationship and obligation. The world is therefore appropriated in a valuing way. Finally, in the third phase, the activity of selection takes place, which is grounded in the vital (i.e., biologically rooted) and spiritual interests of the person. These interests have been cultivated in the course of one's upbringing, and therefore influence this activity of selection.

T'ang correlates these three phases with the three fundamental Confucian values: the self-forgetting world-empathy of the first phase is formally the same as the value of *jen* (love); the valuing appropriation as guest-host is formally the same as the value of *li*[1] (propriety); and the vital-spiritual selective activities are formally the same as the value of *yi* (rightness).

Whether or not this analysis in the specific form given here represents traditional Confucian understandings is not so important. What it rightly puts forward is the Confucian refusal to separate intellectual perception from valuing perception. Moral valuing is integral to human knowing.

The young Gautama clearly began with the factual immediacy of actual life—the encounter with old age, sickness, and death. In his reflections he too agreed that ordinary knowing was never neutral but always evaluative, including within it an act of liking or disliking. This, of course, was a false knowledge, according to the Buddha. Required was a new kind of nonevaluative knowing.

This Buddhist epistemology diverges considerably from the Confucian account. In particular, where the Confucian account (represented by T'ang above) affirms a continuity of natural and moral (transcendent) knowing, the Buddhist account asserts a discontinuity between natural and transcendent knowledge, and therefore posits an epistemological dualism. This becomes the foundation stone for the Buddhist enlightenment or mystic quest.

Marx, too, takes serious account of commonsense knowledge, though in a way heavily influenced by European empiricism. Marx did not articulate a formal epistemology, but the implied epistemology can be described in the following way. The primary fact is the pregiven matter of the natural world. A secondary fact is consciousness or imagination, derived presumably from nature but which has the distinctive power to receive and manipulate sense impressions from the rest of the world about. These are always together dynamically, in human praxis. Human consciousness processes these impressions in terms of its own interests (most fundamentally economic ones) as ideas and concepts, which then become tools of the human mind, which in turn activates the body as the human actively appropriates nature by making something of it (houses, baskets) in terms of the prior human self-interests or needs. On the basis of this knowledge nature is progressively controlled and subordinated to the service of human interests.

The most obvious difference between this account and the Confucian is in the first step. In the Marxist account the knowledge that derives from sense experience is as such morally neutral. Human appropriation of sense knowledge necessarily unites it with human interest and in this secondary sense is therefore moral. Clearly, this tends towards a technical or instrumental morality, which subordinates morals to the interests of human need, and does not allow for the objective reality of values that are prior to, and give definition to, human interest. The reason for this difference is, of course, the materialist and empiricist assumptions of Marxist thought, assumptions that never rest easily with the teleological spectacles Marx also wears.

The Confucian lives differently between matter and mystery than does either the Buddhist or Marxist, as these divergent epistemologies suggest. How differently? We turn to the Confucian experience.

The rectification of names

The "slight difference" is the Confucian point of entry into what it is to be human. Indeed, the entire Confucian tradition is a prolonged exegesis of this distinction: we share body and feelings with animals, but not moral sentiments. The complete passage in Mencius reads as follows:

> Mencius said: That wherein the human person differs from birds and beasts is slight; ordinary folk disregard it, the person of virtue retains it. Shun was clear about things and understood human ways; he acted out of love and uprightness; he did not [merely] act them out.[62]

This is simply to say, as did all within the Confucian tradition, that at the nub of human existence is a social reality, and it is within this social-moral milieu that we find the starting place for discerning what it is to be rightly human.

Confucius, accordingly, also begins in the encounter with our ordinary world. As with Marx, he is not primarily troubled by finitude and frailty, sickness and death, but rather with a disrupted and disrupting sociopolitical order. Sharing with Marx this social milieu as his starting point, he nevertheless develops his critique on very different foundations and makes proposals that latter-day Marxists are often prone to deride.

The general situation at Confucius's time was one of political transition, a transition covering several centuries. Chinese society was in transition from the collapsing feudal-imperial order of the Chou (1122–249 B.C.E.) to the emerging bureaucratic-imperial order first put together by the Ch'in (221–207 B.C.E.) and Han (206 B.C.E.–220 C.E.). The centuries in between the Chou and the Ch'in are called the Spring-Autumn (722–481/480 B.C.E.) and Warring States (403–221 B.C.E.) periods.

From the unified patriarchal world of the Chou, there was a gradual political decay into numerous small principalities, which over a period of time contested for primacy, gradually eliminating and absorbing each other till only eight were left at the beginning of the Warring States. Confucius lived during the latter part of the Spring-Autumn period, as this whittling process was well on its way, as the so-called tyrants, or *pa,* came into political prominence.

For Confucius, "a world without order (*Tao*)" was due to the breakdown of the social institutions of his time. His critique sought to remedy this state of affairs and is encapsulated in the teaching on the "rectifying of names" (*cheng-ming*).[63] The locus classicus in the *Analects* reads as follows:

> Tzu-lu said: "The prince of Wei is awaiting you, Sir, to take control of his administration. What will you undertake first, Sir?" The Master replied: "The one thing needed is the rectification of names."[64]

While this is the only occurrence of the term in the *Analects,* the idea is assumed throughout, and given explicit formulation on occasion. Thus, for instance, when asked how best to govern, Confucius responded to the ruler of Ch'i: "Let the ruler be a ruler, the official an official, the father a father, and the child a child."[65]

A "name" or "term" is not an arbitrary label to designate something, but is a concept that clarifies, if it does not establish, a social relationship. A designation, e.g., "child," implies its counterpart, "father," and thus establishes an intrinsic sociomoral value. A "name," therefore, designates a social role or function, and a value appropriate to that function. To use the name without reference to the value reduces it to a mere tool which can be manipulated at will to one's own advantage. This would be to reduce morals to utility. Conversely, to possess the value without the name that designates a social function would reduce the value to a mere private, internal, intuitively known reality without a public character, transforming morals into mysticism, losing thereby a sociopolitical efficacy. In the above citation the critique was leveled against the former danger.

This concept functions as a critique, for Confucius uses it to show up the contemporary political and social scene for what it is—roles and values fail to correspond, while individual ambition and moral confusion are rife. Nevertheless, this concept is by no means the heart of Confucius's thought, for it serves principally as a formal criterion whereby to critique the present. But as such it does establish a necessary (not sufficient) condition[66] for a rightly ordered social world. The passage earlier cited goes on to indicate that if the social function or name (*ming*) does not bear its proper value (*cheng*), i.e., if the ruler does not truly prove to be a ruler, then one's words will prove inefficacious and ultimately the laws will be arbitrarily applied and the people will be at loose ends.[67] Rectification establishes the social framework, the *li*,[1] that makes social order possible. The sufficient condition, however, is the interior, personal dimension and is summed up in the integral value of *jen*, or love. This concept, more than any other, gives a distinctive and constructive character to Confucius's thought.

The stages of life

It was once asked of Confucius if he had achieved this integral value of *jen*. His response is revealing: "As to sagehood and *jen*, how dare I qualify? If it is to practice without tiring and teach without wearying, to that I can lay claim." The reaction of the disciples was, "This is just what we disciples cannot emulate."[68] In the final analysis social reformation could come about only through personal endeavor, and the Confucian challenge was a summons to lifelong learning and practice in moral accomplishment.

Indeed, in what might be termed the shortest moral autobiography in history, Confucius demonstrates how the commitment to moral learning shaped his entire life. I will utilize this minibiography to summarize Confucius's view of the human person:

> The Master said: At fifteen I was committed to learning, at thirty I was confirmed, at forty I was without any uncertainty, at fifty I comprehended the destiny of heaven, at sixty I understood all I heard with ease, at seventy I could follow my heart's desire without overstepping the bounds.
>
> (*Lun-yü* 2.4)

The most obvious—and superficial—way to take this passage is to simply see this as a comment upon the stages of life and one's own maturation along the way. Thus, 15 is the time at which a youth comes of age and begins serious studies; at age 30 one has a family and has become established within society; by 40 one is experienced and unflappable; one has made one's mark by 50, and by 60 has become thoroughly familiar with the ways of the world so that nothing takes one by surprise; finally, at 70 óne enjoys retirement to the full.

There are those who will interpret this passage in so prosaic a fashion, and it is hardly to be doubted that these correlations have their point.[69] Nonetheless, the concepts dealt with at each stage along the journey are fundamental to the Confucian quest for a satisfying human being in the world and are hardly to be tied to so rigid a chronology and limited to such trivial observations. Perhaps the final message of this passage is that the truly human life begins with the morally committed self, reaches out to embrace the whole human world and in so doing encounters the transcending boundaries of human existence (heaven) as well, so that this life of humanity that begins in great effort properly completes itself in the immeasurable ease that comes from a life congruent with heaven's ways.[70]

The life of humanity begins with a "commitment to learning." This phrase can be compared with several others that occur in the *Analects,* such as "commitment to the Way," "commitment to goodness," and the like. The boisterous energy of youth finds here its focus. There are two aspects to this: the objective aspect of learning, which involves culture and tradition, and the subjective side of willing. The two join, creating a unity.

Learning includes both the appropriation of tradition (history, music, poetry, archery, the rites—all would be disciplines) and the emulation of models. The ideal view of society assumed in this Confucian understanding of learning is well summed up by Munro:

> Three related elements are included in the early Confucian vision of the "social order". . . . The first element is a collection of occupational positions, every one having its own "job description." Second, there is a hierarchical relationship between these positions. Third, a formalized code of behavior, affecting the occupants of each place in the hierarchy, ties the whole together; the social virtues are realized by individuals who abide with this code.[71]

The act of rectifying names, referred to above, was an effort to define the outlines of this order. The "commitment to learning" of this first stage is, accordingly, the determination to realize the social virtues.[72]

The heart of these social virtues for Confucius is *jen*.[73] As such, this learning of *jen* begins close at hand, at home and not at school. "Filial respect and brotherly affection are the root of *jen*."[74] Family relationships are thus the nurse bed of this learning. Furthermore, the goal of this learning has its manifestation outside the home as well, most especially in the political arena. Many of Confucius's disciples ask about precisely this, and to each he gives a personal response. One such student was Tzu-kung. The response to his query shows what *jen* can achieve in the political sphere, but then are added words that perhaps better than any other disclose the meaning of *jen* as the interior goal towards which the commitment to learning strives, a goal which is no longer just interior.

> Tzu-kung said: "Suppose there were one who conferred benefits far and wide upon the people, and who was able to succor the multitude, what might one say of him? Could this be called *jen*?" "What has this to do with *jen*?" asked the Master. "Must he not be a Sage? Even [the sage Emperors] Yao and Shun felt their deficiency therein. For the man of *jen* is one who desiring to confirm himself confirms others, and desiring to develop himself develops others. To be able from one's own self to draw a parallel for the treatment of others: that may be called the way to practice *jen*." [75]

This passage introduces the concept of "confirm," which directs us to the second step, "at thirty I was confirmed." To be confirmed can mean many things, but nothing is more central than to be established in virtue. "The person of virtue is devoted to the root of things, and when the root is confirmed then the Way issues forth." [76] We have already see that this root is *jen*.

To be confirmed in *jen* involves both the self and the other, requiring a plunge that is deeper than the sphere of family relationships and a reach that is more embracing. The plunge is into one's own experience ("to be able from one's own self") and the reach is to all others ("to draw a parallel for the treatment of others").

This rule, the "golden rule," has a negative and positive formulation, both appearing repeatedly in Confucian texts. Negatively, *shu* or reciprocity (or altruism) is the maxim that one "do not do to others what you do not like done to yourself." [77] The importance this holds in the teaching of Confucius is clear, as this passage indicates:

> The Master said: "Shen! My teaching contains one all-pervading principle." "Yes," replied Tseng-tzu. When the Master had left the room the disciples asked: "What did he mean?" Tseng-tzu replied: "Our Mas-

ter's teaching is conscientiousness (*chung*) and altruism (*shu*), and nothing else."[78]

Positively, it appears in the *Analects (Lun-yü)* 6.28, already cited (p. 52).

Integral to this way of linking the self and the other is the idea that self-knowledge includes moral-knowing. Whence then this moral knowledge? Since the *Analects* simply assumes this as a basic human capacity, there is no effort to explain it further. Indeed, Confucius was wary of all explanations and speculative questions, not unlike the Buddha. A slight doorway to later speculation was, nevertheless, left ajar for, despite the fact that Tzu-kung is recorded as saying, "the Master has not been heard to speak about [human] nature and heaven's ways,"[79] there still remains one occurrence in the *Analects:* "The Master said: 'By nature people are close, by custom they are far apart.' "[80] This clearly implies that by nature all are more or less capable of the good whereas in practice there are the good and the evil. As soon, moreover, as the Confucian vision bumped up against other visions, the issue of human nature could not remain unaddressed, and with Mencius and Hsün-tzu the door was swung wide open.

The subsequent Confucian debate, even up to the present, dealt with two moments of human nature. "For both Mencius and Hsün-tzu, these constituted 'original' human nature: man as he is born; and its 'existential' state: man as he finds himself in society and culture."[81] A few words will help indicate the nature of this debate.

In actuality, the views of Mencius and Hsün-tzu, while not identical, were not all that far apart. Both grounded human morality in original human nature, though they grounded it somewhat differently. Mencius treated the issue more directly and simply while Hsün-tzu introduced a more complex psychology with the interrelations of *hsing* (nature), *ch'ing* (emotions) and *hsin* (mind).

According to Mencius, "all things are complete within us."[82] By this he means that our nature (*hsing*) is given by heaven and is the basis for all moral good. He distinguishes between the physical senses which we share with animals and are the lesser part (*hsiao-t'i*), and the mind-heart which is unique to the human, and performs a thinking or evaluating function. It is the greater part (*ta-t'i*).[83] Embedded within the mind-heart are also the beginnings or fonts of all virtue: the sense of commiseration which issues in *jen,* the sense of shame and dislike which issues in uprightness (*yi*), the sense of modesty and yielding which issues in propriety (*li*[1]), and the sense of right and wrong which issues in wisdom (*chih*).[84] These four beginnings, however, must be actively nurtured and developed lest they be stunted. This accounts for the fact that "by nature people are close, but by custom far apart." All possess these beginnings, but not all develop them.

At this point Mencius makes a distinction that seems to prepare the way for Hsün-tzu's emphasis upon *ch'ing.* He speaks of breath, or energy, or force (*ch'i*) which fills one's physical nature. Nature (*hsing*) is a compound made up of the words for life (which is its root meaning) and mind (or heart). Its original sense, therefore, incorporates the idea of vitality, and it is this vitality (*ch'i*) that fills our nature and gives it expressive powers. If one lives by the senses or gives this energy unrestrained sway, then evil will result, whereas if the evaluating function of the mind directs one's being so that the four beginnings of virtue find their development, then one cultivates goodness.

The thought of Hsün-tzu, even though one of his chapter headings is "nature is evil," is not far from this. The basic difference seems largely to be that Hsün-tzu gives greater play to the emotions (*ch'ing*) and depletes human nature of an innate tendency to good (the four fonts of Mencius). The natural tendency, therefore, is the chaotic tyranny of the emotions, which in themselves are not evil, but need to be controlled by the mind-heart. Mind-heart retains its evaluating function and ability to discern the good and guide towards it. That it can choose the good is not given so direct a metaphysical grounding, however. Thus:

> That which at birth is so, is called the nature. . . . The love, hate, joy, anger, sorrow and pleasure of this nature are called the emotions. When, the emotions being so, the mind-heart selects from among them, this is called cogitation. When the mind-heart cogitates and can act accordingly, this is called the acquired.[85]

When the process is complete the human forms a ternion with heaven and earth.[86]

To sum up, Mencius gives a more positive account of "original" nature by attributing to it innate tendencies toward the good while not discounting the potentially disrupting tendency of one's inner vitality; both give an encompassing and governing role to mind-heart which can indubitably lead to the good if permitted to function. This is to be genuinely confirmed in virtue.

"At forty I no longer harbored uncertainties." The term translated "uncertainty" is literally "not in doubt," "not in confusion." Elsewhere in the *Analects* we read that "wisdom is not in doubt,"[87] for it is a sureness of insight.

The first step involved a direction of life, a mindset. The second step gave a value depth to this direction of life, grounding one's life in the subjective moral awareness that is at the same time a social awareness. The third step describes the ability to triumph over circumstances and to use them constructively.

Uncertainty has a variety of manifestations. Intellectually, it can show itself as the failure to discriminate, to misjudge; the antidote is wisdom. It can show itself conatively as indecision when the occasion properly calls for action; the antidote is courage. It can show itself in the realm of emotion as a fickle mind; the antidote is *jen* (love). We read, for instance: "To like someone and therefore desire that one's existence, to hate someone and therefore desire that one's extermination, is to yield to uncertainty (*huo,* also "confusion").[88] As we also read: "The person of wisdom is not uncertain, the person of love is not anxious, the person of courage is not fearful."[89] All one's abilities are brought into play as one acts in all things surely and rightly. This leads directly to the fourth step, "the comprehension of heaven's mandate."

The fact that circumstances can lead to testing and uncertainty, as suggested in the third step, suggests that the ideal and real do not always coincide and may even require, in a not-yet-ideal world, risking one's own life. While there is an inherent optimism within the thought of Confucius, this optimism is not always warranted, especially if one regards circumstances and the common enough triumph of evil. The *Analects* does in fact recognize important limiting circumstances, and it is these that are finally overcome in this fourth step.

Actually, there are at least three kinds of limit situations that are acknowledged in the *Analects*. The one is of an organic kind—sickness, old age, and, above all, death. Confucius, while taking note of these limits, never deals with them directly. He may sigh when dread disease strikes, he may mourn bitterly when his favorite disciple dies at an untimely age, but when directly asked about death he brushes the question aside with the words, "Not yet knowing about life, why inquire about (after) death?"[90] Nevertheless, it was to become a distinguishing mark of the Confucian way that careful and elaborate attention was given to the mourning and ancestral rites without, however, delving into speculative issues.

A second limit is a moral one, reflected in the later Confucian discussions about the goodness or evil of human nature, as mentioned above. Confucius did not claim perfection either for himself or others. It was all too apparent that human achievement fell short of the goal. Even so, despite failure, for whatever the reason, Confucius still maintained the possibility of persons achieving perfection in virtue: "Is there anyone who can exert himself for one day in *jen?* I have never seen any without the ability. Perhaps there is such a one, but I have never seen such."[91] Failure only gave greater reason to urge self-reflection, correction, and renewed effort.

The third limit was a social and historical one. Confucius's own life was a testimony to this. Most of it was spent in seemingly fruitless peregrinations and exhortations before rulers uninterested in his theories. He became known as one "who knew he would fail, yet persisted."[92] "It is heaven that acknowledges me!"[93] he exclaimed in a moment of deep discouragement. Indeed, there were times when his own life was threatened, but this only confirmed his conviction that heaven's mandate lay upon him.[94]

Then, at 60 he achieved a thorough perspicacity—"I understood all I heard with ease." The world about is apprehended through the senses. Here the sense of hearing is specifically referred to, but can be considered to include seeing and the other senses as well. Chi'en Mu suggests that we are more directly involved personally through the sense of hearing, than, for example, of seeing, for in personal address we are called to response and action.[95] In this stage, however, the world of human desires, motives, and plans lies open and transparent before one. Nothing surprises, nothing daunts, and the experience of one's harmony with heaven becomes as well a harmony with earth.

With the world as an open book before one, the life of virtue reaches the final stage when one acts with a complete ease and effortlessness in the moral life—"I follow my heart's desire without overstepping the bounds." The subjective will of commitment and determination, so prominent at the beginning has now so gone beyond itself that one experiences a full, spontaneous, and free correspondence with the objective demand (measure) of a moral universe. The "happiness" that one experiences in the pursuit of learning now becomes a fulfilled joy.

The history of existential nature

This last step raises many questions for the reader concerning the meaning of ultimate fulfillment in human life. Later discussants in the Confucian tradition are to speak in more or less metaphysical terms of a union of the self with heaven and earth so as to form a single moral whole, or ternion.[96] To be sure, this goes far beyond Confucius who, as we have seen, kept his teaching within the mundane sphere of human experience; nevertheless, this claim, as well as many others put forward in the *Analects*, bristles with so many unanswered, indeed often unasked, ultimate questions that his later interpreters in making a case for his teaching to a sometimes quite skeptical world had to find convincing—and sometimes also metaphysical—ways to make his teaching intelligible, while remaining true to his purposes.

As earlier remarked, Julia Ching has observed that, for the Confucian, human existence is seen to consist of two moments, the moments of original nature and existential nature. Thus the *Analects,* as we have already seen, says that "by nature people are close together" (original nature) but "in practice are far apart" (existential nature). Original nature is common to all and enfolds within it the possibility of good. It is "that which at birth is so." The five stages of life discussed above all deal with existential nature, the cultivation of it, and the consequence in life of this cultivation.

For the Confucian tradition the question of existential nature and its right cultivation constitutes the entire human project. Nothing else really matters. In this cultivation process there are at least three moments in the passage from original to existential nature: the stirring up of the self by the world through the senses, the issuance of a response in the affections and the will, the completion of that response in action that leads to sagehood and world harmony or diabolicalness and chaos. We will deal in more detail with these later.

By and large, as this process of self and world cultivation was articulated by the Confucian, three interlocking traditions developed. Mou Tsung-san has characterized them in this way:[97] The one strand stressed moral nature as an objective cosmic reality in which human nature participates. This strand, which I shall term the "objective" tradition, predates Confucius, is transmitted by him (consider his concept of the mandate of heaven), and is represented most characteristically by the later *Chung-Yung* and *Yi-chuan* texts, achieving its richest development in the Ch'eng-Chu school of the Sung (12th century and following). The phrase "the Mandate of Heaven is Nature" sums up this strand.

Another strand is that which stresses moral nature as constituting human subjectivity itself, the human mind, and refuses to objectify this nature. This strand, which I shall term the "introvert," dynamist, or subjective strand, was given classic development in Mencius, flowered in the Lu-Wang school of the Sung and Ming, being dominant in the late Ming (16th century). The phrase of Wang Yang-ming that "Mind is Nature" sums up this tendency.

The third strand, also of ancient origin, is the materialist tendency that assumes a morally neutral material nature, without transcendent implication, and which perceives the moral as in effect a construction of conscious human activity. A representative phrase would be, "the functioning of one's vital energies is nature." Kao-tzu, Hsün-tzu, Wang Ch'ung, and Lin Shao develop this strand, which I shall term the "extrovert" or materialist strand. This tendency has an important influence upon the Ch'eng-Chu cosmology and reasserts itself in a more independent way with the materialist tendencies of the critical historical thinkers of the Ch'ing (1644–1911), passing through K'ang Yu-wei and others, and climaxing as it joins up with Western materialist thinkers in the May 4th (1919) renaissance.[98]

These three strands[99] did not develop independently throughout Chinese history, but rather continually intertwined, with one or another strand being dominant at any given moment or in any given thinker.

In the contemporary scene, there is a conscious effort by Marxist historians and philosophers to establish the materialist strand as the normative Confucian tradition, while outside of mainland China the second in particular, but the first strand as well, has been dominant among the philosophical pace-setters, Ch'ien Mu, T'ang Chün-yi, Mou Tsung-san, and Fang Tung-mei.

In a way these three traditions are not entirely inconsistent with each other but seem to fit somewhat like Chinese boxes, the one within the other. The extrovert emphasis upon strictly sociopolitical matters (the smallest box) is included as a particular expression of the introvert emphasis (the next larger box), in which all human construction is a product of mind. Both in turn are included as concerns in the objective, cosmological emphasis (the largest box), which grounds both matter and mind in an ontology of *ch'i* (breath, energy, active matter) and *li*[2] (reason).

F. Prelude Continued

The five issues identified in the discussion of Buddhist and Marxist views of human being in the world[100] are all present in this Confucian discussion as well. Confucius, too, begins with our matter-of-fact corporeal existence. This existence includes both the physical, shared with animals, and the mental-moral, which marks the slight difference. Similarly, it is the experience of a particular wrong within the world that becomes the starting point for the evolvement of the Confucian teaching. Furthermore, a definite pathos (in this case human empathy or *jen*) is involved, human agency is optimistically affirmed, and the final harmony, the ternion, of heaven, earth, and the human person, is envisioned.

One evident difference between the Marxist and Confucian views on the one side, and the Buddhist on the other, concerns their sense of the wrong within existence. For the Buddha the organic sphere, symbolized by sickness, old age, and death, is the sphere in which this wrong is initially experienced. For the other two it is the social sphere within which initial awareness of the wrong comes about. Wrong is equally encountered; the entree into the experience of it, however, differs enormously.

According to Mencius only a "slight difference" became the doorway to the whole meaning and value of human being in the world. We live as a self with a world between matter and mystery, poised betwixt nature and spirit. The Buddha, Marx, and Confucius all recognize this in one way or another. Human existence is in some sense an open-ended existence; there is a doorway to transcendence. This slight difference, the betweenness of our existence, introduces at least three irreducible ingredients or qualities of transcendence into our experience of a self with a world.

The Buddha, Confucius, and Marx all began with empirical life, with our corporeality. This is correct, for the first irreducible fact with which we have to do is the givenness of life. I am born with a world, and this not by choice but by birth. I thus unavoidably live, and with this gift of life is the awareness of the given itself as something prior to the experience of a self with a world. For the Buddhist *karma-samsara* and its subtle workings is one symbol for expressing this givenness; for the Confucian one such symbol is *t'ien-ming* (heaven's mandate); for the Marxist it is dialectics.

Givenness though there be, we still live in a betwixt and between. Though ever present, this quality of givenness that inheres in the self with a world is nevertheless supremely reticent.[101] Indeed, though given, it is beyond possession. It is beyond possession fully and irrevocably, beyond possession even for the barest moment. Not to be taken hold of, it cannot even be received. Unable to possess it, we might nonetheless choose to lose it—by taking one's own life, for instance. But that only proves the point—we can choose to lose, we cannot choose to gain. We are mortal, a speck of contingency in a world of contingent events. We have seen the Buddha exegete this fact for us quite persuasively.

Being both given and reticent, that which comes to us in this way is experienced as inexhaustibly compelling, as inexhaustibly eliciting respect: it is to be supremely desired, feared, obeyed, or trusted.

These three qualities of transcendence—givenness, reticence, evoking respect—would appear to be universal to human experience. They are inherent in this "slight difference," integral to our corporeal (physical-mental) existence, implicit in our experience of a self with a world.

However, as the second issue we have identified suggests, this only provides the background to another universal feature of human experience, the experience of some kind of irascible wrong within existence. It was precisely at this point, as we have seen, that Buddha, Confucius, and Marx felt it necessary to take account of life and set forth their prescriptions. To the degree that this twofold sensibility is present—the sense of wrong against the background of transcendence—to that degree we are justified in speaking of this experience as religious.

We have seen in the cases of Buddhism, Confucianism, and Marxism that each specifies a present human circumstance (the given world), a final consequence (the goal to which all the penultimate goals add up), and the action that mediates between the two (claims about how to proceed). In all, a sense of predicament becomes part of the description of present human circumstance precisely because of the discrepancy between the actual and the hoped for. In each of these cases the human is seen as the principal intervening subject that mediates the hoped-for passage from the present to a different circumstance.

Implicit in the human intervening will, however, as already indicated, is the question of transcendence. Our next task is to turn to this.

2

THE ELUSIVE PRESENCE

A. Three Religious Families

At least these three, the givenness[1] of reality, the mode of reticence with which it appears as given, and the respect this reality evinces from us, are openings to the experience of transcendence. Presumably these three are modes in which a common reality articulates itself in, upon, and through us, each mode including in itself the others as well. Nevertheless, one can argue that various religious traditions find their primary access to transcendence through one or the other of these modes. I shall argue for that in this chapter.

By and large the religious traditions that derive from a particular cultural matrix share certain striking family resemblances. Three matrices in particular—the Semitic, the Indic, and the Sinic (Chinese)—are foremost in our concerns here. To be sure, the Hellenic, the Iranic, the Japanic, and the multiple primal traditions also deserve treatment, were this to be a truly comprehensive study. Our principal concern here is with the three primary matrices.

The religious traditions that derive from these three cultural matrices share certain striking family resemblances. Judaism, Christianity, and Islam, for instance, show a particular interest in affirming something about God, even though they affirm God differently, and yield strikingly different religious communities. Hindu traditions and Buddhism focus upon the status of the self, affirming the truth about the self in characteristically different ways, while also yielding religious communities of very different kind. The Confucian and Taoist traditions, coming out of the Chinese matrix, show a particular interest in affirming something about the world. Again they do so differently, Taoism affirming the world through nature and Confucian tradition through society, and again the consequent communities they yield have vastly different commitments and norms.[2]

To affirm something about God also includes affirming something about self and world, and to affirm something about the world includes certain understandings with respect to God and self.[3] In the Semitic traditions, for instance, God is affirmed as one and as personal. Self is consequently perceived in the light of this prior affirmation, under such rubrics as covenant, faith, and submission; and the world under such rubrics as creation and history. As Abraham Heschel comments: "In the bible [and one could just as well add the Qur'an] the realness of God came first, and the task was how to live in a way compatible with His presence. Man's coexistence with God determines the course of history."[4] The Semitic traditions consciously differ from all religious traditions that would affirm God as many, or subordinate God to cosmos in some fashion.

It is similar when the prior affirmation concerns self. Buddhism, which argues the absolutely nonfinal reality of the individual self, is characteristically indifferent to the question of the reality of God and of the world, even while it must take these categories into account in some way. Hinduism, which affirms the irreducible reality of the self, either takes God seriously as the supreme instance of the self-reality, as in some theistic systems, or prefers to identify the individual self with an absolutely impersonal self-reality, as in certain nondual systems. The world receives its appropriate assessment in either case. We have already noted the Taoist penchant to view world in terms of nature, and the Confucian penchant to do so in terms of society.

We have so far looked briefly at three traditions, one coming from each family. Marx, of course, denied the experience of transcendence as a valid concern, but his atheism was asserted in terms compatible with the Semitic-Hellenic past from which it ultimately stemmed; this will become more apparent below.

There is, it seems, a certain degree of correlation between the three religious families (obviously they are not exhaustive of religion) and the three pointers to transcendence mentioned above: givenness, reticence, respect. The quote from Heschel already suggests that the dominance of the sense of God in the Semitic tradition cannot be divorced from a sense of a prior givenness. The importance of creation and revelation as positive doctrines in the Semitic traditions is further *prima facie* evidence of this.

The Indic traditions, in their preoccupation with the self and the question of its identity/nonidentity, were driven to the concern with transcendence by an overwhelming sense of finitude, transcience, temporality, becoming. Transcendence, which in this case is experienced in the inexhaustible reticence of final reality, is simply the yonder side of the hither sense of finitude.

The Sinic traditions, as distinct from the Semitic and Indic, are noted for their profound sense of the inviolability of the cosmos, whether in the experience of it as nature or society. The "respect" thus elicited did not necessarily lead to a sense of God—indeed, often it led in the opposite direction—for the obligation to conform to reality as it presented itself in nature and society was immanent within that presentation itself. More on these things later.

In this chapter we shall begin by giving attention to one representative from each of these families insofar as each shows itself open to one of these modalities of transcendence. In Islam, *tauhid* (unity) is a prime symbol of the mode of givenness; in Buddhism *sunyatta* (emptiness) is a prime symbol of the mode of reticence; and in the Confucian tradition *ming*[2] (mandate) is a prime symbol of the mode of respect. We shall look at these separately and together.

B. God as the Given: The Islamic Experience

"Externality is a necessary characteristic of claimed theistic reality."[5] The self-presentation of the divine, the reality of God as given to experience, is a fundamental intuition of all "prophetic" religions, and is surely the supreme intuition of the Islamic faith.

Signs

The givenness of the world, its sheer externality, is basic to this intuition. Theologically stated, it is the doctrine of creation. The world in its givenness is a revelation of the primordial givenness of God (Allah). This conviction is common to the Semitic religious family, "For whoever would draw near to God must believe that he exists and that he rewards those who seek him."[6]

In the Qur'an a term that indicates Allah's theophany is *ayat,* usually meaning "signs" or "tokens." These *ayat* serve as a "manifestation of the deity and as credential of the prophet."[7] Thus we read in Sura 45:

Surely in the heavens and earth there are signs
for the believers;
and in your creation,
and the crawling things He scatters abroad, there are signs
for a people having sure faith,
and in the alternation of night and day,
and the provision God sends down from heaven,
and therewith revives the earth after it is dead,
and the turning about of the winds, there are signs
for a people who understand.
Those are the signs of God that We recite to thee in truth.[8]

Natural phenomena are a sign of God's power and bounty, but so also is history, for God has repeatedly sent his prophets to the various nations (*ummah*) of the earth, most of whom have rejected the signs brought by the prophet and incurred judgment upon themselves.[9] The recitation of the messenger, confirmed by these events, is itself a sign and, indeed, the supreme sign: "Those are the signs of the Manifest Book. We have sent it down as an Arabic Koran; haply you will understand."[10] The recipients of the message, contrariwise, demanded miracles as signs:

We will not believe you until you cause a spring to erupt from the earth, or till you have a garden with palms and grapes in which you can make rivers flow, or till you cause heaven to collapse, as you claim, or bring us face to face with God and the angels, or till you own a house of gold, or ascend into heaven, nor will we believe your ascension until you send down to us a book that we can read.[11]

They were given nothing, however, except the external and all-too-ordinary signs of natural phenomena, of history, and of the recitation of the message by a mere mortal. The compelling force of these phenomena was in their simple, nonmiraculous presentation for all to see, experience, and hear. Even so, "If men and jinn banded together to produce the like of this Koran, they would never produce its like."[12]

Not unlike the Buddha, Confucius, and Marx, Muhammad too begins with the matter-of-fact world present to all. Unlike the Buddha, however, who was struck by the incongruity of an appearing yet evanescent world, Muhammad was impressed by the very fact of its givenness. The phenomena of nature, the history of a people, the word recited impressed upon him their actuality and proved to be signs of the prior (i.e., creating) and posterior (i.e., judging) actuality of God.

The Muslim sense of transcendence finds its truly overwhelming quality in the sense of divine unity (*tauhid*). Thus we read:

> Say: "He is God, One,
> God, the Everlasting Refuge,
> who has not begotten, and has not been begotten,
> and equal to Him is not any one."[13]

This sense of divine unity is, at the same time, experienced in a multifaceted way. God is experienced as both Creator and Judge, being equally absolute originator (*badi'*) and final disposer. "God is the Creator of everything,"[14] who "creates what He will"[15] by a command (*amr*), most simply stated as "Be!" (*kun*).[16] Having bestowed all things, God will also dispose all things in the end, for he is "the justest of judges."[17] God is also experienced as powerful and merciful. Both of these aspects express God's reality as Lord (*al-Rabb*) and human reality as servant (*abd*). The "inscrutable omnipotence of God" demands by right "the total and trusting committal of oneself . . . to this omnipotence." This "committal to God" (*islam*) is indeed the essence of Muslim religion (*din*) insofar as it is human response.

Divine unity comprises the whole truth. "To me it has been revealed that your God is One God," is reiterated without cessation throughout the Qur'an. This asservation is, in the first instance, a denial of the existence of other, competing deities, a rejection of polytheism, rather than a proclaiming of God's existence as such, a fact already taken for granted by Muhammad's fellow tribespeople.[18] In the second instance, the unity claimed is seen essentially as a unity of willing (as distinct from being). God is revealed as the singular will behind all willing. This unity of will therefore calls for a unity of obedience.

Integral to the theistic experience of transcendence is this element of externality: God is other, seemingly "Wholly Other,"[19] over against and acting upon the world and the self. The very awareness of transcendence as given within the experience of self and world includes within it the sense of its reticence—the modalities of givenness, reticence, and respect are not finally separable. The Qur'an "is the Book, wherein is no doubt, a guidance to the godfearing who believe in the Unseen."[20] Thus, the very God who reveals is not revealed. God is utterly unavailable to human scrutiny. Nevertheless, God does *reveal,* and this positive note of givenness is the crux of the matter.

Externality, however, is no mere externality. Indeed, as other, as object, it does not preclude but requires the concomitant subject that is aware—in this case directly aware. There are several symbols in the Qur'an that express the immediacy, in contrast to the remoteness, of the divine will: God is more intimate to the self than one's own jugular vein; God is a presence in every social grouping as the fourth of three or the sixth of five;[21] God is immanent amidst all reality as "the Light of the heavens and the earth," such that

> the likeness of His Light is as a niche
> wherein is a lamp
> (the lamp in a glass,
> the glass as it were a glittering star)
> kindled from a Blessed Tree,
> an olive that is neither of the East nor of the West
> whose oil well nigh would shine, even if no fire touched it;
> Light upon Light.[22]

Similarly, God's face is everywhere, for "whithersoever you turn, there is the Face of God."[23] Thus, immediacy and remoteness are correlative.

Similarly, externality is complemented by inwardness. Regarding the revelation we read:

> It has not been granted to a mortal (*basar*) that God speaks to him, unless through a revelation (*wahyan*), or from behind a veil, or by sending a messenger that he [i.e., the messenger] reveals, with His permission, what He wills.[24]

This suggests a hierarchy within the experience of revelation: "a direct, interior revelation heard as an internal word, the word externally heard from a Messenger, and an intermediate way."[25] Clearly, Muhammad's own experience of revelation was the first of these.

The call of a prophet

In the previous section we have briefly considered the circumstances (at least as preserved in tradition in the cases of the Buddha and Confucius) that preceded the respective insights and teachings. Admittedly, it is not easy to pin down motives that might account for a "revelation," and that certainly is not what we will attempt here.

Certain of the background circumstances of Muhammad's prophetic call are clear enough, though it is hardly possible to determine his own reaction to these. Two circumstances, nonetheless, seem particularly important, the religious and the socioeconomic. Important in the religious background was the polytheism of traditional Arab religion, the presence of so-called *hanif* who held a vague sense of a universal deity, and the existence of Jewish and Christian communities with whom Muhammad had been in contact. The diversity of beliefs was puzzling, and this was no doubt one of the concerns that preoccupied Muhammad during his periods of meditation upon Mount Hira in the environs of Mecca. As recorded by Ibn Ishaq: "The apostle [to be] would pray in seclusion on Hira' every year for a month to practise tahannuth as was the custom of Quraysh in heathen days. *Tahannuth* is religious devotion."[26] The fact that his early message was a clear rejection of polytheism with the assertion of the singular deity of Allah fits with this.

With this religious concern probably also went a social concern. The fact that during his month of meditation "the apostle [to be] would pray in seclusion and give food to the poor" suggests as much. Mecca at the time of Muhammad was going through a considerable material change.[27] Originally a temporary settlement for nomadic groups, it had recently become a major and permanent commercial center. Attendant with this shift from a pastoral, nomadic economy to a mercantile one were many social changes as well. The rules of tribal and clan solidarity no longer applied adequately to the new situation. A powerful group of merchants was arising who, among other things, would take advantage of the economically indigent, most notably widows and orphans. Muhammad, indeed, had direct experience of this, for he himself had been orphaned, though in his case he was cared for by uncles, and he married a woman who had been widowed, though in her case she was prosperous. In any case, tribal solidarity was yielding to the demands of the individual business interests of the merchants, and power became increasingly attached to wealth. Appropriately, care for the poor, the orphaned, the widow, and the needy is one of the most insistent moral themes in the Qur'an.[28] Since, furthermore, Mecca was the center of a principal Arab shrine, the quest for wealth and power would naturally link up with control and use of the shrine, in other words, with religious identities.

Circumstances, however, do not account for the overwhelming vision vouchsafed to Muhammad. His meditations were rudely shattered by a direct perception of the divine will. There are various accounts of this experience, or initial series of experiences. The Qur'an alludes to at least two[29] of these. In Ibn Ishaq's *Life of Muhammad,* the earliest comprehensive biography of the prophet, two incidents are recounted in connection with his initial calling. The incidents took place during one of his monthly vigils and were both visual and auditory. Ibn Ishaq writes:

When it was the night on which God honoured him with his mission and showed mercy on his servants thereby, Gabriel brought him the command of God. "He came to me," said the apostle of God, "while I was asleep, with a coverlet of brocade whereon was some writing, and said, 'Recite!' I said, 'What shall I recite?' He pressed me with it so tightly that I thought it was death; then he let me go and said, 'Recite!' I said, 'What shall I recite?' He pressed me with it again. . . [the command comes twice more and then] I said, 'What then shall I read?'—and this I said only to deliver myself from him, lest he should do the same to me again. He said:

'Recite in the name of the Lord who created, Who created man of blood coagulated. Recite! Thy Lord is the most beneficent, Who taught by the pen, Taught that which they knew not unto men.'

So I recited it, and he departed from me. And I awoke from my sleep, and it was as though these words were written on my heart."

The passage then goes on to relate how Muhammad feared he had become possessed, and accordingly headed for the mountaintop to hurl himself down. But midway:

I heard a voice from heaven saying, "O Muhammad! thou art the apostle of God and I am Gabriel." I raised my head towards heaven to see [who was speaking], and lo, Gabriel in the form of a man with feet astride the horizon, saying, "O Muhammad! thou art the apostle of God and I am Gabriel." I stood gazing at him,. . .moving neither forward nor backward; then I began to turn my face away from him, but, towards whatever region of the sky I looked, I saw him as before.

He was dissuaded thereby from self-destruction, but the experience was a shattering one. He bemoaned his demented state. He cowered in fear before his wife to seek her spiritual aid. "Perhaps you did see something," she comforted. "Yes, I did," he replied. She sought the counsel of her cousin Waraqa, "who had become a Christian and read the scriptures and learned from those that follow the Torah and the Gospel." When he heard of it "Waraqa cried, 'Holy! Holy! Verily . . . there hath come unto him the greatest. . . who came to Moses aforetime, and lo, he is the prophet of this people." With this assurance came also the warning that, "Thou wilt be called a liar, and they will use thee despitefully and cast thee out and fight against thee." These ministrations comforted him not a little, and gradually his confidence returned and he accepted his call.[30]

It was in some such disturbing, yet compelling, manner that Muhammad came to the direct knowledge of the divine unity, that "there is no God but God." And now that the "realness of God" was con-

71

firmed to Muhammad "the task was how to live in a way compatible with His presence." A mere mortal became the bearer of God's eternal word.

When we say that it is primarily through the mode of givenness that the Qur'anic sense of God is to be understood, two meanings of *givenness* should be distinguished. On the one hand is the bare fact, the primal experience of an already-given world and self, the experience that there is something, and not nothing. Givenness can also be understood in a cultural sense. Muhammad did not invent the idea of God on his own—the idea was given by the prior religious traditions, whether Arab polytheism, hanifism, or Judaism and Christianity. What the relation between these two (existential and cultural givenness) might be is surely a complex matter, but in and with the cultural expression is the root experience of the primally given. The witness to Allah is the complex confluence of the two.

C. Gratuitous God and Fortuitous Cosmos

In his study of Christian and Buddhist experience Arapura observes:

> Wherever the unity of God has been stoutly maintained, man's being was apprehended as something given, the result of a gratuitous act on the part of a God who is not only Wholly Other but the true conferrer of being in every instance.

Describing, then, the religious awareness that follows upon this apprehension, he continues:

> Here a sheer feeling of gratuitousness clearly dominated as the conviction had been formed that the world had come into being for no reason at all but merely by virtue of the free act of a Creator who had willed it.

This describes Semitic monotheism, but

> in polytheistic religious views, man's being is not thought of as gratuitous givenness but as fortuitous occurrence. Ontologically, the gods have the same status as men and they are all governed by the same transcendent

law of the cosmos. . .; the only difference is that insofar as the gods in their inner essence have an identity with the supreme law. . ., they hold superintendence over man's conduct as well as over the working of the universe.

The consequence of this "in Vedic and subsequent stages of Hindu religion" is that, though there may be "all manner of fervent gratitude for favours received" from the gods (or God), "the sense of ontological indebtedness to the gods for man's own being, repayable or otherwise, is conspicuously lacking."[31] Something of the same kind of experience of world, self, and gods as all a part of "fortuitous occurrence" characterized Greece. One Greek solution, if it can be called that, was in the idea of fate (*moira*)—all entities were equally subject to its designs.

Indian religion worked towards a different solution. Eventually this fortuitous character of world, self, and gods was characterized as the workings of *karma-samsara,* and the solution was a liberation from this endless cycle of fortuity. As Arapura puts it, "*samadhi,* ecstasy, became the generic means of returning fortuitous existence to Ultimate Reality."[32]

The characterization seems fitting. Yet, one might want to make some slight modifications, or at least clarifications. For one thing, polytheism also formed the background to the Semitic monotheisms. But this is a small matter. More important is some clarification of the term *gratuitous.* When Arapura writes that the Semitic monotheisms lived in the conviction that "the world had come into being for no reason at all but merely by virtue of the free act of a Creator who had willed it," we understand this to be what is meant "gratuitous act."

Much depends upon what is meant by *gratuitous* and *free. Gratuitous* can mean the granting of something without prior conditions or without reciprocity. It then points in the direction of the word *grace.* It can also mean that which appears for no reason at all other than arbitrary, inscrutable will. It then points in the direction of arbitrariness. World is not yet fortuitous occurrence, for it is grounded in an act of will, however opaque. For now, we wish to leave this ambiguity in the term, recognizing, however, that *gratuitous* does not necessarily mean arbitrary will.

This ambiguity conceals an important Muslim-Christian issue. For "one of the first and most important questions about the doctrine of creation is the question of the *contingentia mundi*."[33] It is the question whether world proceeds from divine nature or divine will; is it eternal with God or temporally finite? Is creation an arbitrary or a reliable act? Both Semitic interpretations are, however, in agreement in that both begin with the givenness of world as the primary constructive datum.

In the non-Semitic families it is different. In Buddhism, as in much of Hinduism, world and (empirical) self as fortuitous occurrence were perceived not as gift but as burden. The doorway to transcendence was entered from below, through the sense of fortuitousness, contingency, and finitude. Not that life was given, but that it was transient was the dominating constructive datum.

In Chapter 1 we have dealt with this matter in an introductory way. Since, moreover, this Indic sense of finitude is so closely bound up with the Hindu and Buddhist sense of wrong within existence, it may be better to postpone discussion of it to a later point in this section.

Does the above distinction help us toward the understanding of the typically Chinese experiences of transcendence, most notably in Taoism and Confucianism?

It might, if we slightly modify Arapura to allow for a somewhat more differentiated experience of transcendence. Both Semitic monotheism and Indic absolutism developed out of a polytheistic background. One would have to say the same thing for Sinic "cosmism," if we may use this term. Monotheism returns the world and self to the believer as gift; absolutism transmutes the world and self for the insightful from appearance to reality. In cosmism, world and self are authenticated as parts of the larger whole of which they are constituents.

If we can be somewhat schematic here, it would seem best to say that both the gratuitous and fortuitous find their place in the Chinese experience, but in significantly modified form. Taoism is closer to the fortuitous, but accepting it in a spirit of naturalism, whereas Confucianism is closer to the gratuitous, but accepting transcendence in an immanental, rather than in such a strongly eminental (cf. Islam), way. The continuity between the gods and the world was never so clearly broken as it was in monotheism or absolutism. Transcendence inheres in the world as it is, whether it be the natural or the social world, and the gods or Heaven, insofar as they are real, are simply signs of this inherence.

D. The Immanental Mandate

The place of both God and the gods is ambiguous in Confucian thought, to say the least.

Theistic indifference

Reference has already been made to the three main strands of Confucian tradition—the extrovert or materialist, the introvert or subjectivist, and the objective or substantialist. None of these is theist in orientation. The extrovert tradition is explicitly nontheist, while the other two are essentially indifferent to theism. To be sure, there was an ancient strand that was theistic, and one might well argue a theist strain in Confucius.[34] One would also have to keep in mind state-supported Confucianism which was explicitly theist in many ways,[35] as well as the almost universal theism amongst the Chinese populace; yet, in the reflective, normative traditions there was a studied indifference to the whole subject.

Even Confucius—however much one may wish to point out his belief, whether real or supposed, in a "personal" heaven—was still fundamentally indifferent to theism. Just as Buddha and Jesus had their silences, so did Confucius. He set aside all questions that bore on the issue of theism and the real or fictitious nature of the gods, and maintained a consistent agnostic and pragmatic stance: "Serve the spirits as if they are present."[36] The act was its own justification; the reality of the spirits, if they were so, added nothing essential. Similarly with Heaven, he was interested in its mandate, not its personality.

Though some of his followers took more explicit nontheist—and sometimes theist—stances, Confucianism, when true to its roots and the "as if" approach of Confucius, always remained open to theism without becoming theist. As Julia Ching correctly observes:

Even where the problem of God is concerned, the Confucian tradition has always kept a predilection for starting its reflections with man—with his understanding of the universe and of himself, in each of which he discovers something greater, that which also explains the oneness between self and the universe.[37]

When more absolutist trends developed, under the influence of Buddhism, it continued to be the burden of that interpretation adamantly to "remain related to all that is 'not absolute.' "[38]

T'ang Chün-yi represents one of several contemporary efforts to be faithful to this basic insight of the Confucian tradition. In his final work, *Life and the Realms of the Spirit*, he once again develops the theme. In the latter part of this work, after having dealt with Christian and Buddhist transcendence, he turns to the Confucian sense of transcendence, setting forth the basic idea that transcendence is most directly and basically experienced as moral immanence.

The polarity of givenness and finitude is clearly recognized, to be sure, but only as a more or less vague background. He says, "Human life as a birth into this world is at the outset a bare, naked life that issues as a rending of emptiness."[39] The birth of a natural life bears a double import at least: it discloses a basic goodness in reality in this flowing forth of life, and, in the setting of a limit, birth lays down the condition for spiritual transcendence in this mundane realm, the only realm of which we can speak. This is so, for the total ignorance of what might precede birth delimits human consciousness.

Without denying their functional, and even metaphysical value, T'ang wishes to keep a distance from all Christian and Buddhist notions of transcendence. The reason that the "Confucian teaching speaks of the flow of heavenly virtue but does not attend to divine revelation or mystical experience" is because the genius of the Confucian spirit is "to attend to what can be affirmed, and not to what can be negated," and thus it "speaks only of matters having to do with our present life and the world before us."[40] This is an irreducible Confucian insistence.

While T'ang does indeed recognize a transcendent source for our being born, he will not grant it any specificity, other than this:

Therefore, life thus surely has its transcending metaphysical source, and exists by virtue of the source's existing. However, inasmuch as it negates nothingness by rending emptiness, the existing that is therein accomplished is, still, individually possessed. This. . . possessing is a principle, a way. . . . The meaning of this principle and this way, moreover, is even more important than this source. . . . This metaphysical source is referred to by the Chinese Confucians as Heaven, and this principle as Heaven's principle, and this way as Heaven's way. The possessing in our life of this principle and this way is Nature; that is, heavenly nature which is also human nature.[41]

To say that "the meaning of this principle and this way. . . is even more important than this source" certainly challenges Semitic assumptions. The only heaven that is known is the heaven immanent within my own existence and nature.[42]

As T'ang then exegetes this existence and this human nature, the concept of *ming*[2] (mandate) becomes central. Thus:

Our life and the heaven which is its transcending, metaphysical source are mutually dependent and mutually exist while also relating as mutually separate and mutually distinct. Therefore, this margin between heaven and the human cannot be only conjunctly or only disjunctly expressed. In speaking of this, at once both a conjoint and a disjoint margin, the concept of *ming* (mandate) is set forth. As regards heaven it is the mandate of heaven, as regards the human it is the mandate of nature.[43]

He then goes on to argue that this nature, which is naturally given, is identical with the transcendent ought, *ming*[2]. It is in this sense that the statement of the *Chung-yung* that "the mandate of heaven is nature"[44] is to be understood.

In the succeeding pages T'ang then proceeds to show how the mandate, the ought of existence, is experienced both in the circumstances one encounters in life (to begin with this is the social milieu of the family) as well as in one's own innate, mental-physical constitution. Social and personal existence and the pregiven ontological structures are merely the hither and yonder poles of the same, continuous reality.

Knowledge-of-the-good

Perhaps the most celebrated, if not also the most dramatic, example of a quasi-mystical discernment of this *ming*[2] as immanent in life is the experience of the 16th-century Confucian philosopher and politician, Wang Yang-ming (1472–1529). He represents the subjectivizing strand of Confucian tradition, in contrast to the objectivizing strand as represented by Chu Hsi (1130–1200). The latter preferred to "discover the Absolute in the World," rather than as Wang to "find the Absolute in an experience of the Self."[45] In fact, as already seems evident in the discussion of T'ang, no clear distinction is made between self and world. They are both immanentally intertwined. Nonetheless, for Wang, mind (*hsin*, more properly, "mind and heart") became the locus for the experience of transcendence. As he says:

> The original substance of the mind is none other than the heavenly principle. It is originally never out of accord with what is proper. This is your true self. This true self is the master of [your] physical body. If there is no true self, there will be no body. With it, one lives; without it, one dies.[46]

Though the language here is obviously influenced by Buddhism, the basic understanding is not, for in contrast to Buddhism this mind is not emptiness but possesses definite content, moral content.

Etymologically, the word *mind* is derived from a flame symbol and refers to the psychic principle within that gives unity to one's whole person, both in its vital functioning as well as its conscious activity.[47] It is, therefore, everything that one is as an active, conscious individual, and is identified with one's essential nature.

Throughout much of his life Wang served the government in a variety of official capacities, both in civil and military affairs. As with not a few other officials during this particularly corrupt period of the Ming dynasty, he was in and out of imperial favor a number of times. Nonetheless, he distinguished himself in a variety of ways and soon became known for his scholarship and wisdom, and acquired a considerable following of disciples. Much of his teaching is preserved in records of his conversations kept by various disciples.

Traditionally, Wang's spiritual and intellectual pilgrimage is divided into three stages: his early discovery of his celebrated doctrine of the unity of knowledge and action, a transitional period of special emphasis upon quiet meditation, and the hard-won and climaxing insight, gained through the many trials and testings of his life, into the truth of the-extension-of-the-knowledge-of-the-good (see below).

The earnestness which accompanied him throughout his life is well revealed by the earliest failure and first insight. As a young man he took to heart the teaching of Chu Hsi that heavenly principle was contained within everything in the world. In his ardor and naivete he took the teaching about "the investigation of things," which presumably enabled one to perceive heavenly principle, all too literally, and, in his own words:

> In earlier years [at the age of 20] I discussed the question of becoming a sage with my friend Ch'ien, wondering how a person can have such tremendous energy to investigate all things under Heaven. So I pointed to the bamboos in front of the pavilion, and asked him to investigate these. Ch'ien spent three days trying to investigate thoroughly the meaning of bamboos, working hard day and night and using up his mental energy, until he fell ill. . . . So I myself proceeded to this investigation, working day and night without reaching the principle, until I also fell ill through mental exhaustion on the seventh day. So we lamented together that sagehood is unattainable.[48]

It was not until several years later, when he was about 37 (1508), that he really began to find his spiritual directions. It was at a low point in his career—by no means the last—when, because he had caused displeasure to the corrupt imperial eunuch Liu Chin, he had been exiled to a menial post among the "uncivilized" tribes of southwest China. This exile nonetheless gave him opportunity for meditation and reflection. Thinking back upon that earlier experience, mind and world, subject and object, knowing and doing had been separated. In a kind of enlightenment experience he broke through to an understanding of the principle of the unity of knowledge and action. In his biography we are told:

> Suddenly, in the middle of the night, the meaning of "extension of knowledge through the investigation of things" dawned upon him. Without knowing what he was doing, he called out, got up, and danced about, so that his servants all became alarmed. Now for the first time he realized that for the Truth (*Tao*) of the sages, one's own nature is self-sufficient,

and that it is wrong to seek for Principle (*li*[2]) outside of it in affairs and things.[49]

Finally, around 1521, this idea ripened into the doctrine of the "extention-of-the-knowledge-of-the-good" (*chih liang-chih*). It was a discovery "made through a hundred deaths and a thousand sufferings." It was a doctrine of the radical immanence of moral knowing, which knowing issues in a spontaneous doing of the good. In his own words:

> "Extension of knowledge" is not what later scholars understand as enriching and widening knowledge. It means simply extending my *liang-chih* to the utmost. This knowledge of the good is what Mencius meant when he said: "The [moral] sense of right and wrong is common to all men." This sense of right and wrong requires no deliberation to know, and does not depend on learning to function. This is why it is called liang-chih.[50]

Some years before this one of his best students, Hsü Ai, raised a typical issue: "There are people who know that the parents should be served with filial piety and elder brothers with respect, but cannot put these things into practice. This shows that knowing and acting are clearly two different things." Yang-ming's reply was: "The knowing and acting you refer to are already separated by selfish desires and are no longer knowing and acting in their original substance. There have never been people who know but do not act. Those who are supposed to know but do not act simply do not yet know."[51]

A Phasic Psychology

The distinction made here between "knowing and acting in their original substance" and knowing and acting as impregnated with "selfish desires" is to be understood in terms of the phasic psychology of neo-Confucian thought. All behavior issues forth in a phased process. The initial phase is that of quietude, prior to movement, in which all subsists in an original state of purity and equilibrium. The final phase is the taking of action itself, whether the action be mental or physical. The ideal goal is that of harmony, which is the state of unity, a state that follows upon action which inwardly conforms to the original nature. This original nature is characterized as being one of quietude, a kind of primordial equilibrium.

In between these two—equilibrium and harmony—several additional phases can be distinguished. There is first an encounter with the world; this generates a response within the individual that stirs quietude into movement, and leads then to the final phase. The critical point is this in-between moment of incipient movement. If the transition from quietude to movement is not smooth, and calculation, secondary reflection is allowed its place, selfish desires can creep in and misdirect this movement. As Wang tirelessly repeated, "an infinitesimal mistake in the beginning may lead to an infinite error at the end."[52] Wang's concept of *liang-chih* (the-knowing-of-the-good) was intended to bridge this gap and insure that the passage to and through incipience was an untroubled one. All that was needed was to allow this original goodness to find free expression.

Late in his life Wang enunciated the famous four axioms, which speak of this passage. It reads:

> In the original substance of the mind there is no distinction of good and evil. [This depicts the state of equilibrium before particular goods are contrasted with particular evils.]
>
> When the will becomes active, however, such distinction exists. [This will reflect the moment of incipience.]
>
> The faculty of innate knowledge [*liang-chih*] is to know good and evil. [This assures safe passage from quietude to movement.]
>
> The investigation of things is to do good and remove evil. [This is that movement itself.][53]

The central content of this "knowing-of-the-good" is, of course, *jen,* which is the moral unity of all things. Showing the rootedness of his basic ideas in Mencius, he says:

> When he [that is, any human individual] sees a child about to fall into a well, he cannot help having a feeling of alarm and commiseration. This shows that his humanity (*jen*) forms one body with the child. It may be objected that the child belongs to the same species [as he]. Yet when he observes the pitiful cries and frightened appearance of birds and beasts [about to be slaughtered], he cannot help feeling an "inability

to bear" their suffering. This shows that his humanity forms one body with birds and beasts. It may be objected that birds and beasts are sentient beings too. But when he sees plants broken and destroyed, he cannot help having a feeling of pity. This shows that his humanity forms one body with plants. It may be said that plants are living things too. Yet even when he sees tiles and stones shattered and crushed he cannot help having a feeling of regret. This shows that his humanity forms one body with tiles and stones. This means that even the heart of the [morally] small man must have [in potentiality this humanity which unites him to all things].[54]

In a paean of praise to this innate human capacity for the knowing-of-the-good (*liang-chih*), Wang says in language borrowed from both Buddhism and Taoism:

The vacuity of *liang-chih* is [one with] the vacuity of the Great Void (*T'ai-hsu*). The nothingness (*wu*) of *liang-chih* is the formlessness of the Great Void. Sun, moon, wind, thunder, mountains, rivers, people, and things—all that have figure, shape, form, and color—all operate within this formlessness of the Great Void. None of them ever becomes a hindrance to Heaven. The sage merely follows the functioning of his *liang-chih*. Heaven, Earth, and the myriad things are all contained in its functioning and operating. How can there be anything else transcending *liang-chih* which can become a hindrance [to it]?[55]

As Julia Ching observes, "To him, the extension of *liang-chih* eventually came to represent the continual discovery, within one's entire being, of that which is greater than oneself—the absolute."[56] This subjectivist strand of Confucian experience, for all its borrowings, remains distinctly Confucian in its emphasis upon the primacy of the moral sense and a social constitution of reality.

E. The Causal Gateway

The region of finitude, in contrast to the realm of creation or the moral sense, as the doorway to the human experience of transcendence has probably been most powerfully put forward in and through the Buddhist testimony. The Buddhist experience appeals today, for it takes finitude so radically, and seems to fit so well with the receding of a homocentric world in this post-Copernican age, without at the same time becoming reductionist. The heart of the Buddhist thesis is that in breaking attachment to self and world, all things are revealed in their true reality.

We have already briefly discussed the three marks of all existents—impermanence, unsatisfactoriness, and nonsubstantiality. These three marks point to different spheres of experience: impermanence is a temporal category, nonsubstantiality is a spatial category, and unsatisfactoriness is an axiological category. We have already indicated how it is that existence is judged as unsatisfactory because the individual wrongly takes existents to be permanent and substantial. The Buddha urges a true view of reality as the ultimate solution.

The kernel of the whole Buddhist doctrine, that with which it rises or falls, that which exegetes the ultimate nature of existents as impermanent and nonsubstantial, is its teaching on causality. We should explore some facets of that here.

We have already cited the basic causal formula of Buddhism:

> When this is, that is;
> this arising, that arises;
> when this is not, that is not;
> this ceasing, that ceases.[57]

This formula is not an attempt at a logical analysis of causality in the Aristotelian sense, a concern with efficient, formal, and final causes, for instance. It is, rather, an empirical statement of causality, not unlike that of Hume.

We recall that the Buddha set out upon his quest because of the daunting encounter with old age, sickness, and death, the three most obvious and distressing cases of impermanence within human life. This did not lead him to posit, as was the case in the Upanishads of Hinduism, a permanent selfhood or soul that was beyond the flux of becoming, and which subsisted in the eternal bliss of self-identity. Neither did it lead him to nihilism, and like the Indian materialists annihilate the very concept of selfhood. Much has been made of the Buddha's silences when asked to expatiate on the matter of the eternalism or annihilation of the self and other related issues. When he did speak, his assertions were always couched in the language of causality which affirmed the radical conditioning of all things and the attainment of the nonconditioned state of Nirvana.

The effort to state the case clearly has led to a great variety of formulas and metaphysical speculation throughout Buddhist history. It is not quite true, as Whitehead's famous dictum would have it, that Christianity "has always been a religion seeking a metaphysic, in contrast to Buddhism which is a metaphysic generating a religion."[58] In fact, throughout its history the penetrating insight of the Buddha into conditioning has led to a continual search for an adequate metaphysic.[59]

The causal chain

Without getting into these elaborate discussions, it may be well to identify two understandings of the Buddhist insight into conditioning[60] —or, to put it in different words, its radical affirmation of causality— that seem to best represent this insight and yet do not become explicitly metaphysical. We may term these the empiricist and absolutist understandings.

Murti agrees that causality is the central tenet of Buddhism. Citing the *Salistamba Sutra,* "Whosoever sees the Pratityasamutpada [dependent origination, i.e., causality] sees the Buddha, and whosoever sees the Buddha sees the Dharma (Truth or Reality)," and Nagarjuna, "One who perceives truly the Pratityasamutpada realises the four sacred truths—pain, (its) cause, cessation and the path," he then observes that "Buddhism has always been a Dharma-theory based on the Pratityasamutpada, and every Buddhist system has claimed to be the Middle Path."[61] All Buddhist systems are then simply different ways in which the "original vision" of the Buddha has been systematically formulated.[62]

What was the original vision? The Madhyamika (Middle Way) of Nagarjuna that Murti interprets represents it in absolutist terms. Kalupahana represents the empiricist approach. The concluding words of his study on causality read:

Rejecting an Absolute (such as the Brahman or Atman of the Upanishads) or a transempirical reality, the Buddha confined himself to what is empirically given. Following a method comparable to that adopted by the modern Logical Positivists, he sometimes resorted to linguistic analysis and appeal to experience to demonstrate the futility of metaphysics. As a result of his empiricism he recognized causality as the reality and made it the essence of his teachings. Hence his statement: "He who sees causality sees the *dhamma*."[63]

It is indeed correct to maintain the empirical cast of the Buddha's statements. However, the data available to the Buddha "empirically" was considerably richer than that available to today's empiricists, for the whole range of psychic phenomena and intuitions disclosed in yogic meditation were also allowed. Thus one could "empirically" speak of innumerable worlds and remote past events in this cosmic whirlpool.[64]

Be that as it may, the traditional account of the Buddha's enlightenment is couched in terms of the endlessly repeated 12-fold causal chain, the *pratityasamutpada*. This formula of dependent origination reads:

> On ignorance depend dispositions;
> on dispositions depends consciousness;
> on consciousness depends the psychophysical personality;
> on the psychophysical personality depend the six sense organs;
> on the six sense organs depends contact;
> on contact depends feeling;
> on feeling depends craving;
> on craving depends grasping;
> on grasping depends becoming;
> on becoming depends birth;
> on birth depend aging and death.
> In this manner there arises this mass of suffering.[65]

The presupposition of this elaborate chain of reasoning is the (to the Buddha) indisputable fact that existence is suffering. Without going into elaborate detail a few essentials might be identified with regard to this chain.

The general movement is from ignorance into becoming. The fact that "ignorance" occurs first in the chain does not necessarily mean that ignorance is a kind of absolute beginning to the whole thing. Foucher takes ignorance (*avidya*) to mean simply the inability to know (empirical evidence provides no data), while Kalupahana takes it in an axiological sense as to know in a wrong way. The latter is no doubt intended, and does not exclude the former. However, this not knowing is just as much consequence as cause. Re-becoming simply brings it about once more, and so again becoming, and thus endlessly. Just as becoming permeates the whole chain, so also does ignorance. Nonetheless, there is a definite temporal order, for this chain of reasoning has been empirically derived.

"Consciousness" mediates the passage from metaphysical ignorance to existential personhood or psychophysical personality. "Dispositions" refers to the preconscious conditions antecedent to consciousness. Here, apparently, consciousness (*vijnana*), which is also one of the five aggregates that make up the composite "psychophysical" (*nama-rupa,* see above) personality, is given a somewhat privileged role in agency. The traditional Buddhist accounts of rebirth, in fact, posit three conditions: coitus, female fertility (the periods), and the *gandhabba* (*hsiang yin*). The first provides the physical characteristics, the latter, which is identified with consciousness, the psychic characteristics. Thus consciousness serves both as a psychological concept as one of the aggregates, and also as an eschatological concept as the factor that bears continuity between lives.[66]

Once the psychophysical personality is in place the description turns to its functioning. A critical transition point is the passage from "feeling" to "craving." Another text which describes this functioning somewhat more fully makes clear that this is a transition from an impersonal process to a personal one involving volition. This passage reads:

> Depending on eye . . . and visible form arises visual consciousness; meeting together of the three is contact (*phassa*); because of contact arises feeling or sensation (*vedana*); what one feels, one perceives (*sanjanati*); what one perceives, one reflects on (*vitakketi*); what one reflects on, one is obsessed with (*papanceti*); what one is obsessed with, due to that, concepts characterized by such obsessed perceptions (*papancasannasankha*) assail him with regard to visible form cognizable by the eye, belonging to the past, the future, and the present.[67]

At the point of craving, then, ego-consciousness has clearly intruded.

In an effort to stress the circularity of this causal chain, these 12 steps have often been correlated with the 3 times of past life (1–2), present life (3–9), and future life (10–12). This use simply points out more directly the essentially temporal character of the experience of conditioning to which this schema bears testimony.

During his night of meditation the Buddha-to-be reflected upon this formula, both in its forward order of production (birth gives rise to aging) and its reverse order of cessation (when there is no birth, aging ceases). The two-directional meditation agrees with the basic causal formula that with "this arising, that arises" and when "that ceases, this ceases." If this causal formula discloses the heart of reality as impermanent, conditioned, it also itself stands forth as a constant, verifiable, and permanent truth. One need only examine one's own existence to ascertain this.

This peering into the radical conditioning of existence leads to a breakthrough of sorts, for by insight one unravels this whole web of necessity. As a corollary, one with such an insight develops a "revulsion for (*nibbindati*) the physical form (*rupa*), feeling or sensation (*vedana*), perception (*sanna*), dispositions (*sankhara*) and consciousness (*vinnana*). Having revulsion, he is not attached (*nibbindam virajjati*); being non-attached, he is freed." Thereby, "destroyed is birth; lived is the higher life; done is what ought to be done; and there is no future existence."[68]

According to Kalupahana this is the end of the matter. Nirvana is the state of detachment the enlightened one has attained: "Hence nirvana comes to be characterized as the end of suffering. . . and a state of perfect happiness." In other words, nirvana is the description of a state to be experienced in the causal nexus when that nexus is perceived for what it is. The Buddha was silent when metaphysical questions were posed, because further speech was unwarranted (no empirical data to go on). The Buddha did not say there was nothing more, but neither did he say there was anything more. Nirvana climaxes meditation upon the causally conditioned character of reality. It is indeed a psychological reality. Beyond this nothing more, either by way of limitation (nothing but) or expansion (more than), can or ought to be said. "The idea that nirvana represents a transcendental reality beyond any

87

form of conceptualization or logical thinking"[69] has only produced confusion. Nirvana cannot be spoken of further, not because it is inherently inexpressible (beyond conceptualization), but because it is unwarranted (beyond empirical verification).

Beyond metaphysics

Buddhist tradition has, nonetheless, said more, much more. Metaphysical theories abound. Among the earliest were those who accepted the fact that a self was merely a fiction, a name applied to the aggregates, but then granted substance to the aggregates or prior elements. This radical spatial or elemental pluralism was matched by an equally radical pluralism of moments. Stcherbatsky states this view eloquently:

> The elements of existence are momentary appearances, momentary flashings into the phenomenal world out of an unknown source. Just as they are disconnected, so to say, in breadth, not being linked together by any pervading substance, just so they are disconnected in depth or in duration, since they last only one single moment (*ksana*). They disappear as soon as they appear, in order to be followed in the next moment by another momentary existence. Thus a moment becomes a synonym of an element (*dharma*), two moments are two different elements. An element becomes something like a point in time-space. The Sarvastivadin school makes an attempt mathematically to determine the duration of a moment. It, nevertheless, admittedly represents the smallest particle of time imaginable. Such computations of the size of the atom and the duration of the moment are evidently mere attempts to seize the infinitesimal. The idea that two moments make two different elements remains. Consequently, the elements do not change, but disappear, the world becomes a cinema. Disappearance is the very essence of existence; what does not disappear does not exist. A cause for the Buddhist was not a real cause but a preceding moment, which likewise arose out of nothing in order to disappear into nothing.[70]

This effort "to seize the infinitesimal" was only one of several attempts to make a metaphysical assault upon the Absolute (or the silence of the Buddha). The efforts persisted, and still do, to give some basis for continuity (such as the *pudgala* person theories) or to dissolve all in discontinuity (as above). Preeminent amongst the efforts to articulate the meaning of the Buddha's silence without offering an explicit meta-physic, whether substantialist or pluralist, was the absolutist *prajna* school and its main defender, Nagarjuna of Madhyamika fame.

The emphasis in our discussion of causality above has been upon the temporal aspect. Because things are caused, they are impermanent (*anicca*), and therefore there lacks a substantial self (*anatman*). However, it is also evident that the 12-fold chain can be interpreted in nontemporal or spatial terms. Because existents are dependent upon other existents, and these upon yet others, and so on ad infinitum, therefore empirical reality is in essence a web of relativity, and therefore devoid (*sunya,* empty) of any own-being. Murti states the position clearly:

> In the *Prajnaparamita* and the subsidiary Canonical (Sutra) literature of the Madhyamika, the one basic idea that is reiterated *ad nauseum* is that there is no change, no origination, no cessation, no coming in or going out; the real is neither one, nor many; neither atman, nor anatman; it is as it is always. Origination, decay etc. are imagined by the uninformed; they are speculations indulged in by the ignorant. The real is utterly devoid (Sunya) of these and other conceptual constructions; it is transcendent to thought and can be realized only in non-dual knowledge— Prajna or Intuition, which is the Absolute itself. . . . The Absolute in one sense transcends phenomena as it is devoid of empiricality, and in a vital sense is immanent or identical with it as their reality. . . . Pratitya-Samutpada is *not the temporal sequence* of entities but their *essential dependence.*[71]

The upshot of this thorough relativity is the identification of the empirical with the absolute, or what Murti refers to as the "phenomenalisation of the absolute."[72] If there is a difference, and there is, it is a purely subjective or epistemological one: either one knows only the empirical and is ignorant of its true reality, granting substance to that which is devoid of such, or one knows the absolute as the empirical, the empirical as the absolute, and, possessed of this insight (*prajna*), self and world are experienced in their own true nature as the absolute.

This wisdom (*prajna*) would seem to be quite consistent with the famous Udana utterances of the Buddha, one of which reads:

> Monks, there is a not-born, not-become, not-made, not-compounded.

Monks, if that not-born, not-become, not-made, not-compounded were not, no escape from the born, become, made, compounded would be known here. But, monks, since there is a not-born, not-become, not-made, not-compounded, therefore an escape from the born, become, made, compounded is known.[73]

The Buddha's experience of reality as radically reticent to give itself into our possession ultimately overwhelms thought. Nagarjuna's was a determined effort to keep thought at bay. The thought that seeks a metaphysic is no longer so overwhelmed.

F. The Marxist Denial

In the passage from the actual world to the hoped-for world the principal intervening will is the human will—we are the subjects.

Or are we? The three traditions we have looked at come up with three different ways of viewing the human as subject. For the Muslim, God stands before, behind, and above the human subject; human subjectivity is realized in *islam,* human committal to God-as-Subject. For the Confucian, the human subject is intrinsically moral, and human subjectivity is realized in heeding the mandate (*t'ing ming*) and in according with the immanent moral order, letting this immanence penetrate one's own subjectivity. For the Buddhist the human subject is finally no subject, but an instance of the subjectivity of totality itself. Each in its own way seems to be saying something about a transcendent quality that inheres in human being in the world and constitutes our true subjectivity.

The Marxist is not impressed.

The human subject is the only subject that can be human, and therefore it must be said that *"for man the supreme being is man."*[74] It is not God, it is not the immanent moral order, it is not reality in its transcendence, but the concrete human subject—individual and corporate—that alone is the subject. Anything else demeans and debases the human.

Religion (that is, whatever posits a transhuman referent), therefore, is without any content it might call its own—its content is simply and plainly a human content. As he writes to Ruge in 1842: "Religion, in

itself without content, lives not from heaven but from earth."[75] Therefore, the stuff of religion is nothing other than the stuff of human
earthly experience; religion possesses only a parisitic life.

If this is granted, what then is this human content that goes by the
name of religion? The rationalist answer would be that it is the stirrings
of the prerational mind in its effort to cope with the world about.
Reason, which has the power to bring all areas of life gradually under
its sway, will replace this unreason, this ignorance of the primitive
mind. Thus, according to Engels who repeats this position, "religion
arose in very primitive times from erroneous. . . conceptions. . . about
. . . nature."[76]

This theme of natural ignorance as the basis for religion—though
so prominent in later Marxist-Leninist rationalizations—was not that
prominent a consideration for Marx. "Marx," Gardavsky comments,
"was aware that there are religious ideas abroad which are both child-
ishly naive and obscurely fanciful. But he was opposed to the arrogance
of the enlightenment."[77] Is the content of religion, then, human feeling,
as Feuerbach might suggest?

Feuerbach's humanist thesis, as we have already seen, transforms
Hegel's unearthly subject (Spirit, Idea) into the earthly subject (the
human person) and makes religion entirely the predicate of the human.
What is the content of this predicate? The human essence is the love
relationship. In love the ego gives itself over to the other as its object,
and thus in the love relationship the role of subject and object is mutually reversed, so that I become your object, with you as subject, and
you become my object with me as subject. Thus we realize the fulfillment of our species-identity. God is the ethereal image of our unfulfilled humanity. We do not find full human love, and therefore project
our quest onto a fictional deity, who is really only the externalization
of our own individual essence. The more we make this fictionalized
God a subject, and become objects of this fiction, the farther removed
we are from experiencing truly human relationships.[78] "Thus Christ,"
he writes, "as the consciousness of love, is the consciousness of the
species. . . . [But] when there arises the consciousness of the species
as a species, the idea of humanity as a whole, Christ disappears, without, however, his true nature disappearing; for he was the substitute
for the consciousness of the species, the image under which it was

made present to the people."[79] On this reading, all theology is nothing more nor less than a category mistake.

As much as Marx accepts this description, it is still for him an inadequate treatment of the content of religion—it is too abstract; it does not reach deeply enough into concrete human life.

For Marx, religion reflects an inverted social, not merely psychological, reality. As he sought to demonstrate throughout his life, this earthly existence as it now is, is a dehumanized existence of a debased humanity. Because the world of our economic and social relations is without decency, therefore a decent counterreality is sought. But, should the indecency of the world be overcome, the need for a counterreality will disappear. Thus, he continues to Ruge, as for religion: "with the dissolution of the reverse reality whose *theory* it is, it will collapse in itself."[80]

Religion, therefore, expresses the suffering of our inverted world: "*Religious* suffering is at one and the same time the *expression* of real suffering and a protest against real suffering. Religion is the sigh of the oppressed creature, the heart of a heartless world and the soul of soulless conditions. It is the *opium* of the people."[81]

Religion, therefore, is entirely without its own content, and when the conditions of suffering and cruelty which give rise to it cease, then religion itself will pass away.

This argument raises a number of questions. With what is religion here to be compared, and why? Is it a purely escapist device such that it "ranks with other types of escapism, so that the fanatic, the prostitute, the alcoholic are all its illegitimate brothers and sisters"? Lenin surely thinks so, for "religion is a sort of spiritual booze."[82] Or is the most appropriate comparison with the state, whose content, as we have seen, is also society and which too shall wither away after the disappearance of class? Or, again, is it not the case that art and literature are just as surely also without their own content? Why is it that after the revolution they shall have a full flowering but religion shall die a natural death? It is not at all clear why art and literature are granted this relative autonomy but religion is not. Indeed, even the withering of the state will not take place without some residue, for something that takes over the function of law, polity, and philosophy will continue on or, as Althusser says, there will be "a shift of their functions to neighbouring forms."[83] Why is religion alone of all the ideological forms to find no postrevolutionary counterpart? Perhaps Lobkowicz is correct that it is, after all, not the social explanation that accounts for Marx's belief in this disappearance but rather the hidden assumption—explicit in Engels and Lenin—that religion is simply erroneous.[84]

Nevertheless, it is no trivial fact to give religion this social content. Illusory solution that it may well be, it is yet the case that religion is an effort to transcend the present circumstance. It articulates the longings of the oppressed by its construction of an otherworldly perfect order—and thereby serves to pacify; but it also constructs a vision of better things that may even stir to protest—and thereby serves to motivate. If this double possibility is taken seriously, then how religion functions in any given situation is not preordained. Marx's disgust with Prussian Christianity clearly shows up religion in the former light; Kautsky's account of religion in the Roman Empire is closer to the latter. "The only societies," he writes, "that maintained themselves under the Empire were religious ones, but it would be taking a mistaken view of them to let the religious form. . . obscure the social content underlying all these associations which gave them their strength: the desire for a solution to the hopeless existing conditions, for higher forms of society, for close co-operation and mutual support on the part of individuals lost in their isolation who drew new joy and courage from their coming together for high purposes."[85] Nonetheless, one wonders if this account still takes the social and human content of religion with sufficient seriousness.

It may just be that the human content of religion ought to be probed much further than Marx was inclined to do. We have already noted his great silence with regard to the question of individual and social mortality. On what grounds, furthermore, is the human quest for a right social and truly human order to be based? What is the primal motivation? Why is there hope, rather than indifference or despair? In what way might atheism provide this fuller human content?

Gardavsky has explored this question, and we might benefit by hearing his words. "For the Marxist," he states, "atheism is of its very nature the sole dimension of his thinking, of all his questions and answers. In this sense, one could see this type of atheism as the *first philosophy* in the Aristotelian sense, as Marxist metaphysics."[86]

The territory covered by this "atheology," as we shall term it—an atheist Marxist metaphysic that does not make the category mistake that theology does—is succinctly summarized:

> Mankind evolves by transcending itself, and by transforming the limits set for it by nature into historical limits, thanks to man's many-sided practical activity. This means that metaphysics represents the reflective aspect, or alternatively the theoretical aspect, of practical behaviour. This statement may well give an indication of the subject-matter with which metaphysics is concerned. It deliberates on the problem of the type of subjective identity which transcends itself, and yet at the same time is constantly threatened with being changed back into something dead, with being swallowed up once again by insatiable nature, and thus losing its meaning for mankind. Yet at the same time it is also menaced by another danger: that of being so afraid of ending up like this that it will withdraw into its own exclusiveness and gamble away all its opportunities.[87]

This seems to say that a Marxist atheology is concerned with interpreting *(a)* the already-given subject that affirms itself by going beyond itself, *(b)* which in the end is to be extinguished and knows this, and *(c)* which yet has its reasons for persisting in this process of continual affirmation. These three points deserve our further attention.

Atheology is concerned with "the type of subjective identity" that affirms itself by transcending itself. This identity is both a personal and a social one. The individual ego is a subject because it constitutes the focal point in which all other relationships cohere and are given shape. But society too has a subjective identity (though no ego as such) which is constituted by the continual flow of its many distinct egos. Society's identity is like "an everlasting fire in which new flames are constantly blazing up to replace the old ones which have burnt themselves out." Each individual is experienced as "gift" to the other, just as society is experienced as gift to the individual and the individual as gift to society. Neither is dispensable, not least the individual, for "the *irreplaceability* of the individual is virtually the precondition of society, and may not be done away with."[88] In the long run, the relation of individual to society and society to individual is as cause to effect in perpetual succession.

The subject affirms and transcends itself in practical activity. "The practical, active subjective identity," writes Gardavsky, "divides up the cosmos by stepping out of its own narrow framework, discovering new continents, climbing up to the heights, and digging down to the depths. It hoists its flags on the mountain-tops and deposits its emblems on the celestial bodies. The scope of its power expands from day to day, and it feels that everything is attainable. It is merely a question of the means of doing so. It surveys the space it has conquered and experiences the delightful sensation of victory: power, greatness, glory."[89] To be sure, there are natural limits—and we shall hear more about that—but the historical project itself of the human subject is to transform "the limits set for it by nature into historical limits."[90] The goal of this endeavor is not technological but human, the achieving of "a community offering a life worthy of man," a goal going by the name *communism*.[91] By practical activity nature is made to serve human purposes and goals, and thereby is made over into history.

But there are limits. The final inevitable limit is our mortality—certainly individual, perhaps also social. It is because of mortality that the self must transcend the self in order to confirm itself in the face of predestined death. "I die—i.e., I will not complete my work, I will no longer see those I have loved, I will no longer experience beauty or sorrow. The unrepeatable music of this world will no longer find an echo in my senses; I will never again transcend myself, in any direction." Thus my "innermost heart ceases to be the point of inter-section where things come together."[92] Nevertheless, "society will sur-vive," and "live, evolve and become more humane." Therefore he writes: "Because I am mortal, I am . . . social."[93]

Our mortality leads to another feature of our transcendence: the present takes its meaning from the future. "The thought of the future, of socialism, represents for the Marxist the structural principle under-lying this conscious creative act."[94] But how secure is this future? It is no absolute, guaranteed future, but only an open possibility whose achievement always remains uncertain. But it is work towards this future that gives meaning to the present in the sense that "the value of the present, as an end in itself, lies in what we make of it."[95] It is precisely in the midst of this uncertainty, which nevertheless offers this possibility, that one takes up one's human responsibility and be-comes thereby truly human. "I do not have. . . hope. So I see all my

relationships with transparent clarity. . . . Each of my relationships
. . . has a unique value in my eyes. . . . Every encounter. . . is . . .
a gift, for it may be my last . . . . And I too am a gift for anyone,
provided that I have something to offer."[96]

Thus, the givenness and reticence of reality are thoroughly and clearly articulated. But what of that third category, the inexhaustible invitation to respect?

Or, putting the question into Gardavsky's words, "What is the driv-
ing force which moves man inwardly to take the tragedy of his own
defeat consciously upon himself, for the sake of a communal hope for
mankind?" "What were the deep-seated inner motives which inspired
a man to enter the Communist Party in difficult times?"[97] Not merely
"rational awareness," nor "the study of the inherent laws underlying. . . history," nor "scientific deliberation," but something more
basic yet, namely, "love."[98]

Love? Yes. But it is not the love of myth, as in Christianity (see p.
117), nor is it the compassion of a Buddha, nor the deification of
feeling, as in Feuerbach, nor an innate "moral law within us" of the
Confucian, nor yet the undifferentiated love of some utopia. Rather,
it is "the imperative Existential precondition of all human relationships." "I understand love," Gardavsky continues, "as one element
in the make-up of the subjective identity, whenever it decides to perform an act of immediate interest and endeavours to give this decision
the optimum human form. This can consist equally well of pronouncing
the death sentence over somebody else, or of sacrificing one's own
life; everything which lies between these two extremes will do."[99] This
love is "bottomless." "It is unfathomable in that the man who resolves
to perform an action for the good of society can never say that he got
to the bottom of it."[100] This love is the principle that underlies all
human creation; "it suspends the causality of nature" and therefore
makes the human act a truly free and autonomous act, giving us culture
and history. Because of this human faith, "we do not believe in God,
although it is absurd."[101]

In this account, atheology has confirmed the threefold structure of
human transcendence—givenness, reticence, respect—to which we
have already referred. The Marxist, too, acknowledges our complex
existence between matter and mystery.

We return, then, to our earlier question. Has the content of religion as nothing other than the content of human experience been adequately described?

Within the Semitic traditions, religion, it would seem, contains a double referent: a referent to the human reality and a referent to the reality of God. This latter referent is, for Marx, spurious. If one must choose, then Marx's choice would (given biblical—or at least New Testament—assumptions) undoubtedly be the right one, for that is the choice God presumably made. But is the choice itself a spurious one? In the account of Gardavsky it is clear the human does live between matter and mystery. It is so precisely because "the Marxist theory of subjective identity and transcendence is materialistic and dialectic."[102] It is materialistic, for human thought is grounded in the concrete struggles of material and social life (givenness). It is dialectic, for it is a continual process of affirmation—negation (reticence), amidst which operates the "imperative Existential precondition," the "bottomless" activity of "love" (respect).

May it not be that these three windows to transcendence— givenness, reticence, respect—are just that, windows? It is as if the Marxist acknowledges the presence of these existential windows, but then draws thick curtains over them. Only one referent is possible. The monolatry of the human is the only truth—and one idolatry is substituted for another. What if these windows were left open? What if existence is not a closed room? What if God, or Nirvana, or Mandate are not simply "projective constructions" but rather "structures of discovery?"[103] Is it not precisely a double referent that best resists a double idolatry?

"Atheism," Gardavsky says, "represents an attempt to formulate a theory of subjective identity which would not be subjectivist, a theory of transcendence. . . which would not be objective."[104] A direct subjectivist correlation of human desire with God would be one form of idolatry—it would be hard to deny that Semitic faiths have not sometimes in their practice been guilty of this. A direct objective identification of concrete socialism with absolute goal would constitute the other—it would be hard to deny that Marxist states have not sometimes in their practice been guilty of this. But why must it be the case that human existence is open in only one direction (towards the uncertain future), and not to both the eternal "from" of God as source and the eternal "whither" of God as possibility, to speak in a Semitic sort of way? Then monolatry of both kinds becomes truly a questionable act, and human reality receives a larger affirmation.

G. A Summing Up

Transcendence is clearly elusive; yet, at the same time, it is insistently present within human experience. Even in the determined Marxist effort to deny transcendence, its footprints seem to show a kind of eternal "Bigfoot" presence. Matter does not yield its mystery up to scrutiny; our scrutiny seems to deepen the mystery.

We have attempted to demonstrate in the above discussion that *(a)* the awareness of transcendence is complex, or multimodal, *(b)* the three religious families come to the awareness of transcendence each in a characteristic way, and *(c)* there is a fundamental coherence at least to the degree that the awareness of givenness, reticence, and respect are always present in one form or another whenever there is the experience of transcendence. We can therefore assume a certain degree of coherence or complementarity among the divergent religious convictions.

Nonetheless, a more fundamental issue remains to be examined. The awareness of transcendence is one thing; how the transcendent reality is seen to relate to the mundane world is quite another. Here there is profound difference not only between the families, but within the families themselves. The question as to how reality in its transcendent quality relates to reality in its mundane character is most fundamentally posed by suffering. To this we turn.

3

THE SUFFERING PRESENCE

A. Kinds of Pathos

One might wonder, given these three modes of access to the experience of transcendence, whether in fact it is the same reality being experienced? Is this reality itself multivalent, and appropriately experienced in this plural way, or is the pluralism the sure sign of a merely fragmentary, and therefore faulty, knowledge?

Whatever the answer to this question, it is evident that the Muslim, the Buddhist, and the Confucian are concerned to articulate the essential unity of human experience. The quest for transcendence is at bottom a quest for unity, for coherence. Whether in fact these articulations cohere with each other is one matter, the matter of adequacy; that they each in their own ways strive to identify the subsisting factor—that than which nothing greater can be imagined—that unifies the entire range of human experience is another. Without this factor life fails to cohere.

Contrasting the Indic (particularly Buddhist) and Semitic apprehensions of transcendence, T'ang Chün-yi suggests that the former seeks a horizontal integration while the latter seeks a vertical:

> In general, the manner whereby monotheistic religions lead humanity to a realm that transcends subjectivity and objectivity is to go by way of ascent from the sublunar realm of subject-object opposition to the divine

realm that unifies subject and object. This is based upon the spirit's self-transcending (activity), which accomplishes a vertical integration from the lower to the higher. Attaining a confidence in the existence of God, one advances in understanding through faith in God, contemplation, prayer and the like. Buddhist thought, however, by destroying the various obstructive clingings of our spirit in the subject-object world, enlarges thereby the capacity of the spirit, and achieving the horizontal integration of the dharma-realm with all (particular) dharmas enables the progressive enlargement of the spirit. Thereupon, from above to below, it penetrates into the core of all sentient beings of the world of [particulars, dharma] and, because of the sufferings which stem from the clingings, joins them in a common feeling of sympathy which gives rise to a mind of compassion; furthermore, by wisdom it shows that the clingings at the core of sentient beings are in their original nature empty, and by this wisdom roots out this suffering and accomplishes the salvation of sentient beings. This is definitely different from the spiritual aspirations of the world's monotheistic religions, and its teachings are likewise distinctly different.[1]

A number of things are of interest in this statement—though we need not agree with the particular ascent/descent formulation that appears. First, transcendence is represented as just this attainment of the unification of reality; second, and of more interest, is the role of pathos in achieving this unification. Here T'ang speaks only of Buddhist pathos, though he is quite well aware of Christian and Confucian pathos as well. Pathos, in all its forms, is also at root a thrust towards unity. Pathos, moreover, is an active experience which does not accept the status quo but recognizes, rather, the transformative possibility of present circumstance—it is a structure of mediation between the mundane and transcendent. Third, as such, pathos, or what Scheler termed the *ordo amoris,* is the key to the way one's values are ordered. Finally, T'ang identifies two interrelated aspects in the structure of pathos, one which is characterized by "sufferings," the other by "compassion." If these things are in fact so, then we have not dealt adequately with transcendence until we have dealt with the question of the pathos structures of the different religious Ways.

We earlier suggested that a twofold sensibility is integral to what we refer to as religious experience: "the sense of wrong against the background of transcendence." These two sensibilities seem integral to each other. But this is not sufficient for defining religion. Neither transcendence, which is a background, nor a sense of wrong, which is a feature of the concrete foreground, constitute or provide the content for "religion." This honor goes to the third feature, pathos, which not only argues for the possibility of change, but fills in the content of that change. We should now add a third criterion for a definition of religion—the sense of transformative possibility.[2] In the play of the sense of wrong against the background of transcendence a quality of pathos is disclosed as integral to present human experience, disclosing both the pain of existence as well as the possibility of transformation. Religious experience includes all three, and it is in this sense we use the term *religious*.

This pathos, T'ang indicates, has a twofold character, one aspect of which is characterized by "obstructive clingings" or "sufferings," the other by "compassion." In a similar vein, Murti identifies two pathos structures in the "phenomenalising activity" of the absolute, as represented in Madhyamika thinking: "one through ignorance, through avidya and its satellites, the klesas; and the other . . . the free conscious assumption of phenomenal forms activitated by prajna and karuna. The former is the unconscious activity of the ignorant (prthasjana), and the latter is that of the Enlightened Buddhas and Bodhisattvas."[3] The first of these, the *klesas*[4] and the "mass of suffering" that accompanies them, we shall term *predicamental pathos;* the second kind, the liberating *karuna* (compassion) we designate *reconciling pathos*.

A not entirely dissimilar pathos structure is present in the Semitic and Sinic traditions as well. While for the Confucian, the sense of wrong is not anywhere near so prominent as in Buddhism, that sense is still there, perhaps most profoundly in what Metzger has described as "elusive immanence" (*Escape from Predicament*, p. 111). Reconciling pathos is present in the Confucian tradition in its distinctive sense of humanity (*jen*). In the Semitic theisms, predicamental pathos is clearly present in the story of the primal Fall and the host of teachings that derive therefrom. For Islam reconciling pathos is most adequately designated as mercy (*al-Rahman*), in Christianity as *agapē*.

Confucian *jen* (humanity) is that empathy which begins from the human sphere but embraces, as we saw in Wang Yang-ming's description of it, all spheres of the known cosmos—organic and inorganic.

Its etymology is a character that combines the words for "human person" and "two." It is, thus, a unitive empathy. Mercy is the most common Quranic ascription of God. God is "the Merciful." Revelation itself is an act of mercy. It bespeaks an attentiveness of the divine towards the human. This mercy becomes a part, then, of the human response to the divine. While the analogy fails at important points, mercy is a personal term, one that identifies the quality of a relation.

Mercy, compassion, and humanity are all forms of empathy, though they are rooted differently in reality. Mercy is given in revelation; humanity is immanently and naturally given; compassion is given transcendently through intuitive insight. In the latter case, wisdom discerns the disorder of the apparently orderly, and in an all-embracing act of good will is moved to seek the release from suffering of all sentient beings.

As we consider the differing pathos structures, it is well to keep in mind the integral character of each of the intuitions of transcendence we have referred to. The trifold sensibility (transcendence/wrong/pathos) is an integral one. But the modes in which transcendence itself is experienced (givenness, reticence, value modality) are also integral to each other, even though transcendence is mainly apprehended through one or the other mode. This complex interrelatedness must constantly be kept in mind.

If, for instance, the always creatively given (and God therefore being that which is always creatively giving) is the dominant element of the experience of a self-with-a-world, then the ensuing conviction acknowledges this creative givenness in some way, perhaps by striving to share as fully as possible in that creative activity. If this givenness is predominantly experienced as reticence, then the ensuing conviction will acknowledge that reticence, perhaps by acknowledging the utter finitude of the empirical self. If that encountered in a self-with-a-world presents itself primarily as an immanent sense of inexhaustible value, the ensuing conviction will grant the respect due in some specific way, perhaps, as in Confucianism, in a seriousness of life, respect being translated most immediately into filial piety. Pathos has its proper place in these interactions between intuition (of transcendence) and conviction (about the way to be that is appropriate to it).

B. The Axiological Frameworks

The experience of transcendence yields a specific form of conviction and an appropriate mode of behavior. Thus it is that the Muslim submits, the Buddhist meditates, and the Confucian acts with due respect. The structures of pathos inform and shape conviction and action.

However, the frameworks—and we shall term these the axiological frameworks, that is, the frameworks within which values are ordered—are different in each case. To take the three principal traditions we have been dealing with, the Sinic, Indic, and Semitic, the axiological frameworks can be characterized as follows.

The Confucian framework is one of replication. One might wish to argue the same for Taoism. But, to limit our discussion for now to Confucianism, one might envision two distinct planes, the ontological and existential. As Julia Ching suggested, Confucianism differentiates original nature and existential nature. Or, to put it in terms of neo-Confucian phasic consciousness, there is the state of equilibrium which belongs to prior heaven, and the effort towards harmony of posterior heaven. By replication we mean that, in the Confucian tradition, the effort is always to replicate in actual life the ideal state that precedes life. This precedence might be simply ontological (prior heaven or original nature), or it might be historical (the ideal past of the sages). To be sure, the conditions of the present or existential state are different from the past or the original state. There is no mere imitation. Confucius would consider one who attempted such to be a moral bumpkin. The concern is a dynamic one of replication on a different plane—whether temporal or spatial—and fitting to the context.

For instance, Confucius was once queried about the nature of change thus: "Can one anticipate ten generations hence?"

> The master replied: The Yi dynasty was inheritor of the rites of the Hsia; there were modifications [losses and gains] which one can still discern through investigation. The Chou was inheritor of the rites of the Yin; there were modifications which also can be discerned through investigation. In the future there will arise one that will be successor to the Chou; even though it be a hundred generations hence we yet ought to be able to have an anticipatory discernment.[5]

The basic idea here is that there is the unchanging amidst the changing. While historical conditions do change, the moral content does not; nevertheless, the articulation of that content is appropriate to the context. Each age replicates the same fundamental content, but under changing circumstances. It is in this sense that the past functions in an exemplary way. The Taoist response to nature (rather than to social mores) may, as we shall later see, be thought of in a not dissimilar way. The model may be depicted as two parallel circles in separate planes thus:

DIAGRAM 1

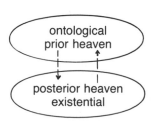

The equilibrium of the ontological mode is to be expressed as harmony in the existential mode. Each individual and each age is equally distant and equally near to the ontologically prior and historically exemplary.

The Indic framework, represented here by Buddhism, is one of return. This may be depicted in the form of a closed loop, indicating three phases. There is the Absolute Reality which logically, if not temporally, precedes phenomenal reality. Phenomenal reality is represented by the loop. The loop itself is entirely bound up in ignorance; it is the realm of delusion, of *samsara*. In enlightenment, however, one escapes the loop and returns to Absolute Reality.[6]

In Buddhism the passage into nirvana is indicated in the technical term *parinirvana, pari* here meaning round, complete.[7] Similarly, the commonly used, but also technical, term for becoming a Buddhist is the "triple returning" (*saranagamana, san-kvi*), returning by committal to the Buddha, the Dharma, and the Samgha.[8] These serve well to symbolize the model indicated here. It might be noted that an important difference between the Confucian and Buddhist models is the

DIAGRAM 2

enlightenment

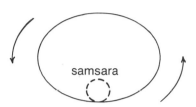

threefold structure of the Buddhist, in contrast to the twofold structure of the Confucian. A distinct concept of "fall" and "redemption" is not present in the Confucian model.

The Semitic framework can perhaps be termed one of representation. An appropriate diagram might be an irregular line that has both a beginning and a terminus. The wandering line indicates the historical adventure, or misadventure, of humanity through the vissitudes of mundane existence, but this passage is under the guidance and enabling of God, who is both beginning and end.

DIAGRAM 3

The term *representation* is well indicated by the Quranic designation of humanity as God's vice-gerent (*khalifa*). This is humanity's essential destiny. At the same time, in Islam this destiny is fulfilled by the degree to which the individual and society exercise this destiny in the "servant" (*abd*), not "master," mode, for, while we are indeed designated as God's vicegerent, we are at the same time under God's exclusive lordship. Christian and Jewish considerations are differently put, but the fundamental destiny of being God's representative amidst God's creation remains, and to that end humanity is made in God's "image." Distinct from both the Confucian and Buddhist models is the presence of a definite teleology of a temporal, historical kind in the Semitic traditions.

The nature of predicamental pathos in each case is accordingly different. In Buddhism the loop clearly indicates a fall from essence into existence. The return is back to "essence." Attachment, or ignorance (which is to say the same thing in different words) characterizes the fall of existence, and nonattachment, ontological freedom characterizes the return. In Confucianism the error is manifested as a disjunction or miscorrelation between the two planes. There is, so to say, a field of tension between the two planes, and as one moves from the ontological to the existential plane, mishaps might occur. The mishap is an error either of excess (*kuo*) or of insufficiency (*pu chi*). To use Wang Yang-ming's happy phrase once again, "an infinitesimal mistake in the beginning may lead to an infinite error at the end." If things are allowed to go that far, then the disjunction is nearly complete. Be that as it may, there is no "fall" when movement occurs from one plane to the next. There is tension, nonetheless, and the continual need for exertion and effort. Confucius's attainment of freedom in the final stage of his biography indicates the close correlation between planes.

In Islam, there is a doctrine of fall that closely corresponds to the Genesis account of the fall in the Bible. This fall, however, is no more than a proneness to misguidance. To use mythological language, it is the devil, Iblis, that is the ultimate agent behind this misguidance. It is evident, however, as also the centrality of the notion of *islam* (submission) indicates, that this proneness is at least in part due to a weakness, if not a flaw, in the sphere of human will. It is in Judaism, and much more in Christianity, that a stronger doctrine of fall occurs. This fall, however, is never a fall from essence into existence, nor is it essentially a reflex of the tension between two planes, but always a fall within existence, regardless of how catastrophic the consequence might be drawn. It is also a fall in the sphere of will, of personal relation, of historical action, and for Judaism and Christianity in particular the fallen one is implicated in guilty responsibility. There is a struggle of wills throughout the historical meanderings, a meandering marked off by creation and judgment.

C. Predicamental Pathos

The nature of wrong

There is good reason for us to begin with the Confucian perspective. It would be hard to find a clearer, more direct expression of the intermediacy of human being in the world than we find here. It is a truism of the Confucian worldview to speak of the human world in the same breath with heaven and earth. The human world is intermediary between the two, and the ideal is for the human world to form a ternion with that of heaven and earth. But the Confucian sense of intermediacy is by no means only external; it is also internal, as we shall see.

In *Fallible Man,* Paul Ricoeur has argued that the whole question of human fallibility and suffering is to be seen in the context of human existence as one of intermediacy. This intermediacy is the experience of existing between the infinite and finite, as Ricoeur puts it:

> If man is a mean between being and nothingness, it is *primarily* because he brings about *"mediations"* in things; his intermediate place is *primarily* his function as mediator of the infinite and the finite in things.[9]

Being of both heaven and earth we experience a kind of "unstable ontological constitution."[10] Ricoeur speaks of this as a "disproportion" in our existence. This intermediacy is not, however, to be viewed as something external. He finds the term *between* misleading since it suggests a locality, a static insertion between two other realities. The Confucian heaven-humanity-earth would also on the surface seem to suggest this. Rather, Ricoeur argues, the human individual "is intermediate within himself, within his *selves*."

This interior intermediacy is precisely the neo-Confucian concern, and in at least this sense represents an important advance over earlier Confucian thought. We have already spoken of their concept of "phasic consciousness." Even though it be the case that the concept of wrong does not have so high a profile within Confucian considerations as it does within Buddhist and Christian, it is perhaps also the case that the intermediacy of human being in the world receives no clearer (not necessarily fuller) expression than it does within the Confucian tradition.

Wrong as fragility

It is often said that the Confucian tradition has little sense of human fault, being thoroughly optimistic in its view of human nature. This is in fact far from the case. From the time of the Chou to the late imperial age the Confucian was in search of a remedy for human moral ills. Nor was the early Confucian philosopher Hsün-tzu entirely uncharacteristic when he entitled one section of his major writing with the words "human nature as evil."[11]

At the same time, the Confucian tradition never gave up the inward confidence that the doing of good was humanly possible, that human nature was ultimately malleable, and that instruction could promote the good and eradicate the evil.[12] All that was needed was the effort to do good—and it could be done.

It was precisely this confidence in the infinite possibility for doing good of human nature which, in the face of the continual failure to realize this possibility, led to the deep predicamental pathos that one finds within this tradition—we recall Wang Yang-ming. "The Confucian belief that the individual can and should summon a godlike flow of moral power within himself," Metzger writes, "was paradoxically combined with a fearful realization that he would be unable to do so, trapped in a fundamental predicament."[13] In a word, the Confucian was caught in the disjunction between possibility and probability, between infinite appreciation of moral value and finite fumbling in making it actual.

We have already broached these themes in our earlier discussion of the Confucian tradition. As there indicated, Confucius was not unaware of the problem of discrepancy between possibility and probability: he himself was a wandering teacher, never fully accepted anywhere; he denied that he himself had attained the perfection of *jen;* while ever affirming the possibility,[14] he could never point to a living example. One gets the impression that for Confucius the possibility of achieving the good, because it was just a handbreadth away, beckoned the individual onward, despite the almost universal evidence—evidence of which he was fully aware—suggesting that the probability was in the other direction.

Mencius and Hsün-tzu, as we have already seen, developed some-what differing traditions on the matter of evil and the human possibility of good. While neither denied the possibility, the emphasis was mark-edly different. Put simply, Mencius stressed the possibility[15] while Hsün-tzu stressed the probability. For Hsün-tzu the chaotic power of the emotions (not in itself evil) tipped the scales in the direction of probable failure unless constrained from without by teaching and ritual. As Julia Ching comments:

> In describing human nature as good, Mencius was looking at it from its "substance" or source, as principle of its activity. In describing it as evil, Hsün-tzu was speaking mostly of abuses occurring in its activity. Mencius was anxious that efforts be made to keep nature-in-itself clear and manifest. Hsün-tzu desired that measures be taken to correct the abuses of its activity.[16]

It is much later in the development of the Confucian tradition that the problem of this disjunction received considerably more attention without, however, arriving at a clear solution. Julia Ching speaks of the "definitive acceptance" of what she terms "the new Confucian *credo*" by all neo-Confucian philosophers from Chu Hsi (12th century) to Wang Yang-ming (16th century). This "cryptic formula" was taken directly from the Book of Documents (*shu-ching*), considered to be one of the most ancient of the Chinese classics. Containing only 16 Chinese characters, it reads:

> The human mind (*jen-hsin*) is prone to error, [While] the mind of the Way (*Tao-hsin*) is subtle. Remain discerning and single-minded: Keep steadfastly to the Mean [or Equilibrium] (*chung*).[17]

This "duality between the fallibility of the human mind-and-heart, and the subtlety and evasiveness of the 'Way' "[18] provided the basic as-sumption from which all neo-Confucian moral reflection proceeded. As such, these lines present the "core" of the "orthodox transmission" (*tao-t'ung*).

As discussed earlier, two moments in human nature were differen-tiated, namely, original nature ("the mind of the Way") and existential nature ("the human mind"). Because of the former, "by nature people are close together," but because of the latter they "in practice are far apart." [19] It was the gap or fissure between these two, the metaphysical and the experiential, the ontological and the historical, and the problem of their linkage that now became the focal point of the quest for sagehood and the problem that had to be solved in an effort to change the world. How might the possibility of our original nature become a probable, if not a certain, actuality in life?

The classic division that developed during this period (13th–16th centuries) between the Ch'eng-Chu/Lu-Wang schools of thought [20] recapitulated in some ways the old division between the emphases of Hsün-tzu and Mencius. Not unlike the emphasis of Hsün-tzu on the use of external constraints such as education, the Ch'eng-Chu line of thought laid emphasis on the active cultivation of a right frame of mind, whether this be by ritual, [21] by quiet sitting, [22] or study. Sincerity (*cheng*) and seriousness (*ching*) and the way to achieve these became central themes. The intent was by means of a disciplined self-cultivation (embracing intellect, feeling, and will, as these issue in behavior) to heighten the probability of acting on the basis of one's original nature. The Lu-Wang line of thought sought to collapse the gap between these two moments of one's being, placing an emphasis on possibility and on direct, unpremeditated action as the immediate expression of this original nature. Yet, the gap between the two planes of reality—the ontological and the existential—was there, and it was this that generated the pathos of Confucian effort.

These planes were related in such a way that the metaphysical was immanent in the existential, infusing it with the power for good. Even where the difference between the two could be emphasized, this immanence of good was consistently affirmed: "True principle is not a distinct thing; it inheres in the ether of materialization." [23] But this inherence (the "is") was a matter of possibility, not yet actual. There was also, therefore, an "ought" implicit in this inherence, so that the good possible to human nature ought to become actual in human behavior. This metaphysically given good, the "is," was to be replicated in the existential plane or, to put it in somewhat different words, the equilibrium (the pregiven wholeness) of original nature was to be replicated through action so that it became harmony (an antecedent wholeness) in existential nature.

The human agent is the crux, the point of linkage that mediates between these two. We have already seen this intervening will analyzed in terms of the temporal sequences of a phasic consciousness. These phases, leading from original nature (*tao-hsin*) to existence (*jen-hsin*), are five: "total stillness, sensation of an outer object, imminent issuance, incipient issuance, and accomplished issuance." [24]

The first three phases of this sequence occur within the plane of ontological good (*tao-hsin,* "the mind of the Way"), that is, in the sphere of the good, immanently given. But as one takes passage into the last two phases a moment of great danger and fragility transpires. Anyone who has handled a butterfly coming out of its chrysalis, only to be chagrined at the deformation brought about by even the most gentle touching of the not yet fully developed wings, can perhaps get a sense of the fragility of this moment of transition. To be sure, the incipiencies (*tuan-ni*) or feelings are there, but they await development. As Chu Hsi said: "When we inquire into the source from which the principles of the world have come, there is no badness. How can delight and anger, grief and joy ever be bad in the form which they have when just on the point of being issued?" [25]

It was the passage from imminent to incipient issuance that was pivotal, and the zone of greatest risk. At the moment of incipient issuance the mind (*jen-hsin,* that is, "the human mind" or the moral will) becomes active. Again, as Chu Hsi says: "the mind controls [that process of issuance involving man's] heaven-conferred nature and his feelings." [26] Wang Yang-ming also comments upon this moment: "When a good thought arises, recognize it and make it pervade the mind. When a bad thought arises, recognize it and stop it. It is the mind's ability to decide on its goal, a heavenly intelligence, which enables one to know thoughts and stop them or make them fill the mind." [27]

If life is interpenetrated by the goodness of original nature, and if the mind shares in "heavenly intelligence," whence then this fragility and danger? Whence comes the evil?

A wrong choice occurs at the fragile moment of transition—but that still begs the question. At the same time there seems to be an inherent weakness in the human will which, at the least, needs continual encouragement. Beyond this, as we have seen, there is the suggestion of a "cosmic shortcoming"[28] that lies behind this weakness. This cosmic fracture requires a bridging of the gap, and it is in the cosmically determined necessity of bridging, linking, mediating that the risk of failure lies. Moreover, the subtle and elusive "mind of the Way" is seemingly disadvantaged by the more bold and assertive movements of human desire. Chu Hsi comments on this question of relative power, observing that on the metaphysical level "it is very easy for heavenly principle to be victorious over human material desires," but that on the experiential level "it is . . . very easy for human material desires to be victorious over heavenly principle."[29] One thing is certain, however: evil as such does not inhere in human nature, whether it be knowledge, feeling, or will. Its location is external, environmental, a function of the circumstance of life. At the moment of fragile transition, things (*wu*), whether objects or events, have power to contact the senses and perhaps to misdirect. As Mencius says, "When external things contact the ear or eye, they lead them astray."[30] This sensation stirs the will and brings response. The possibility of evil lurks there in the fragility of this moment. And once this has occurred infinitesimal error leads to infinite error. Beyond this, Confucian speculation cannot or will not go.

Metzger sums up what he terms the Confucian "pathos of power":

What I call the metaphysical bias of Neo-Confucians comes down to the key point that for them, the individual was not a self-sufficient moral agent, and ethical purity was not enough. They needed to feel supported by an immense power transcending the immediate ego, and they wanted this power in order to transform the world. Even when they suspected it was unavailable, they still sought the pathos of this power.[31]

It seems evident that wrong does not have a very secure and stable ontological status in the Confucian tradition. Was it metaphysically grounded? That was not clearly granted. Was it existentially grounded? There was more plausibility to this, but even here nothing in human nature was itself evil. Wrong is not supposed to be there, yet it is, so that the natural goodness inherent in human possibility is continually frustrated.

Quite in contrast to the Confucian tradition, there is no comparable hesitancy to speak of suffering or evil in the Buddhist (or Indic) and

Christian (or Semitic) traditions. Indeed, suffering is a fundamental axiom of Buddhism, being the most pervasive characteristic of human existence.

> The Noble Truth of suffering is this: Birth is suffering; ageing is suffering; sickness is suffering; death is suffering; sorrow and lamentation, pain, grief and despair are suffering; association with the unpleasant is suffering; dissociation from the pleasant is suffering; not to get what one wants is suffering—in brief, the five aggregates of attachment are suffering.[32]

In Christianity, likewise, suffering is central. In this case it is epitomized by the cross, its most characteristic symbol.

The Buddhist and Christian traditions deepened the understanding of suffering and evil, each in a different way. Both chose to give them a deeper existential rooting, though the choices did have metaphysical implications. For the Buddhist the pain of existence was a sign of one's existential (not metaphysical) exile within reality, and the way out was return from this exile. Existence as we typically know it is a faulty construct, a product of ignorance. Thus, suffering and evil have an unambiguous epistemological root. For the Christian, evil was attributed to an existential fault in the act of human intending itself, and the way out was repentance from sin and the forgiveness of guilt. Evil became a category of relationship and personal will.

Wrong as existential exile

The Buddhist framework of existential exile and return—a framework shared with almost all the Indic systems—may be depicted in the form of a closed loop within a larger circle, as we have suggested (see pp. 104-105). As noted above, the Buddhist model has a threefold structure, the Confucian a twofold one. In the Confucian tradition there is no sense of a thoroughgoing "exile" or "fall" which calls for "redemption."

The Confucian experience, as noted above, discovers a gap between the infinite possibility and the finite probabilities of human life, and interprets this as an interior feature of all individuals. What to the Confucian appears as a gap that can theoretically be bridged—thus linkage becomes the problem—in Buddhism becomes a chasm of infinite proportion. Samsara is the very antithesis of Nirvana, and the two are not to be linked or bridged in any way whatsoever. The gap is in fact no gap, but absolute difference. Predicament belongs entirely to the sphere of samsara, of phenomenal existence. The pathos that the Confucian experiences as tension between two spheres the Buddhist experiences as bondage within a single sphere. This single sphere—samsara—has its own peculiar form of epistemic tension. We have already seen that the Buddha felt compelled to choose between a cosmology of impermanence and an epistemology of permanence, and that he rejected the latter while embracing the former.

In what then does the conflict or dis-ease consist? Is it a conflict in things, or a conflict in thought? Murti rhetorically asks, "Do appearances quarrel and contradict each other? They do not do so."[33] The world about us is clearly without contradiction, else it would not be about us. But what then of "pain, evil, ugliness, and finitude?" Are they not actual? To this Murti replies:

> Is the discord constituent of the nature of things or not? If it were, it can never be dissolved without dissolving things at the same time; then nothing remains to be taken up in the Absolute. If it were not constitutive of the real, then our viewing of things as contradictory and discordant is our error, a mistake that cannot find a place in the real. It has just an epistemic status, not an ontological one.[34]

All discord, then, is discord within reason, within mind itself. It is entirely subjective, with no objective foundation. The subjective ground, as we have already seen, is the positing of a self. Thus:

> He who frames conceits, bhikkhus, is a slave of Mara, the man without conceit is free from the Evil One. "I am", bhikkhus, this is a kind of conceit; "This I am", bhikkhus, this is a kind of conceit; "I shall come to be. . ."; "I shall not come to be. . ."; "I shall become one endowed with consciousness. . ."; "I shall become corporeal. . ."; "I shall become one who possesses neither consciousness nor unconsciousness. . . ." All conceit, bhikkhus, is a disease, a tumour, a dart. Therefore, bhikkhus, you should take this resolution, "Let us dwell with a mind which does not frame conceits". Such is the way, bhikkhus, you should train yourselves.[35]

Conceit yields craving, which determines the emotional texture of human life. Thus:

> These three cravings and these three kinds of conceit ought to be given up. . . . The craving for sensual pleasures, the craving for becoming, the craving for de-becoming. . . Preoccupation with self, thinking lowly of self, thinking highly of self. . . .

The act of positing a self is in effect to superimpose a finite image upon reality—infinitude—and then to compound this confusion in the attempt to make this finitude—the individual self or entity—permanent, unchanging, infinite. Our experience of self and world is the result of this twisted and twisting subjective projection upon reality. All the qualities of samsaric existence—attachment, pain, hope, and fear—are merely the outflow of this false construct. This constitutes our exile into finitude. The only escape from this samsaric loop of unending disappointment and grief is the complete extinction of this false infinity. Only then can reality, which is appearance, be what it is—absolute.[36]

No mediation is in the final analysis possible between this false construction and reality in its true nature. The only possible relationship is that of its extinction. In this sense we can say that predicamental pathos occurs as the result of an "exile" from essence into existence.[37] The return is back to "essence." Attachment or ignorance displayed in its variety of forms characterizes the exile into existence, and non-attachment, or ontological freedom, characterizes the return.

The Buddhist has deepened the understanding of evil in a way that the Confucian did not and would not. The Confucian may have been troubled by the seemingly elusive quality of immanent good—possibility and probability were forever in tension—but this never led to a rejection of ordinary life as the proper sphere of human activity. The Buddhist had no such hesitations. Perceiving the sorrow of life, Gautama left wife, infant son, and princedom to seek for a truth that transcended these entanglements. Such a self-exile from society and its concerns forever drew the scorn of the Confucian for whom the social group, epitomized by the family, was precisely that which could never be given up. The Confucian was tied to phenomenal existence and had to work out solutions in that sphere.

Not so the Buddha. So profound was the sense of human fallibility and error that the whole human project of phenomenalizing activity— the act of mind which implanted a subject/object image upon all reality; the act of feeling which became attached to self as subject and in turn became satisfied or dissatisfied with objects; the act of will which imposed its determinations upon objects and other subjects—was rejected as itself the very core of error. With so thoroughgoing and devastating a critique of that which the Confucian took for granted, no area of experience was left untouched and what the Confucian experienced as tension the Buddhist experienced as revulsion.

Wrongness is the phenomenalizing activity of the mind itself as a differentiating knowledge, feeling, and will. Therefore wrong is universally present wherever this activity takes place. If universal, it is nevertheless eminently capable of being overcome. The Buddha demonstrated this.

Wrong as distrust

1. Introduction

The Semitic tradition deepens the understanding of wrong in a rather different direction. As with the Confucian, in the Semitic traditions the involvements of life are the proper sphere of activity. Yet, like the Buddhist, these involvements are themselves entangled in inescapable error. If for Buddhism wrong is essentially the double-twist of finitude exiled from the totality, in the Semitic traditions wrong becomes a category of a misconstrued relationship, a violation of communal wholeness.

We have termed the Confucian framework that of replication, the Buddhist one that of return, and the Semitic framework that of representation. The presence of a definite idea of temporal and historical purpose is distinctive of the Semitic framework, we suggested.

Indeed, this difference is quite fundamental. In an important sense mythical speech is not to be excluded from biblical discourse. Bound as they are to the categories of personal relations, the Semitic faiths are more closely tied, or tied in a distinctly different way, to such speech than is either the Confucian commitment or Buddhism. For the Confucian, mythical speech was never important. The neo-Confucian concern throughout was with one's relation to an immanental, largely impersonal, power for good in the cosmos. Buddhist literature is, if anything, more replete with myth and legend than biblical texts, but it is not the quantity but the quality of mythical speech that is important. The abundance of myth in Buddhist texts is due largely to the rhetorical and instrumental, not intrinsic, value of such material. Myth is penultimate. But in the Semitic traditions, mythical speech or, if one prefers, analogical or metaphorical speech about God and world is never entirely expendable, for here one is in the sphere of personal relation, of historical action, of willing and counterwilling, of address and response.[38] When dealing with transcendence, this seems to require the category of myth—God sits on a throne high and lifted up; Jesus shall come again; God speaks.

As a consequence, the deepening of the experience of "disproportion," to use Ricoeur's word, moves in a very different direction from the Buddhist deepening. It is a deepening that intensifies rather than explains the experience of fracture. What the Confucian experiences as a weakness of the individual in appropriating cosmic powers ready to hand, and what the Buddhist experiences as a faulty construction of mind and heart, the adherent of a Semitic faith experiences as guilty responsibility, as a failure to heed aright the speech and address of God. The "disproportion" is cast into personal categories, and history is experienced as the struggle of wills.

The Christian perspective is one version of the Semitic tradition (we shall later speak of a family quarrel involving the Jewish, Christian, and Muslim views), and goes farthest in addressing the question of suffering and evil.

We might amplify the diagram on representation to accommodate the Christian view as follows on page 118:

DIAGRAM 4

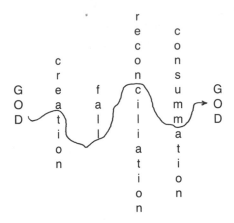

In this view the four terms, creation, fall, reconciliation, and consummation, are all of one piece, a single movement that mediates from God to God.[39]

Each of these moments introduce novelty, each is irreversible, each qualifies that which precedes and each defines the conditions within which future action is to take place. A few words about this.

In the biblical symbol of creation God posits an ordered reality outside of God's own self. We need not discuss here whether creation is to be interpreted as *ex nihilo* or simply the ordering of a primal chaos.[40] What is important is that God establishes God's own reality as in relationship with that which is not God. This is irreversible, for God could no longer be as though there were not a world in relationship with God's self. It qualifies God's reality, for relationship with not-God becomes a factor for God. Creation also establishes the conditions for that which is not yet. Without ambiguity, this creative act, and its consequence, is deemed "good."

The fall introduces the novelty of evil.[41] Apparently one of the "goods" of creation was freedom, with humanity being the prime bearer of that good. But that good could be misused in freedom. Such, the fall says, has become the case. This too is irreversible. It is a corruption, a distortion, a thwarting, a misconstrual of creation. God and world can no longer be as if evil had not been. Evil qualifies creation, and introduces forces into it that are contrary to its original and intended goodness. It sets conditions for the future. Human history becomes the principal arena within which this play of contrary wills works itself out. The primeval history of Genesis 1–11 begins that narration.

God, creation, and fall establish the conditions for reconciliation. God's good intention for creation remains, despite the added conditions of fall. It works within (not against or outside of) the conditions already established.[42] Thus, "when the time had fully come, God sent forth his Son, born of woman, born under the law, to redeem those who were under the law, so that we might receive adoption as sons."[43] This is a complete statement of historical revelation.

Reconciliation, in turn, is also irreversible.[44] God and world can no longer be as if reconciliation had not been. This reconciliation qualifies evil (judges) as well as creation (restores), and qualifies even more profoundly the inner life of God, as the doctrine of Trinity seeks to make clear.[45] And again, a new mixture of conditions prevails for the making of the future.

Finally, consummation—the hope set into motion by reconciliation and the biblical faith in the final competence of God in the divine intention—sums up the past, creates a thoroughly new set of conditions devoid of evil, and opens up into a continuing future of unobstructed fellowship with God. "Then comes the end," Paul reminds, "when he delivers the kingdom to God the Father after destroying every rule and every authority and power. For he must reign until he has put all his enemies under his feet. The last enemy to be destroyed is death." But this only marks the prelude to the consummation (*anakephalaiosis*), for "when all things are subjected to him, then the Son himself will also be subjected to him who put all things under him, that God may be everything to every one."[46]

2. The biblical deepening

What then is the Christian manner of deepening the category of wrong? It is, first of all, entirely dependent upon Israel's prior experience. Let us then turn briefly to this.

If we might speak of secular history as the story of events as they arise from the interplay of human purposes and counterpurposes, then sacred history would be this same story in the light of its interweave with divine purposing. This latter is certainly the essence of the biblical understanding of history. "Man's coexistence with God," writes Abraham Heschel, "determines the course of history."[47] It is in the matrix of this interweave of manifold purposing that sin is disclosed.

Covenantal dialog and the prophets

We have referred in our diagram above to creation and fall. Israel did not, of course, experience "sin" because of these doctrines; rather, these formulations developed because of her sociohistorical experience. They sum up; they do not explain.

Israel's experience of sin as disobedience (distrust) takes shape within the experience of covenant. The saga of Israel reaches back to the remembrance of deliverance from Egypt, which constituted Israel as a people, and back through this to the stories of the patriarchs. The human-divine dialog—from Abraham to Moses—is integral to this saga. In the deliverance from Egypt this dialog becomes explicit in covenant: "You have seen what I did to the Egyptians, and how I bore you on eagles' wings and brought you to myself. Now therefore, if you will obey my voice and keep my covenant, you shall be my own possession among all peoples; for all the earth is mine." This dialog projects back to the deepest root of Israel's historical remembrance— Abraham: "Go from your country . . . to the land that I will show you. . . . So Abram went, as the LORD had told him." This memory is to be constantly cultivated: "A wandering Aramean was my father; and he went down into Egypt and sojourned there, few in number; and there he became a nation, great, mighty, and populous . . . and Yahweh brought us out of Egypt. . . and he brought us into this place and gave us this land."[48]

The greater part of the Hebrew Scriptures is an exploration of the ensuing covenantal dialog. In dialogic terms this history is a tale of fitful efforts to make the covenant arrangement of mutual trust and obligation a historical reality. Each attempt inevitably unravels, due to the untrustworthiness of the people. This unraveling reaches its dread climax in the piecemeal destruction of Israel and Judah by Assyria and

Babylon, in turn, and the accompanying exile of the leading citizens of both the Jewish nations.

Because of the covenantal dialog this is not simply another history, but the history of God's relations with his people. It is the prophets who entered supremely into the crossroads of this dialog. As Heschel puts it: "The prophet claims to be far more than a messenger. He is a person who stands in the presence of God (Jer. 15:19), who stands 'in the council of the Lord' (Jer. 23:18), who is a participant, as it were, in the council of God."[49] At this crossroads, the prophet experiences "a fellowship with the feelings of God, a *sympathy with the divine pathos,* a communion with the divine consciousness."[50] This "sympathy is the prophet's answer to inspiration, the correlative to revelation"; which is to say that the prophets see things "from the point of view of God."[51]

As they look at their people they see not faithfulness but disobedience. Entering into the pathos of divine disappointment Jeremiah exclaims:

> Be appalled, O heavens, at this,
>   be shocked, be utterly desolate,
>   says the Lord,
> for my people have committed two evils:
>   they have forsaken me,
> the fountain of living waters,
>   and hewed out cisterns for themselves,
> broken cisterns,
>   that can hold no water.[52]

But to forsake God is an ethical, just as much as a religious, act of defiance, and calls for the outflow of divine wrath:

> Will you steal, murder, commit adultery, swear falsely, burn incense to Baal, and go after other gods that you have not known, and then come and stand before me . . . and say, "We are delivered!"—only to go on doing all these abominations? . . . And now, because you have done all these things . . . I will cast you out of my sight.[53]

What is called for is clear: "Let justice roll down like waters, and righteousness like an everflowing stream."[54] All that is said is said in terms of the covenantal dialog:

> Hear this word that the Lord has spoken against you, O people of Israel, against the whole family which I brought up out of the land of Egypt:
> "You only have I known
>   of all the families of the earth;
>   therefore I will punish you
>   for all your iniquities."[55]

The prophetic indictment is sweeping:

> Run to and fro through the streets of Jerusalem,
>   look and take note!
> Search her squares to see
>   if you can find a man,
> one who does justice
>   and seeks truth.[56]

The search, of course, is in vain: "Every one deals falsely."[57] And so say the other prophets: "There is no faithfulness or kindness, and no knowledge of God in the land."[58] The indictment even becomes a part of Israel's own hymnody: "There is none that does good; no, not one."[59]

After the onslaught of the prophets, the Genesis account of the fall almost becomes anticlimactic. But it is not. It may well be that the "sweeping allegations, overstatements, and generalizations" of the prophets "defied standards of accuracy. Some of the exaggerations reach the unbelievable."[60] Yet, "exaggeration is often only a deeper penetration."[61] Indeed, in the Genesis account of the fall the exaggerations of the prophets occasion the insight into human sin as a universal, a reality that stands at the very gateway to history. By exaggeration the prophet thrusts into the depths; and by myth the writer of Genesis thrusts into the primordial. Sin is coterminous with history.

Jesus' critique of Pharisaism

For all the intensity of the prophetic message, yet one more intervening phase in the experience of covenantal dialog is presupposed before we can arrive at the New Testament understanding of sin. This intervention is the Pharisaic movement.

Exile was followed by return, and the lesson of national failure led to the intensification of individual effort. The prophets prepared the way by individualizing the concept of sin.[62] The Pharisaic movement offered that intensified effort a field of potentially unquantifiable legal stipulations.[63] To be sure, we know little of the actual origins of Pharisaism and of its institutional continuity with the past; nevertheless, there appear to be many links of an intellectual and religious kind with Israel's past. In terms of the continuity of ideas, it might be said that Nehemiah and Ezra provided the pivot that linked the two ethical movements—prophetic and Pharisaic—together. "What is certain is that Ezra opened an historical epoch of conscience 'as important as the rise of prophecy, and only less important than the work of Moses.' This epoch is that which is properly called the religion of the Torah."[64]

It would simply be impossible to understand the event of Jesus without this intervention. As recent New Testament studies make clear, Jesus did not appear on the scene as a full-blown egomaniac, proclaiming his divinity and messiahship—these honors were ascribed to him by the early Christians[65]—but rather as a prophet who spoke for God, seemingly directly, without the need to appeal either to Moses or Torah for backup authority. The struggle over authority and Torah which Jesus posed became, then, one further and climactic stage in the ongoing covenantal dialog.

Our concern here is with the implications of this dialog for our understanding of sin. What advance, if any, did the Pharisaic movement give to the understanding of sin, and what understanding of sin emerged from the climactic dialog with Jesus?

The roots of the Pharisaic movement are preexilic and ultimately reside in the same ethical and historical monotheism in which the prophetic movement resided.[66] To say that ethics is bonded to history is to say that its authority lies not in reason or in some supposed moral universals but that it is always bound to events. "The sign of the distinction of Israel among the peoples is that it has the Law, *this* Law."[67] Ethics was bonded to the event of the Exodus and the revelation on Sinai. As such, ethics is always event-oriented, historical, contingent. The initial impulse that led to the Pharisaic movement was a will

123

to take the radical contingency of ethics and law with utter seriousness and to realize the will of God in every conceivable contingency—in short, to achieve comprehensive obedience. "Pharisaism is this will to follow heteronomy all the way to the end, to stake daily existence without reserve on the 'statutes of God.' "[68] The ethical question was: "How will God be truly served in this world?"[69]

The "logic of scrupulousness" that follows from this, a logic that is clearly present also in the much later Muslim appeal to *hadith* and *sharia,* is quite clear. The Torah, that is, the divine instruction given by Moses, is revelation. However, a once-for-all revelation cannot accommodate all contingencies. Thus, as life is lived, the original Torah must be applied to ever new situations. This requires interpretation and application. Thus, in the desire to do the will of God in all circumstances (*mitzvah*), a body of legal interpretation invested with authority second only to the original Torah itself arose, the *halachah.*[70] Life became the labor of devout service to God by the application of this law in all activities. It was an act of joyful service, as the Psalms so well display.[71] Thus, the divine will is enabled to have an effective impact upon daily life: "The heart of the God-man relation is an instruction concerning what is to be done; even if this instruction is more than law, it is inscribed in a voluntaristic context: God is ethical and the bond between man and God is a bond of obedience to instruction."[72]

There is, to be sure, a problem here—a deadly one for Jesus, and a fateful one for Paul. This is the infinity of the demand of the law. There is no absolute limit either to this demand or to its contingent relevancies. The mountains of prescription are mute reminder of the human endeavor to encompass this infinity.

Infinity of demand implies infinity of transgression. Yet, the Pharisaic mind did not quite see things so. As the book of Psalms bears witness, the scrupulous mind of the Pharisee was accompanied by a penitential spirit. To be sure, perfection in its entirety was not to be gained; yet a relative perfection could be, for the entirety was in the end the sum of its individual parts, and one could achieve an obedience that relative to the parts was a more or a less. The scrupulous mind aimed at such relative gain, rejoicing therein, while mourning as well the relative fault. In this way the intent could remain infinite while the accomplishment remained finite. Much more than the Confucian, the

124

Pharisee recognized the improbability of perfection, yet by faith in God had a recourse not available to the Confucian: confession and mourning of failure. The divine mercy would complete what was lacking.

For all the grandeur of this structure, and its seeming unassailability, it was perceived by Jesus as a domestication of the divine will. As he strove to expose this domestication, authority was pitted against authority, with both claiming biblical grounding, and one or the other had to give way.

Jesus, it is clear, perceived the covenantal dialog in very different terms from the Pharisaic movement. To be sure, the central question of Pharisaism was also the central question for Jesus: "How will God be truly served in this world?" The Pharisaic answer was: "By identifying the will of God for every contingency and carrying it out." While Jesus certainly affirmed the latter portion of this understanding— "doing" the will of God—the first part clearly did violence to that will.

At least four principles, in tension with the Pharisaic commitment in this regard, become clear from the ministry of Jesus. First, he rejected the idea that a graded response to the divine will, implicit in the system of halachah, was acceptable. God's will could not be broken up into pieces and responded to bit by bit, made to fit the contingency. The response to God's will was right only if entirely free and complete in each moment, in each contingency. The contingency merely provided the occasion to see, experience, and do the will of God in a total and complete way: "You, therefore, must be perfect, as your heavenly Father is perfect."[73] Second, the doer was not to be separated from the deed. One is, rather, what one does: "Not what goes into the mouth defiles . . ., but what comes out of the mouth." This is so, for "what comes out of the mouth proceeds from the heart," and it is "out of the heart" that one thinks and acts, so that as for "evil thoughts, murder, adultery, fornication, theft, false witness, slander," "these are what defile."[74] A tree is known by its fruit, and bad fruit means a bad tree. With this, all notion of merit—a corollary of graded response—is excluded. Third, the Shema (Deut. 6:4-9) is realized only in shalom; that is to say, love to God is known only in love to the neighbor. The effort to identify the specific divine will in each instance must give way immediately and utterly whenever the welfare of one's neighbor is at stake. That demand was absolute: "The sabbath was made for man, not man for the sabbath."[75] To be sure, the Pharisaic movement itself recognized the supremacy of the dual command "to love God" and "to love neighbor" as the essence of the entire Torah.[76] Nevertheless, the Torah and its authoritative interpretation, mediated between command and practice, and the accepted, indeed inviolable, exegesis of that dual demand, in effect obscured and domesticated it, at least in the interpretation applied to the matter by Jesus. The infinity of demand remained in the many (of an indefinite number of stipulations) as it did also but differently in the much (taking the law as a single whole): "I say to you, till heaven and earth pass away, not an iota, not a dot, will pass from the law until all is accomplished."[77]

Finally, Jesus' challenge of the Pharisaic tradition was not benign in its presentation. Whether directly, as above, or implicitly, Jesus claimed to speak for God, directly interpreting Moses without an appeal to the middle term of tradition, thus placing himself in effect above both. It is hardly likely that such language, most notoriously his claim to forgive sins, is the product of secondary invention. For others to have credited Jesus with such words would have been the best way to discredit his monotheism. It only makes sense that he is credited so because he spoke so. Jesus was, not surprisingly, deemed a blasphemer. Thus, Jesus' implied claim to speak for God was the only, and blasphemous, authority that buttressed his challenge to the "tradition of the elders." In the portrayal of the Gospels, the conflict of authority lay in the background of Jesus' rejection and death.[78]

Culmination of the dialog in Paul

Of the New Testament writers, it was Paul who most directly and fully comprehended the implications of this conflict between Jesus and the Pharisaic movement—perhaps in large part because he came out of that movement himself. For Paul, too, the central issue was the right service to God. But he had experienced a profound sense of the inability of Torah and its tradition of interpretation to provide the needed access to that service—it pointed to the way of works, which in actual fact was the greatest obstacle to that service. To the way of works he counterposed the way of faith. In this way Paul began and completed an exegesis of the conflict between Jesus and the Pharisaic movement that has become the basis for all later Christian interpretations of sin.

The Torah was a pedagog (*paidagogos*) "until Christ came."[79] Paul accepts fully the contingency of the law, that it was a revelation tied to a specific event.[80] Nevertheless, in Romans 1 and 2 he is at pains to demonstrate that there is "a correspondence to the Israelite law in the conscience"[81] of the Gentiles.[82] What Torah does for the Jew, conscience does in a somewhat analogous way for the Gentile. All are thereby tutored into the knowledge of disobedience before the will of God and are "inexcusable."

But Paul was only able to speak of the universal function of the law (Torah and conscience) out of the depth of his own experience of the inward penetration of the Torah's pedagogy.

What was at stake for Paul was not the infinity of intent but the finitude of the deed. No doubt his own experience—having been a persecutor of Christians in good conscience—instructed him. His Damascus encounter exposed to him the infinite gap between intent and deed. Paul is hardly indulging in a spasm of psychological self-depreciation in his loud complaint of Romans 7. He is mourning the objective circumstance: "For I delight in the law of God, in my inmost self," he writes, and refers to this as the "law of my mind." But there is another "law" or principle at work within him, "in my members," such that by following through on the good intent (the law of the mind) it leads in fact to the very opposite of that which was intended. He speaks of it as a "war," and of the entire situation as "this body of death." The fracture spoken of here is not psychological but ethical: "I do not do what I want [i.e., service to God], but I do the very thing I hate [i.e., transgress the divine will]" (vv. 22-24). This strange dialectic is a law of our existence as the children of Adam.

It is as if the Torah, as pedagog, "incites" to evil. By its promise of life it mightily intensifies the effort towards self-predication of the good. But this effort is self-defeating, for the law of inverse relation is at work: the more intense the intent to do good, the more the result proves to contradict that intent. In Paul's intent to serve God, he in fact rejected God. The dictum of Wang Yang-ming, referred to thrice already, finally does come to haunt—an infinitesimal error leads to an infinite error.

127

What was the infinitesimal error? The doing of the good was a predicate of the self as subject—"works," to use Paul's heavily laden word. Yet, good could only be a predicate of God—the divine act of "justification" speaks of that. And then God is finally the subject. Here the issue rests: of whom or what is good finally the predicate? If of God, then trust is the way; if of self, then effort (cf. the Confucian) is the way. The Paul of faith could only mourn the Paul of works thus: "Wretched man that I am! Who will deliver me from this body of death?"[83]

Wrong as tragic necessity

Wrong, however, is a concept broader than sin. To be sure, the Adamic myth attributes not only human strife to sin (Cain and Abel), but even death (the extremity of finitude), not to mention pain—whether physical pain (childbirth) or the Sisyphean struggle with nature (weeds). Paul picks up the same theme in his revival of that myth, and suggests that the whole range of cosmic pain (Rom. 8:19-22) has its reason for being in the human action of disobedience. Somehow this seems to overreach. Is it really so that the fate of bugs and burned-out stars is to be accounted for by human fault?

It does not seem that the question of wrong can be so easily dealt with. This "extreme attempt" indeed does seek radically to separate the origin of evil from the even more primordial origin of good.[84] Even so, the primordiality of evil still lurks close at hand. The ambiguities of the Adamic myth itself show that evil cannot be so easily "rationalized." The dimension of mystery continues to attach itself to evil. The initiatory action of Satan in the Adamic myth, the protest of Job over the suffering of the innocent, the struggle of Paul with the complexities of predestination—all disclose that in the biblical experience of sin this further dimension is not lost. Is God evil? Predestination at least hints at this. Is evil a power that is opposed to and as primordial as God? The figure of Satan is surely at least a shadow of this thought. Or is evil an essential aspect of the cosmic structure? The failure of God to explain things to Job does not exclude that thought. These three suspicions would call into question the biblical effort to "rupture" the ontological and historical[85] so as to place evil on the side of the latter.

These are by no means novel thoughts, and have been affirmed in an almost infinite number of ways. The theogonic myth in its various forms seems to say that evil and God are equally primary. Did the gods themselves emerge as the consequence of a primeval battle with chaos, and are they really able to hold chaos at bay? The several varieties of the Indo-European myths would seem to suggest so. Or did the order of the cosmos come into being by the gradual emergence of a pair of complementary principles—as in an egg, for instance—which in their mutual interactions gave birth to diversity? A wide range of myths worldwide, including the Chinese *yin-yang* pattern, would seem to suggest this.[86]

We have seen that the Confucian tradition does not make the same kind of ontological/historical-existential rupture (although there was a less awesome fracture) that the biblical and Buddhist traditions make. It does not, however, risk the question of origins other than to suggest that the likelihood of evil is to be attributed to the basic constitution of the cosmos. But it is still at most only likelihood.

Marx, we have noted, was strangely silent about the ills of cosmic scope, of sickness, suffering, and death. The ills that exercised him were social ills, in his earlier career covered by the term *alienation*.

Perhaps there was a reason for this somewhat awkward silence. Perhaps Marx simply accepted evil in the organic realm as part of natural necessity. Perhaps, as we noted regarding Gardavsky, he simply accepted death as a natural but necessary condition for there to be history. Or perhaps he was so mesmerized by the sufferings whereby Prometheus sought to win human liberation that there was no room left for more speculative thoughts about evil. He had no need of a theodicy, since he had no God to defend.

Implicit in Marxist historical materialism is the logic of necessary, unmourned suffering. Class struggle is an instance of this in the historical realm; sickness and death is an instance of this in the realm of nature. Marx mourned the victims of revolution no more than he mourned victims of disease. Both are subject to a natural necessity.

There seems to be here a different mythic approach to evil than in the religious Ways we have just been considering. Implicit in the Marxist vision seems to be some form of the cosmogonic myth, in which order (read "history") comes about only by the brutal subduing of chaos. Only those elements which are moving towards an intensification of history enter into his consideration of pathos.

A Chinese Marxist thinker has briefly raised this question of tragic necessity. Pondering the historical development of China, he takes note of both the winners and the losers. Regarding Confucius's time he writes:

> This was a great social advance. On this foundation were to appear the brilliant culture of the Warring States and the powerful and prosperous Ch'in and Han empires. But at the same time, the remnants of democracy, love, and humanity internal to the class and largely contained in the primitive ceremonial system of the early slave order, as well as the democratic political order of the city-states such as were present in the many middle and small sized tribal nations of the Ch'un-Ch'iu, were completely discarded and destroyed by this advance. History always likes to proceed through this sort of tragic antinomy.[87]

He thus reflects Kant's puzzlement over the antinomies as well as the similar Hegelian concern:

> Social advance, the raising of production, and the increase of wealth is bought at the price of the heavy sacrifice of the great majority. For instance, in primitive society and class society, warfare is a normal and important factor in pushing history forward, but anguish, grief, and the opposition to the suffering and sacrifice brought on by war are also always the just cry of the people. Both sides have their reason, and therefore it can be said that there is an unsolvable tragic character to the antinomies of history.[88]

And again:

> History, reality and humanity are from the beginning always complex and contradictory, and to expect to use a simple method to critique the good and bad, the positive and negative of all things, is to "cut the feet to fit the shoes" and simply does not accord with the facts. For Confucius to uphold the *Chou-li* was conservative and backward, even reactionary; but to oppose the cruel and exploitative pressures, to demand the preservation and return to the relative mildness of the ancient clan system

of government, and to give prominent emphasis to this, was to be democratic and humane. Confucius's intellectual system of *jen* learning was built on just such a contradictory and complex foundation.[89]

To mourn the fact, of course, is not to solve it.

D. Reconciling Pathos

The pain of reconciling

Rescue from wrong does not come easily or without pain. We have looked briefly at predicamental pathos; what then about reconciling pathos?

The reconciliation offered will have to be commensurate with the predicament disclosed. However, this should not be interpreted to mean that the idea of wrong necessarily determines the kind of reconciliation sought; it would seem much more appropriate to say that the kind of reconciliation intended ultimately governs the notion of wrong experienced. In the end, of course, one should say that neither is without the other, for there is a constant moving back and forth between them.

In the preceding section it appears that the Buddhist and Christian explorations of wrong as a distinctively human experience are the most developed or, we might say, present the most grim view of human failure. If so, it would not be surprising were one also to find that their respective visions of the pathos that reconciles is also the most developed. For this reason we shall focus our discussion upon the Buddhist and Christian understandings of reconciling pathos.

The bodhisattva cycle

Karuna (compassion) has already been briefly characterized for us by T'ang as one of the structures of mediation. Let us look at it a bit more closely.

The critical passage is the following:

Thereupon, from above to below, it penetrates into the core of all sentient beings of the world of [particulars, *dharma*] and, because of the sufferings which stem from the clingings, joins them in a common feeling of

131

sympathy which gives rise to a mind of compassion; furthermore, by wisdom it shows that the clingings at the core of sentient beings are in their original nature empty, and by this wisdom roots out this suffering and accomplishes the salvation of sentient beings.

T'ang here describes the *bodhisattva*. A bodhisattva, as the term itself indicates, is a being of enlightenment. In the history of Buddhist ideas there have been two dominant interpretations of this symbol. In many of the texts that reflect earlier tradition, as well as in Theravada Buddhism today, the principal meaning is that of an individual who has made a vow to achieve enlightenment. Such an individual may be described as a "bodhisattva," in the sense of being animated in all saying, thinking, or acting by that vow. In this sense the historical Buddha was a bodhisattva up to his final nirvana. Not only was he such in this present earthly life but, as the tradition became ever more elaborate, he was such for a seemingly endless succession of previous existences, reaching back to that time when he first made the vow for enlightenment during that remote age of the Dipankara Buddha.

The second dominant understanding of the bodhisattva built upon this. According to the principal earlier sutras, upon the decease of the Buddha, the Buddha and his powerful influence was no longer available, either directly or indirectly. All that was left behind was his teaching (*dharma*). Popular piety, to be sure, saw efficacy in the bone fragments (relics) left over from his cremation. Be that as it may, this idea of the Buddha's virtual absence did not seem adequate to the reality of the Buddha. Eventually the Bodhisattva became a universalized concept, as did the Buddha, the cosmos being populated by numerous bodhisattvas who were active as agents of salvation in the equally numerous Buddha-fields (realms wherein a Buddha's influence perfectly prevails). These functioned to mediate the reality of the Buddha to the beings of this world. In Mahayana Buddhism it became a truism that all actualities were inherently nirvanic (possessed the Buddha nature), but not all were enlightened. The bodhisattvas were those beings who had realized their Buddha nature and even after death were active towards the world, manifesting the Buddha reality to the less fortunate, so as to awaken and save all beings.[90]

Three features are of particular importance in the itinerary of the bodhisattva. One is that the bodhisattva has coursed deeply in the liberating insight or wisdom (*prajna*) that the Buddha also attained. At the same time, the bodhisattva turns in attention towards the world, moved by an all-embracing compassion (*karuna*). Furthermore, so as to achieve the goal of liberation for all, the bodhisattvas are known for their skillful use of all kinds of mundane and marvelous means (*upaya*) to convey the truth. These three aspects constitute what I am terming the "bodhisattva cycle."

This threefold correlation is made explicit in the texts. In the *Treatise on the Perfection of Insight*, for instance, we read:

> Skilful means *[upaya]* involves knowing that all actualities are void because of a thoroughgoing completion in the perfection of insight *[prajna]*, and taking pity on living beings because of a great compassion *[karuna]*. By the power of skilful means no deep attachment arises with respect to these two truths *[prajna, karuna]*. Even though knowing that all actualities are void, because of the power of skilful means there is no abandonment of living beings. Even though no living beings are abandoned it is still known that all actualities are in reality void.[91]

This threefold affirmation—*prajna, karuna, upaya*—can be readily joined with the samsaric cycle as we earlier treated it. With this addition it will appear as follows:

DIAGRAM 5

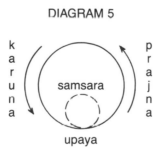

upaya

Prajna represents the upward swing of the solid line which indicates reality seen in its nirvanic (void) character and is the coursing in insight; *karuna* represents the downward swing of the same insightful movement but is now directed towards the world. *Upaya*, which synthesizes the two into practical, soteric action, occurs at the juncture of reality experienced as samsara and as nirvana.

Were we to take *upaya* in its narrowest sense, as Dayal does, then it would be defined as, "skilfulness or wisdom in the choice and adoption of the means or expedients for converting others or helping them."[92] In this definition Dayal has Buddhist preaching and teaching specifically in mind. As such, *upaya* (literally, "means") or *upaya-kautalya* (literally, "skill in [the use of] means") is little more than skillful preaching, good hermeneutics, or effective propaganda. This narrow meaning, however, hardly accounts for the role played by this concept in Mahayana Buddhism.

Pye takes us beyond this. The historical Buddha's resolve to preach does in fact lie at the roots of this concept, but does not limit it. According to this tradition, the Buddha, having attained enlightenment, is inclined not to teach the truth he had discovered. The reason is that people, steeped in ignorance and drowned in sensual pleasure as they are, will not comprehend this deep and subtle *dharma*. Fortunately, the god Brahma Sahampati senses this and in a miraculous appearance appeals to the Buddha to preach the *dharma* for the deliverance of those in suffering. Having reconsidered, and perceiving the different levels of understand among the living, the Buddha does in fact resolve to preach.

Upaya (skillful means) is a principle of accommodation or correlation: the teaching and practice engaged in are provisional means meant to benefit the unenlightened. *Upaya* "is about the way in which the goal, the intention, or the meaning of Buddhism is correlated with the unenlightened condition of living beings."[93] When this principle is extended, as it was in Mahayana Buddhism, then, "Almost anything in the whole range of Buddhist teaching and practice can be described as *fang-pien* or skilful means."[94] So extensive did this principle become, and so congruent with the inner meaning and intent of Buddhism was it that, in Pye's opinion, "Buddhism taking a form *is* skilful means, and nothing else."[95] In short, as a soteriology, Buddhism is a means, a vehicle, a raft, to lead ignorant beings as skillfully as possible, and in ways that they can comprehend, to accept the fundamental truth of Buddhism concerning the inherent voidness of all actualities.

If we were to search for concepts more familiar to us from the Semitic circle of faiths, *upaya* would include all events of disclosure, whether it be a theophany, a prophetic message, a word of forgiveness, a sacrament, or any person, place, event, or thing that discloses, even if only in a provisional way, the truth about things. In the Christian faith, of course, the life, death, and resurrection of Jesus might be described as the supreme *upaya,* just as the entire event of the Buddha is for the Buddhist.

Two of the many parables in the Lotus Sutra will help to illustrate the principle. The one parable is that of the burning house. The Buddha is preaching to a huge throng (the setting is partly historical, but mostly mythical), which shows difficulty in grasping the intent of his words. He is trying to interpret to them what we might term the "upayanic" way of understanding his teaching and his life. Let us suppose, he suggests, that a man returns to his home which he notices has caught fire. In a short time he knows it will be engulfed in flames. His children are within, unaware of imminent disaster, playing happily. As sometimes happens with children, his warning shouts elicit no response. His children are many, and it would not be possible for him physically to search and find them one by one. Suddenly he falls upon a strategem: he will shout to them that he has bought all of them gifts of goat and deer and bullock carts, and they are outside waiting for the asking. The word about gifts draws the immediate attention of the children, and they rush out headlong to be the first to get their fabulous toys. But, alas, there are no carts. Nevertheless, the father in his joy went into town and bought each of them a chariot, far more splendid than the carts originally promised.

The point of this parable is, of course, clear. By dissembling, the father rescued the children from the flames. Even had he not given them either carts or chariots, the father was justified in his action, for it brought salvation to his children. As the father had said to himself, "I will get my children to escape by a skilful means." That they are not only rescued but given even more glorious gifts only adds emphasis to the superabundance of the salvation offered.[96]

In the parable concerning the son who did not recognize his father we have a Buddhist parallel to the biblical prodigal son. This son has left his home and wandered aimlessly for many a year. In the meantime his father has become a wealthy merchant. Eventually the son happens by the town where his father now lives in wealth and, despite his rags and care-worn features, is recognized by the father. When the father tries to approach the young man in the desire to accept him as his true heir, the boy is struck with terror at this unexplained attention. Realizing the psychological state of the son, the father then devises a strategem. The servants are to release the boy and offer him a menial task. In this they succeed. Meanwhile, the father takes off his noble garb and dons workers garments, and so is able to get near to his son as though one of the workers. Gradually the son is given increased responsibilities until he is eventually made the chief steward of the whole estate. Hitherto the father has not revealed their true relationship. Finally, when the time of his death draws near, he summons witnesses, and divulges the entire story to the son, who now enters into his inheritance.

The text interprets this story allegorically. The rich man is the Buddha and the son is his disciples. Just as the son was not psychologically prepared to receive the full truth until there had been a long preparation, so the Buddha has had to lead his disciples on little by little, not able to teach them the full truth of non-self all at once. There is no falsehood or deceit in these contrivances, for the lasting truth proves to be richer and fuller than any of the forms in which it had been partially conveyed. Not anger, but joy, surprise, and gratitude is the consequence.

This principle of *upaya* is radically applied. In this same sutra there is what can only be called a "buddhaphany." This buddhaphany is set within a fabulous mythological setting which includes the manifestation of countless Buddhas and their worlds. The inflated language only enhances the expectation of the moment. One of the earthly postulants, Maitreya by name (who himself is reputed to be the Buddha of the future), begins a description of the preaching of the Buddhas thus:

> And then I can see all the buddhas,
> The holy masters, the lions,
> Expounding the sutra
> Mysterious and supreme;
> Their voices are clear and pure
> And send forth softly sounding tones,
> Teaching the bodhisattvas
> In their innumerable myriads;
> Their divine voices, deep and wonderful,

> Give joy to those who hear.
> Each in his own world
> Proclaims the true Dharma;
> By various karmic reasonings
> And innumerable stories
> They reveal the Buddha-Dharma
> And awaken the understanding of all the living.[97]

As do all Buddhas when they are about to preach the true *dharma*, so now does "the" Buddha, that is, Shakyamuni, send forth a brilliant ray that illumincs the deepest recesseses of all the worlds. It is then that he proclaims the doctrine of the Lotus Sutra, specifically its teaching concerning *upaya*. Lest there be any doubt about the authenticity of this teaching a manifestation appears in the skies. As Pye comments, "the impression which it makes cannot be conveyed adequately at second hand."[98] A stupa (a shrine supposedly containing the remains of a Buddha) appears from out of the void bedecked with marvelous jewels. The great throng is filled with wonderment as Shakyamuni explains that this contains the "whole-body" of the Buddha Many-Jewels who lived in another world aeons ago. He had vowed that he would make his body appear whenever the Lotus Sutra was proclaimed. The eager throng beseeches to view the "whole-body." Slowly Shakyamuni opens the door of the stupa and within, seated in a position of meditation, is the Buddha Many-Jewels. From his meditation throne he attests to the veracity of the Lotus Sutra, and then invites Shakyamuni to join him in the stupa on his seat of meditation. Such power is generated by this event that the entire throng, including the innumerable multitude of other Buddhas of other times and worlds, are raised into the sky to meet before the stupa, once more reassured of the value of this proclamation. In the verses of exhortation that conclude this buddhaphany it is declared that

> By this skilful means·
> I cause the Dharma long to abide.[99]

This phantasmagoria of innumerable Buddhas, including Shakyamuni, joined in this dramatic way by yet another Buddha who expounds on "skilful means" as the ultimate truth, does not detract from the

significance of Shakyamuni himself as the Buddha. It in fact supports
the truth of his Buddhahood:

> The present sign is like the previous omen;
> It is the skilful means of all the buddhas.
> The present Buddha sends forth a ray of light
> To help reveal the meaning of true reality.[100]

By this emphatic multiplication of Buddhas is revealed in an "upayanic" way that Buddhahood itself lies at the fundamental level of reality
as void. Skillful means, one and all, point finally to this single truth.

The Lotus Sutra specializes in these external dramatizations. No new
content is divulged, only demonstrations of the means whereby the
truth is conveyed, which itself is the truth.

Another text important for the understanding of *upaya* proceeds
instead by means of insightful and penetrating discourse: *The Teaching
of Vimalakirti*. Once again the setting is projected back onto an occasion
within the historical life of Shakyamuni—as is the case with all the
sutras, even the most fantastic. Vimalakirti is in fact a wealthy layman
well placed in the society of his day. To the cenobitic followers of the
Buddha, even the best among the monks, Vimalakirti, is a forbidding
partner in "theological" discourse. He has worsted them all. It so
happens that he now lies ill, and the Buddha asks who of his followers
will go to console him. One after another they decline—even in such
a state of disadvantage on his part, they hesitate to risk humiliation by
his insight. Finally Manjusri, the disciple most noted for his insight,
agrees to pay the sick man a visit. In reading the sutra one knows that
two near equals are engaged here in discourse. The opening greeting
of Vimalakirti already challenges Manjusri as to the degree of his
insight: "You come well, Manjusri. With the mark of non-coming,
you come, and with the mark of non-seeing you see."[101] As a matter
of fact, his illness is no real illness despite his actual illness. Insightful
as he too is, Manjusri is probably on to the "upayanic" character of
this illness. The reader need not be so insightful, because the first
sentence of the narrative already informs us that "as such a skilful

means he showed himself ill in body." [102] In any case, the stage is set for Vimalakirti's discourse on the meaning of illness.

The illness, we find, "arises from great compassion," and illustrates how "the bodhisattva enters birth-and-death [i.e., *samsara*] for the sake of living beings." Vimalakirti's illness, while feigned, is nevertheless real. It, however, does not arise from his own body, but from a sympathy with the ignorance and craving of the world. When there is no longer illness among living beings then his illness too will pass. Likened to the love of parents this "upayanic" compassion is described thus:

When the son becomes ill the father and mother become ill too. If the son gets better, they get better too. It is the same with a bodhisattva. He loves all living beings as if they were a son. If the living beings are ill, then the bodhisattva is ill, if the living beings get better, the bodhisattva gets better too." [103]

As such, this illness is signless, without marks, devoid of its own being; however, it still bears the marks of the yet unrelieved sufferings of the samsaric order.

Manjusri rightly wonders how to go about consoling one who is sick in this manner. Perhaps the less enlightened are not able truly to "comfort" such a one. In any case, Vimalakirti enters into a detailed discussion of the relationship between *upaya* and *prajna*, skilful means and insight. Ultimately, self and nirvana are equal, for both are void. There is no attachment to (i.e., no discomfort in) illness as a skilful means, nor to insight (the truth of nonattachment) as the experience of final release. Each reciprocates with the other in the penetrating experience of the bodhisattva:

Yet again, seeing the body in terms of impermanence, suffering, emptiness and non-self, this is called insight.

To stay in birth-and-death even though the body is sick, bringing benefit to all and not getting disgusted or tired, this is called means.

Yet again, when seeing the body, to see that the body is never without sickness, and that sickness is never without the body, to see that the sickness is the body and that there is no renovation and no passing away, this is called insight.

To recognise that the body is sick and yet not to enter eternal cessation, this is called means.[104]

This reciprocity of insight and action is at root soteric. The bodhisattva recognizes that there is no salvation for one that is not salvation for all, and that the ignorance and delusion of even one implicates all other actualities in that sorrow. Vimalakirti's own salvation is in fact contingent upon the salvation of all. The life of Vimalakirti confirms his teaching for, being a person of insight into the voidness of all actualities, he yet lives immersed in the actualities of social life. For the bodhisattva, life in its entirety is a skillful means.

This applies to all the central practices and teachings of the Buddhist faith, including the historical life of Shakyamuni Buddha himself. It was an *upaya*.

Indeed, the Buddha's life and ministry were in their own reality a contrivance. So the Buddha explains it in the Lotus Sutra:

> Seeing that all living beings take pleasure in lesser teachings and that their virtue is slight while their vileness weighs heavy, to these men I declare that I left home in my youth and attained supreme, perfect enlightenment. But I have really been like this ever since I became a Buddha. I make this proclamation only as a skilful means to teach living beings and get them to enter the Buddha-way.

And his death is no different:

> Although it is at this time not a real extinction, nevertheless I announce my impending extinction. It is by this skilful means that the Tathagata teaches and transforms the living.

This principle applies to the entire span of the indeterminateness of time—past, present, and future:

> Thus it is that since I became a Buddha in the very far distant past [there is in fact no time "when"], my lifetime continues to persist without extinction through immeasurable *asamkhyeya kalpas*. Good sons! The

140

lifetime which I attained originally by practising the bodhisattva-way is even now not yet finished and will still be twice what it was so far [there will in fact be no time "when"].[105]

Buddhism would seem to provide a truly comprehensive answer to the question of wrong in its every size and shape, dispelling in one grand sweep the theoretical problems that seem to plague every form of theism. The Buddhist solution is complete, with no nasty leftovers to come around and worry the faithful. Wrong is an epistemological mistake. The majesty of the Buddhist solution lies in the willingness to take the charge seriously—that wrong is an epistemological mistake—and thereby daring to take up all imagined and imaginable suffering without leftover, and by taking suffering up in an upayanic way, that is, in the spirit of wisdom, to expose its illusory character and at the same time penetrate to the unitive character of reality as such, a reality which is truly devoid of any suffering at all.

The Jesus cycle

Christian assumptions do not permit so grand a solution. It is not permitted, because there is a faith in creation. Wrong is a real feature of human being in the world, not because it was created, but because it is a disruption of the created; and suffering is actual, not hypothetical. The commitment to matter precludes a Buddhist solution.

As we turn to the Christian experience of reconciling pathos we might ask whether T'ang's analysis provides a point of entry here, as it did for our Buddhist exegesis. He suggests that "monotheistic religions lead humanity to a realm that transcends subjectivity and objectivity," and that they do so "by way of ascent from the sublunar realm of subject-object opposition to the divine realm that unifies subject and object." This ascent is accomplished from the human realm by virtue of "the spirit's self-transcending [activity]." What is finally accomplished is "a vertical integration from the lower to the higher."

T'ang's analysis is not adequate as a point of departure. The structure of the biblical experience is not fundamentally vertical—that is spatial—but temporal, directional. God is not a reality inexplicably floating outside of time who saves us from time. The integration of the biblical tradition is not from lower to higher but from the first through to the last. We have outlined that framework earlier.

It is within this framework that we must understand the Christian experience of our betweenness and the structure of reconciling pathos. Its elucidation is grounded on at least three assumptions.

First, wrong, as we have suggested, proves to be coterminous with history. This is so, not because history as such is wrong, not because temporal passage as such is problematic, but because history is that eventfulness which is always open to a further future. Every present decides the conditions of future possibility and, since that possibility is freely decided in the present, the opportunity for wrong lurks in the very womb of history. At this point the Christian perspective does not seem too far removed from the Confucian.

Second, if the only possible integration available within the biblical perspective is one that takes place through time, and if God is the principal term of that which is first and that which is last, then that integration must be one that involves God in that which lies between first and last, in temporal process.

Third, if not even God can escape history if there is to be a future consummation that includes the creation, then it is also so that God cannot escape the impact of wrong if wrong does occur. Wrong will then inevitably become a part of God's own reality.

We have said God cannot escape time, history, wrong. We should rather say God wills not to escape time, history, wrong, for God is love. This love, we might say, is the divine life that wills a world in relation to Godself. Included in this will is the will that there be an eternal consummation of this relation, a relation of mutual joy.

It is only within some such set of assumptions that the New Testament testimony concerning Jesus begins to make sense. What are some features of that testimony important for our considerations here?

A preliminary feature, upon which everything else is grounded, is the real humanness of Jesus. He was a human among humans. He was born, and he died. Finitude and mortality marked the boundaries of his life. Without prejudice to either birth narratives or resurrection stories, this commonsense acknowledgment of Jesus as a bit of historical matter like us is universal throughout the Gospels and the New Testament.

In the Gospels, the life of Jesus is witnessed to as a life lived in an intimate awareness of a filial relation with transcendence—with that which gives life. This transcendence he addressed as "Abba, Father." Central to this sense of filial relation was a delight in the will of God, and a complete commitment (*islam*) to that will.

But if Jesus was one who lived thus before God, he was also one who equally lived towards others. It is this life towards others that the Gospels document, providing the fodder for endless Christian preaching.

It is clear from the teaching and the healing of Jesus that his life towards others made some fateful differentiations. Towards some he acted by way of judgment; towards others in infinite mercy. The criterion for this differentiation was derived from Jesus' perception of the divine will. This divine will was a will for universal reconciliation, for a truly human community dwelling within God's love. His designation for this was "the kingdom of God." At every point where society proved to be a failed community, at every point where community failed to be a reconciled community, at that point Jesus directed both his wrath and his mercy. To the rich, the powerful, the responsible persons within society he directed the summons to repent. To the outcast, the rejected, and beleaguered he addressed an invitation of hope. The touchstone of Jesus' life towards others was his attitude towards the excluded, for their presence—as the poor, the hungry, the imprisoned, the hated—was the irrefutable demonstration that community was not yet reconciled. And a community that was satisfied with reconciliation for some but not for all, was a community unreconciled not only in itself but also with God.

It was the combination of Jesus' stance "before God" and "towards others" that ultimately rocked the religious sensibilities of his day. So real was his sense of filial intimacy that he assumed what could only be interpreted as divine prerogatives—he contravened ritual prescriptions founded upon revelational-rabbinical authority, he forgave sins directly and without apology. So insistent was his quest for reconciled community that the threatened social, economic, and political disruptions led the leaders of his day to shower their human wrath upon his head. Death was the logical outcome, taking a form appropriate to the culture—crucifixion.

This is the human story of Jesus, more or less shed of Christian theological judgments. But it is precisely these judgments to which we now must turn.

Throughout the New Testament there seems to be a twofold view of Jesus, a twofold Christology. There is what has been termed an "ascendance" and a "descendance" Christology.[106] An ascendance Christology is one that understands Jesus above all as a man of faith who fully entrusted himself and his destiny to God. It is what we have already briefly described. A descendance Christology, however, is constituted by the judgments that the followers of Jesus made respecting his person and mission in the light, above all, of his resurrection. In this Christological perspective Jesus is the one sent by God and, indeed, is finally also seen as God's own presence.

As for the ascendance: "Abraham 'believed God, and it was reckoned to him as righteousness,' " Paul writes.[107] The same will apply to Jesus. Jesus, we read in Hebrews, "learned obedience through what he suffered," and was thereby "made perfect."[108] He is the "pioneer and perfecter of our faith," to whom we are to look.[109] Just as Abraham, as well as all the other heroes of faith, believed in spite of appearances,[110] so too Jesus amidst the suffering of shame and ignomy continually "offered up prayers and supplications, with loud cries and tears, to him who was able to save him from death, and he was heard for his godly fear."[111] Jesus believed, i.e., entrusted himself to, God. Might we also say then that "it was reckoned to him as righteousness"? I think we may do so.[112]

The entrustment by Jesus of himself to God is clear throughout all the Gospels, though there is no more profound meditation upon this entrustment from a post-Easter perspective than in the Gospel of John, except perhaps for Hebrews. In all the Gospels, this entrustment reaches its utter depth in Gethsemane and the cross. In the midst of total abandonment Jesus ends his life. Whether or not the cry of dereliction from the cross is historical, it rightly portrays the fate of one who trusts all to God and then encounters, even more deeply than Job, and certainly like the suffering servant of Isaiah, the apparent and utter inactivity and unconcern (or willful connivance?) of God.

It is only in the context of this "before God" of Jesus' faith, which reached its tragic culmination in death, that we can understand the "for others" of Jesus' life, as already indicated. Jesus' faith is active through love.[113] Entrusting himself entirely to God, and in the "obedience of faith," he lived from out of God's love towards all. The Gospels are the later believing community's remembrance of this. As such he was both "the one who was open to the absolute mystery," which is God, and "the one who received from the absolute mystery what he had to hand on to others."[114]

Thus, the faith of Jesus and its sorrowful completion in death is this ascending, trusting, response towards God. The descendance is God's action, God's gift, God's love.

Where then is this act of descendance, the completion of divine love to be seen in the life of Jesus, if indeed "God is love"?

The life of Jesus in its entirety, of course, is seen as "an event of disclosure," not unlike the way the Buddha event is viewed. It was not, however, the life and death of Jesus in and of itself that made it a moment of disclosure but, as the New Testament documents seem at pains to make clear, God's act of raising Jesus from the dead. In this act God is seen to confirm the work of Jesus as God's own work, and the death of Jesus as an event of divine condescension. Summed up in Paul's words, this disclosure was that "God was in Christ reconciling the world to himself."[115]

It would not serve our purposes here to enter into a detailed discussion of the resurrection from a critical, historical perspective.[116] The Christian faith is, in fact, incomprehensible without the faith in the resurrection. More particularly, the authoritative claim of Jesus to forgive sins and his seemingly pretentious demeaning of the tradition of the elders, and his doing so without an appeal to Moses to buttress his position, would have become a dead letter together with his body in the grave.[117] As Paul writes: "If Christ has not been raised, your faith is futile and you are still in your sins."[118] There can be no question but that this conviction was central to the New Testament experience.

Without the resurrection as the great descendant act of God, Jesus would have been a failure or, at best, remained an enigma. The nirvana followed as a natural and entirely logical outcome of the teaching of the Buddha. His death posed no problem beyond the very human sense of loss. All the disciples had to do—and it was not easy for them—was to understand. The tragic death of Jesus, on the other hand, called into question the legitimacy of his words and deeds. Perhaps he had indeed overdone it! At the most he could be understood as a tragic figure who meant well, but who could not speak or act for God.

For the early followers of Jesus the resurrection meant that God had in fact been acting in Jesus. Pannenberg has shown how these early believers worked backwards from the resurrection as they sought to understand the meaning of God's act in Jesus. The formulation of Paul in Rom. 1:3-4 is obviously early: "the gospel concerning his Son, who was descended from David according to the flesh and designated Son of God in power [two-stage ascendance Christology] according to the Spirit of holiness by his resurrection from the dead [descendance Christology]." In the movement from early to late Christologies within the biblical documents, we see a gradual development from this descendance Christology of an essentially eschatological kind (the giving of the Spirit as a sign of the end and pointing to the future fulfillment) to an increasingly protological Christology. We need only think of the backward progression through transfiguration, the giving of the Spirit in baptism,[119] birth traditions, to incarnation and other concepts of preexistence. In the late Christologies, most notably in Ephesians and Colossians, we see the protological, creational, and cosmic functions of Jesus amplified.

The soteriological impact of this Christological logic upon the early Christian community is clear. The resurrection established "the permanence of Jesus' relation with God."[120] Moreover, if it is efficacious for Jesus, is it not also efficacious for us? It must be, on the basis of the principle already stated, that Jesus' living "before God" necessarily included a living "toward us." Therefore, the permanence of Jesus' relation with God (the "before God" of Jesus) must include within it the permanence of our relation with God (the "toward us" of Jesus).

The reality of this soteriological permanence is expressed in the New Testament in many ways; certainly one of the most comprehensive and powerful is Paul's theology of the Spirit, his *pneuma*-Christology. The Spirit is always understood as "the creative power" of God.[121] Or, perhaps better still, we should speak of the Spirit as mediating the power of God in God's primordial character with God in God's consequent character.[122] At the same time it is Jesus who is also given that mediating role. The basic structure is outlined in 1 Cor. 8:6—"There is one God, the Father, from whom are all things and for whom we exist, and one Lord, Jesus Christ, through whom are all things and through whom we exist." That Christ—the risen Jesus—plays the role between the "from" (*ek*) and the "to" (*eis*) of God can make sense in the Pauline corpus only by his equation that "The Lord is the Spirit."[123]

When Paul identifies the risen Jesus (Lord, Christ, Son) with the Spirit it seems that no closer or greater association of Jesus, the risen Jesus, with God could possibly be made. The consequences are fundamental: this earthly Jesus who was raised is the revelation of God who in this concrete person has, from out of the divine depths, become a real participant in real time. God's reality is now impacted by time. The ascent Christology of Jesus' human faith has been completed in its seeming opposite, the irreversible divine self-giving of love. Jesus who believed is God. Therefore it can be said, "God is love (*agapē*)."[124]

Karuna and agape—the dynamics of the cycles

It is time now to bring our two discussions together. We shall do so, but limit our discussion to the following considerations. First, what leads us to treat the individual terms of *prajna* and *pistis* (faith), *karuna* and *agapē* (love) in a parallel way? Second, in what ways are the dynamics of the two cycles comparable and not comparable? Third, what insights for our study hitherto do these considerations provide us?

The first question will be dealt with most briefly. We might define *prajna* as the insight that all actualities are essentially empty of any own-being. *Pistis* (faith), is entrustment of the self to an other. For us this other is God.

These two are not entirely antithetical. Among other things both reject an ontology of radical pluralism as well as of a monism that obliterates particulars. From the perspective of *pistis* this is clear, but it is also the case with *prajna*. Here the many subsist as a totality, and the totality functions as the many. Both understand human meaning as lying in some kind of a denial of the self. The nature of this denial, however, differs. For one the denial is achieved by means of an ontological relativism; for the other by means of an ontological relationalism. For *prajna*, the individual entity really is empty, inherently

147

devoid of any self-identity, whether from itself or from others, and to discover this is gain (totality). For faith, the individual entity does have a self-identity, but this identity is not from itself, and to discover this is gain (mutuality)

Karuna is the compassion that arises in one actuality with respect to another so long as all actualities do not equally experience totality. To put it more simply, it is compassion for sentient beings that suffer due to attachment. *Agapē* is the outflow of care by one actuality on behalf of an other as it seeks to maximize the fulfillment of that other in a creative future of freedom and mutuality. In short, it is the free giving of self to enhance the other.

The limited parallelism of these two concepts is again important. Both entail an openness to the other, and issue in deeds that call for the sacrifice of self. However, the sacrifice of self means something different because of the different groundings (*prajna, pistis*). As for love, enhancement suggests an advance towards something richer. The whole is always on the way to becoming a whole. *Karuna* embodies what already is. It is already a whole without any leftover. Attachment to the other as the other is real in *agapē*, attachment to the other as the other is without substance in *karuna*. Clearly, *prajna* and *karuna* are correlates as are *pistis* and *agapē*.

A fundamental flaw in most theological assessments of Buddhism is that this correlation has not been seen in its full seriousness. Most assessments have been inordinantly intrigued by the *prajna* side of things, expatiating endlessly on *nirvana, anatman,* and *pratityasa-mutpada* (causality or dependent co-origination). In fact, and here we take Mahayana Buddhism as the point of reference, there has been no Buddhist interest in *prajna* that has not been a simultaneous interest in *karuna*. The concepts are inseparable.

This leads us, then, from a static definition of terms to make a statement or two about the dynamics of the two cycles, the bodhisattva and Jesus cycles.

The concept of *upaya*, or its equivalent, is necessary to do this. It is in the event, the deed, the revelation, the act of disclosure that we see the dynamic relations between *prajna* and *karuna*, faith and love at work. Let us look at each circle separately, and then jointly.

The ideas of *karuna* and *prajna* are mutually interpenetrating. The first truth in Buddhism states that all existence is *dukkha,* suffering. From the viewpoint of predicamental pathos it is taken to mean that all existence is undesirable. However, from the view of *karuna* (reconciling pathos), it means that the truth of existence is penetrated into only by the deepest experiencing of suffering. If the experience of suffering posits an ultimate unity in things, which it necessarily does, then the deepest experience of that suffering leads to experiencing reality as, at its deepest, a totality. It leads, in other words, to the same conclusion as *prajna.* After all, it was the experience of suffering that led the Buddha on the pathway to discovery. *Karuna* is *prajna* in its active side, *prajna* is *karuna* in its attainment side. This coincidence of the two concepts becomes apparent through the upayanic event.

According to Diagram 5 (p. 133), these events of disclosure occur at the juncture or occasion where *nirvana* and *samsara* meet. The Buddha takes on a fleshly body, which at the same time is not a fleshly body. That body is real, as real as the suffering of sentient beings is real, yet in taking on that body of suffering which is not in itself really a body of suffering the deeper truth is revealed that reality is in fact void of actual suffering. As long as there are suffering beings—that is, beings that experience reality as suffering—so long is there the upayanic disclosure of the Buddha, so long also is there what we have termed the bodhisattva cycle of *prajna, karuna,* and *upaya.* Should there be none that experience reality as suffering, then all would be subsumed into *prajna.* Only the antipodal ground of suffering otherness occasions the manifestation of *prajna* as *karuna* in specific events of disclosure.

Faith and love likewise share in an inner affinity. Faith is a dying to self-attachment that commences as a response to love. Love is faithful action which forgets the self so as to establish the other. Love is fulfilled in faith, in the trust which it evokes, just as faith fulfills the love which has evoked it. Faith can be active only in love, if it is faith that is active, just as love always activates faith when and where it is recognized. Jesus is the supreme upayanic event for the Christian. This is so, for the faith of Jesus was the disclosure of the love of the Father. The inner content of the faith of Jesus was nothing but the love of God as its source and its outcome. Love empties itself in care for the other; faith cares for the other as love empties it of self.

How then do we see the two cycles together? At least this much is clear: what *upaya* is to the Buddhist, incarnation is to the Christian. At the same time, one of the most profound differences between the supreme Buddhist and Christian upayanic events is the multiplicity of the former and the singularity of the latter. In Buddhism the buddhas and bodhisattvas are in principle innumerable. In contrast, in the New Testament perspective there is only one God and one Christ: "For although there may be so-called gods in heaven or on earth—as indeed there are many 'gods' and many 'lords'—yet for us there is one God . . . and one Lord, Jesus Christ." [125]

For Buddhism it is a question of the one and the many. One might appeal to the Buddhist concept of the *trikaya,* the three bodies of the Buddha, to clarify this. In this concept the historical Buddha (*nirmana-kaya*) the enjoyment- or mythological-imaginary Buddhas (*sambhoga-kaya*), and the absolute Buddha (*dharma-kaya*) form a single construct. All of reality is at root Buddha in nature, and therefore the particular manifestations of the one Buddha reality at these several levels are in principle many. The many are the one, and the one many.

It is, so to say, in the middle category—mythological Buddhas— that much of Mahayana Buddhism has specialized. In this category has occurred one of the most striking Buddhist convergences with Christianity. We refer of course to the most prominent of such specializations, Pure Land Buddhism. The Amida (Amitabha) Buddha, the decisive *upaya* of Pure Land, at some point in the past rounds of existences made a series of breathtaking vows motivated by a deep-going compassion. Among these vows was the vow that Amida not attain enlightenment unless by the attaining of such enlightenment all sentient beings could thereby find liberation. Another, similar vow made Amida's attainment conditional upon the guarantee that by simply calling upon Amida's name any and all sentient beings could attain liberation. Amida did attain enlightenment, and thereby all the conditions were guaranteed. In more radical forms of Pure Land, salvation is therefore entirely dependent upon the other power of this Buddha and the enabling power of these vows. Salvation is by the grace of Amida and dependent only upon faith. [126]

We have already tried to speak of the thoroughgoing historical perspective of the biblical material. Here history is taken so seriously that even God is implicated in time. The only liberation that can be envisioned biblically is that which occurs in personal relatedness and implicates God in the process.

Now, the Amida Buddha is plainly mythological. Priest Bando, a Japanese Pure Land monk, in exegeting the Pure Land experience, rhetorically asks this question: Since the Amida Buddha is not historical, does this mean that Amida is simply imaginary, or is Amida in fact actual?[127] Imaginary, actual, historical—what do these mean? Can something be actual without being historical?

"Actual" here means, of course, that the Amida captures a fundamental truth about reality, and about us. Compassion, of the kind represented in the Amida Buddha, is actual in human existence, for it is inherent in the structure of reality as we have already discussed it. This Buddha captures that actuality in symbolic form and mediates it to us. Amida is instrumental to our own salvation by compassion. Amida personifies the deep-rooted compassion that is our own ultimate reality. Once we are so saved we no longer need an external Amida, for we ourselves become concrete loci of compassion—actual Amidas, so to speak. This is the Pure Land way to realize our Buddha nature.

How, then, can we penetrate into the real meaning of the difference between the Buddhist and Christian experience of redeeming pathos? It is perhaps simply this: In Buddhism time and history have a purely instrumental value. They can be means that allow the disclosure of what already is. In the Christian faith time and history have a constitutive role, and are the possibility of that which is really new, of that which is not yet but will be. In Buddhism the many particulars disclose a universal; in the Christian perspective one particular constitutes that which is of universal relevance. In the former, the criterion for universal meaning is hidden, private, interior; in the latter it is public, an ingredient of history.

The Buddha identifies a feature of reality that is permanently so (thusness); Jesus anticipates a feature of reality that is in the making (prolepsis). The final claim of the Buddhist is ontological; the final claim of the Christian is personal. Jesus is God's becoming, God's becoming for us. God's reality is still in the making, for God's reality is meant to include us without being us.

The dynamisms of the two cycles are almost in reverse to each other.

All returns in the bodhisattva cycle to *prajna*—the emptiness of all forms. Beyond this truth there is no further truth. There is no gain or loss, there is no category of newness.

All returns in the Jesus cycle to love. Love evokes faith which leads to deeds of love in an eternally creative movement. This movement never ceases, but abounds in a permanency of ever greater and richer newness. Faith always leads back to love as source and forward to love as aim, whereas *karuna* leads always back to *prajna,* which in essence is the quiescent acceptance of reality in its "thusness" (*chen-ju*).

Is there any meaningful way in which these two cycles, so different as they are, might speak to each other? Perhaps.

Prajna corresponds to *pistis* and *karuna* to *agapē*. It is the reversal of priorities (*prajna* for Buddhism, *agapē* for the Christian) that marks the most basic theological difference between Buddhism and the Christian faith.

If there is to be any mutual learning between Buddhist and Christian it is necessary to go beyond difference without denying difference. For the Christian the understanding of *prajna* can aid in a deeper understanding of faith. Faith, after all, is an emptied self, and in the New Testament can be understood only in the light of the injunction to "take up your cross daily" (Synoptics), and the affirmation that "it is no longer I that live" (Paul). For the Buddhist the Christian understanding of love can deepen the understanding of *karuna*. Cobb, in *Beyond Dialogue,* has begun to explore this two-way learning process.[128]

Prajna is a form of faith, though there is no way in which it can be confused with Christian faith. It is a trust—a trust that persists while yet experiencing existence as thoroughgoing pain—that reality is primordially beneficent. This trust is so radical that an identity for the self is not clung to. It is not yet (could it ever be?) Christian faith, for the polarity of dialog—real subjects—is excluded from its worldview, as is hope, an essential ingredient in Christian faith. Hope is faith as confidence, not only in the primordial good of reality, but in an eschatological consequent goodness, a gift of God's love, achieved through history and which sums up history.

A *family quarrel*

Something has been asserted in the discussion about *agapē* that needs to be made more explicit, for it is an assertion that brings the Christian affirmation into disjunction with its partners in the Semitic faith tradition—Judaism and Islam.

All three of these are what we have termed axiologies of representation and, as such, fundamentally unlike the Buddhist axiology of return. Nevertheless, the role of reconciling pathos in each works out quite differently.

Our basic thesis is this: in the Christian tradition reconciling pathos is in the end an event for God. By the act of creation the divine relationship with creation becomes a part of the divine reality itself—God cannot be as if there were no world. Reconciling pathos is the event of divine vulnerability to creation, to the other—Jesus is that event. The idea of triunity (of which the traditional dogmas are merely one manifestation) is the inevitable Christian theological statement of that event insofar as it preserves Christian faith from collapsing into simple monotheism or dissipating into polytheist pluralism.

This is clearly an assertion repugnant to Islam and troublesome to Judaism. If for Islam it is problematic inasmuch as God is invulnerable to the creation as creation—which would be to associate creation with God (*shirk*), for Judaism the event of Jesus is problematic because the supposed divine involvement has brought no apparent, and therefore no real, change to the human condition of wrong. As a kind of shorthand one can say that, for one, the idea of Jesus as the event of divine reconciling pathos is unacceptable for theological reasons; for the other, the reasons are anthropological or, perhaps better, messianic in nature.

A simple typology may help to clarify further dimensions of this family quarrel. All three, we have said, are re-presentational faiths. Both God and world are to be taken seriously as aspects of reality, even though the reality of world is logically (or theologically) subordinate to God. If we envision the two (God and world) as two circles, we may then designate the relationship between these two circles somewhat in the following fashion:

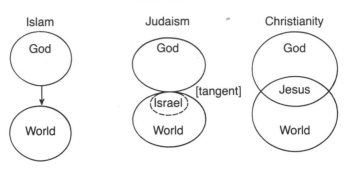

DIAGRAM 6*

In the case of Islam the circles must be kept separate—the only relationship to be posited between the two is that of divine revelation, divine guidance (*hudan*). To be sure, the relation is also immanent, as we have seen, but that is finally an immanence of power. The response of the world is without any necessary implication for God, since God's reality is of a totally distinct order. The world is without claim upon God, though God lays claim upon the world. This is clearly the case in Sunni Islam. Even in Shi'ite Islam the probing reflections upon the passion of Husayn do not violate this barrier.[129] We will not remark upon Sufism, which at least in some of its forms collapses world into divine unity—just as radical a unity (*tauhid*), but worked out in a way that is, so to say, the inverse of traditional Islam.[130]

In the case of Judaism, if we take the covenantal theology of the Hebrew Scripture as our guide, the two circles are at least tangential. The upper circle is tangential to the two lower circles. This means that God and world are associates in a profound theological sense—God is with world in covenant and theophany in a way that binds God's reality to the created, and human order. The so-called Noachian covenant[131] may be seen, for instance, as the tangent between God and the Gentile

---

*The two circles do not intend to suggest that God and the world are two substances that need to come into relation with each other. We agree with Robert C. Neville, *The Tao and the Daimon* (Albany: State University of New York Press, 1982), p. 82, where he says, "I reject the Aristotelian substantialist mode of God and world as separate and conjoined." Rather, "the connection between God and world is internal to God." The Christian view represents, we think, the most emphatic statement of this. We are dealing with degrees of difference, perhaps more than kind of difference.

world. However, within this larger circle is a smaller one. This represents Israel, and the tangent is God's distinctive covenant with Israel, which bonds the divine to a particular human community. Covenant is commitment, and on the basis of the covenant—but the covenant only as God's prevenient act of grace—does Israel have a claim, a real claim, upon God. The classical prophets in particular—prophetic figures are notably absent from the Quranic and general Muslim consciousness—with their deep exploration of divine and human pathos, are the disclosers of the depths of this irreversible relationship.[132]

In the case of the Christian experience, the two circles interpenetrate. Jesus Christ signifies the event of overlap, which for the Christian understanding is a deepening of the divine involvement with creation, which discovers that the world itself impacts upon God. The cross is the symbol of this relationship. It is an event for God—God suffers; it is an event for us—we are suffered (endured), and in that suffering reconciled. At the same time it is an event from us—the human Jesus entrusts himself completely to God; and it is an event from God—the divine act of resurrection confirms the entrustment of Jesus, confirms him as the Messiah. Reconciliation, or the cross as symbol of this, is the limitless deepening of the God-world relationship, posited in creation, under the conditions of wrong. In this event God becomes triunity, that is, suffering relatedness.

Other religious ways

We have here dealt only with examples of Indic and Semitic reconciling pathos. What about the Sinic tradition?

Since we have not yet touched on Taoism only a few words about the Confucian tradition are in order. A detailed discussion of the Confucian concept of pathos would have to move in at least three directions. On the one hand it would have to take into account the centrality of the mourning and ancestral rites for the Confucian self-understanding. The pathos of this ancestral complex constitutes a profound reconciliation of the living with the dead, and through the dead with a moral cosmos. The interpretation of Hsün-tzu can be considered paradigmatic here. The ultimate significance of the mourning rites is not supernatural—that is, having to do with spirits—but cultural.

You pray for rain and it rains. Why? For no particular reason, I say. It is just as though you had not prayed for rain and it rained anyway. The sun and moon undergo an eclipse and you try to save them; a drought occurs and you pray for rain; you consult the arts of divination before making a decision on some important matter. But it is not as though you could hope to accomplish anything by such ceremonies. They are done merely for ornament. Hence the gentleman regards them as ornaments, but the common people regard them as supernatural. He who considers them ornaments is fortunate; he who considers them supernatural is unfortunate.[133]

Were one to follow out this discussion it would lead directly into a discussion of Confucian humanism and the naturalistic cosmology of organic harmony.

Li [rites] is that whereby Heaven and Earth unite, whereby the sun and moon are brilliant, whereby the four seasons are ordered, whereby the stars move in their courses, whereby rivers flow, whereby all things prosper, whereby love and hatred are tempered, whereby joy and anger keep their proper place. It causes the lower orders to obey, and the upper classes to be illustrious; through a myriad changes it prevents going astray. If one departs from it, one will be destroyed. Is not *Li* the greatest of all principles?[134]

Human culture replicates the harmonious rhythms of the cosmos. The ancestral rites bring this harmony into human affairs at the most elemental point of disharmony, that of life and death.

A second direction would be to probe the aesthetic sense of Chinese culture. In the *Analects* of Confucius there are the so-called "sigh" (*t'an-tz'u*) passages. These are passages in which Confucius encounters the death of a beloved friend or disciple or some other human sorrow. When his favorite disciple died an untimely death it led to a simple but profound sigh on the part of Confucius. When a dear friend was ravaged by a loathsome disease, Confucius could only respond with a sigh: "Such a man and such a death; such a man and such a death." The role of emotion and grief in Chinese culture would seem to be intimately related to this grieving, yet accepting, response to tragedy.

Finally, one should note the Mencian emphasis upon the reconciling role of the emotive dimension of life. We saw that work itself out in Wang Yang-ming. The classic Mencian passage reads as follows:

> Mencius said, "It is a feeling common to all humankind that they cannot bear to see others suffer. The Former Kings had such feelings, and it was this that dictated their policies. One could govern the entire world with policies dictated by such feeling, as easily as though one turned it in the palm of the hand.
>
> "I say that all people have such feelings because, on seeing a child about to fall into a well, everyone has a feeling of horror and distress. . . . Not to feel distress would be contrary to all human feeling . . . . This feeling of distress (at the suffering of others) is the first sign of Humanity [jen]. This feeling of shame and disgrace is the first sign of Justice. This feeling of deference to others is the first sign of propriety. This sense of right and wrong is the first sign of wisdom. People have these four innate feelings just as they have four limbs. . . . They are like a fire about to burst into flame, or a spring about to gush forth from the ground. If, in fact, a ruler can fully realize them, he has all that is needed to protect the entire world. But if he does not realize them fully, he lacks what is needed to serve even his own parents." [135]

Mencius locates the reconciling pathos between self and world (the reality of Heaven being exhaustively immanent in both), and thus cosmos or all of reality, in affective (rather than the rational or conative) human nature. The four fonts are perceptible feelings which, if left to follow according to their own internal logic, will rage forth like a fire in the whole range of moral attributes.

It is easy enough to correlate these affective moral promptings with the phasic psychology discussed earlier. These promptings are fragile, yet real. But, as the promptings emerge into the realm of activity, the pathos that would bring reconciliation can be subverted. It is in yielding to the promptings that reconciliation takes place. It is in part this thesis that has made "human feeling" (jen-ch'ing) such a central category in Confucian social psychology.

To sum up: Reconciliation as an act of replication is an act that fills up the gap or space between two planes, the ontological and the existential. The ancestral rites, the aesthetic urge, and the emotive fonts of moral feeling all play their part in reconciling the two planes. These affections link the equilibrium of "prior heaven" with the harmony of "posterior heaven," that is, the realm of society and history. The life of Confucius and, in varying degrees, the lives of many others exemplify this linkage.

Reconciliation as an act of return in Buddhism is an act in which original nature is discovered to be the true reality of which empirical reality is its reflex, or vice versa. Through the pathos that leads to intuitive wisdom, a pathos which in a profound sense is indeed that wisdom, there is no longer any disjunction, for each is transparent to the other; between them there is no difference. The enlightenment of the Buddha is a realization of this logic of identity, an identity of the particular with totality.

Reconciliation as an act of representation is action that is constituted in and through history, through human willing and doing, in a world of relationships. It is creative, for events are the medium of real change, real difference. So far as this willing and doing conform to the divine intent, so far is reconciliation achieved. Jesus, we have said, was that event of full and complete conformity, anticipating the final summation when all things will conform to the divine intent that is love.

We move now to the consideration of human history as the anticipation of a final consummation.

4

THE TRANSFORMING PRESENCE

A. Introduction

In the preceding chapters we have considered the question of transcendence and the question of pathos in both of its forms, predicamental and reconciling, as well as the relationship between them. It is this pathos that above all gives specific and decisive content to religious experience, a content that is appropriate to the respective axiological frameworks. This pathos enables one to experience reality as a unity, to one degree or another, and it establishes an order of valuing.

The religious history of China has its distinctive character. For one thing, here, perhaps more than in any of the other principal civilizational centers, all three religious families and their specific orders of valuing have exerted a profound and transforming historical effect. In the West, Indic religious influences today play an increasing, though still relatively minor, role in society as a whole, while the Sinic religious impact is much less. India has been profoundly shaped by Islam from outside, and in a very different way by Christianity and the West generally, but has been virtually untouched by Sinic influence. In China, and regions influenced significantly by Chinese influences, all three—Sinic, Indic, Semitic—have had a profound and lasting impact. For this reason, if for no other, the Chinese religious experience provides a helpful occasion for theological reflection.

159

We shall take a closer look, then, at the Chinese religious experience, and on the basis of that reflect theologically from within the Christian perspective that we have begun to develop. Might this lead to richer theological insight?

As we do so, however, we need to broaden our treatment somewhat, and at least include the Taoist tradition in our considerations. We have argued that both the Confucian and Taoist traditions belong to a common family, the Sinic. However, their reading of experience is significantly different, the Confucian taking a reading from social existence, the Taoist from natural existence. Thus, our treatment will not be complete until we turn to Taoism and incorporate it into our discourse.

B. Taoist Naturalism

To speak of Taoism is to speak of a diversity of ideas and movements that go under that name in the Chinese tradition. We need not lament the problem of that diversity here, but need only draw attention to it.[1]

The textual tradition that is recognized as standing close to the font of the movements that can be called Taoist and that is universally recognized as authoritative in all such movements, no matter how diverse they are in the way they recognize it, is the *Tao-te-ching*. Authorship, traditionally attributed to Lao Tzu, as well as the formation of this tradition is hidden in the obscurities of history, providing fruitful ground for legend and myth. The early Chinese historian Ssu-ma Ch'ien, writing around 100 B.C.E. in the first serious effort at sorting out the historical facts concerning the reputed author Lao Tzu, concludes his account thus: "No one in the world can say whether all this is true or not. Lao Tzu was a hidden sage."[2] There were, both before and after Confucius, sage hermits who adopted a rustic way of life and critiqued the way society was being run. Some of these developed followers, as well as traditions—mostly oral, but in some cases written. The *Tao-te-ching* no doubt developed in some such fluid context. About all anyone can really say is that it "appears to be an anthology of apothegms borrowed partly from the common stock of wisdom, partly from various proto-Taoist schools. The anthology was built up gradually and did not take on a more or less definitive form until the third century B.C."[3]

We have referred to Taoism as a naturalism. As such, it represents a considerable contrast to Confucian "societism." Ssu-ma Ch'ien again, in a tale that is surely apocryphal, describes a meeting of Lao Tzu and Confucius. Confucius, the expert in ritual, beseeches Lao Tzu, oddly,[4] "to instruct him in the rites." Lao Tzu obliges, so to say, but not quite as Confucius might have hoped. Lao Tzu informs Confucius that "a good merchant hides his wealth and gives the appearance of want," and that "the superior man has the outward appearance of a fool." He then chides him: "Get rid of that arrogance of yours, all those desires, that self-sufficient air, that overweening zeal; all that is of no use to your true person. That is all I can say to you." Confucius, always the gentleman, later remarks to his disciples that, "the dragon is beyond my knowledge; it ascends into heaven on the clouds and the wind. Today I have seen Lao Tzu, and he is like the dragon!"[5]

Whitehead refers to the Taoist view of life as the "clutch at vivid immediacy."[6] While in some ways that may fit better as a description of Chuang-tzu than of the *Tao-te-ching,* there is in Taoism generally, an unmediated acceptance of the world as it happens to one. The Taoist scorns all effort at artificial construction (*yu-wei*), epitomized by the Confucian effort to set right the social relationships, in preference for spontaneity and immediacy.

The text of the *Tao-te-ching* can be read from two directions. One might read it from its admittedly abstruse metaphysics, and then try to apply it to life, or one might read it in terms of its religious and moral function, its soteriology, and then inquire concerning its metaphysical hints. It is in the function that the substance is to be seen.

One of the most complete summations of the *Tao-te-ching's* message appears in chap. 25. We read: "Humanity conforms to earth, earth conforms to heaven, heaven conforms to Tao, and Tao conforms to self-so-ness." Human being in the world is a process of replicating ever more deeply the way in which the Tao itself functions. How is that?

This "summary" can provide a pattern for examining the message of the text. These levels, or degrees, of conformation are ultimately all of a piece, yet can be distinguished.

"Humanity conforms to earth." It is an interesting point to note that virtually all of the imagery of the *Tao-te-ching* is taken from the natural order, not from human activities as in the *Analects*. In spite of the later celebration of "the great clod"[7] in Chuang-tzu, earth is here not to be taken in the sense of matter, or primal stuff, but in the sense of its specific mode of existing or functioning. At least two things can be learned from the way the earth functions. The movement of water, for one, reveals this functioning. Water always follows earth to the lower place. Water seeks the gaps of the valleys, not the peaks of the mountain tops. It follows the rifts and cavities, the hollows and holes of the earth, seeking always the lowest place. There is an eternal constancy in this functioning, and therefore it can be said that, "the valley spirit never dies."[8]

A second way in which one can see earth function is in the manner of its nurturing all things, so that they are filled with vitality. For instance, among the beasts, as in many mating rites, one sees that "the female by stillness overcomes the male"; or, to take water again, "that which under heaven is the most soft, overcomes that which is the hardest";[9] or, "in birth the human [infant] is supple, in death the human is stiff; living plants are tender, but dead ones are brittle." "Thus, the soft and weak are the disciples of life; the hard and forceful are the disciples of death."[10] As tendencies inherent in that which is of the earth, lowliness and weakness will also be the signs of human conformation to the functioning of earth.

But "earth conforms to heaven." At least two things are being said here. The first is that heaven, that is, the cosmos in its overall aspects represented visually by the sky, deals with the whole of things. It is not simply that each particular follows out its own inner tendency, so that one is dealing with a cacophony of tendencies, but that a unifying principle of reversal is the inner logic of all tendencies. The second, a corollary of this, is that heaven is impartial, treating all alike without distinction, regardless of what the subjective need, desire, or wish might be. Thus it is that heaven universalizes. The particularities of the earth become participants in a universal rhythm.

Heaven, in turn, is not the end, for "heaven conforms to Tao." Perhaps the basic idea here is that the Tao is inexhaustibly immanent in its own activity, but as such is ultimately elusive—"it gives rise [to all things] but cannot be possessed." [11]

There is a wealth of passages in the *Tao-te-ching* that speak of the ineffability of the Tao. In the opening passage, to cite it more extensively, we read:

> The Tao that can be spoken of is not the eternal Tao. The name that can be named is not the eternal name.
> That without name *[wu-ming]* is the origin of heaven and earth.
> That with name *[yu-ming]* is the mother of the Ten Thousand Things [the phenomenal world].
> These [the "without" and the "with"] proceed from the same source, yet have different names.
> Both together are called the dark.
> Dark and even darker,
> It is the gate of all hidden-wonders. [12]

This unnamed obscurity is the ground and principle of the birthing of all things, as this clearly cosmogonic passages reads:

> The Tao gives birth to the one.
> The one gives birth to the two.
> The two gives birth to the three.
> And the three gives birth *[sheng]* to the Ten Thousand Things.
> The Ten Thousand Things carry *yin,*
> And embrace *yang;*
> And achieve harmony by the mixing of *ch'i.* [13]

The principles of obscure wholeness (one), differentiation (two, *yin* and *yang* energies) and mediated unity (*ch'i* or breath as third term) are the creating principles intrinsic to Tao and which mysteriously yield the fecund diversity of the "Ten Thousand Things." Again we read:

> That thing which is the Tao is eluding and vague.
> Vague and eluding, within it are the forms.
> Eluding and vague, within it are things.
> Deep and obscure, within it is the life force.
> This life force is truly real; within it are the evidences. [14]

Nevertheless, this generative cosmogony, or *creatio continua* as Girardo aptly uses the term, cannot be stressed in a unilateral sort of way, for to speak of birth or production (*sheng*) is even so only to speak of one side of things, the front (*cheng*) side. Equally, if not more fundamental, is the inverse principle of reversion (*fan*) intrinsic to the Tao. "Reversion [*fan*] is the movement of the Tao."[15] This is so, because that which has being (*yu*) proceeds from that which is without being (*wu*), and has no being in separation from that which is without being. This reversion is a *reversio continua* to the empty, fathomless, obscure, and unnamed. To be attuned to the truth of reversion one must "stop the mouth and shut the eyes," that is, break off the tyranny of sensory stimuli so as to experience the Tao's "obscure penetration."[16]

But even this is not the end of the trail, for "the Tao conforms to self-so-ness." Not only is the Tao immanent in reality, it is absolutely free in its immanence. The category of *tzu-jan*, self-so-ness, spontaneity, excludes all notions of causality lying behind the origin of things. The Tao, as we have already seen, fades into the obscure and the dark, into the nameless and the wordless. In the end the Tao is not a something, it is a somehow, the spontaneous functioning of the cosmos behind which there is no other principle than its own spontaneity.

What is Tao? It is a moving, changing, pervading, birthing. The Tao as molten energy eternally "goes out" without exhaustion, giving birth to all things; as solidified thing it eternally "reverts" without loss, being without its own form.[17] Perhaps we can say that Tao is the cosmos perceived as function, and thus totally without form or name, and thus more like a gap, a hollow, an emptiness, an obscurity, a chaos. It is the cosmos as absolutely immanent to itself.

The action of Tao, and thus so also the *tzu-jan* of the way things are, the self-so-ness of things, which emerges from the depths of obscurity is this action of oscillation between production and reversion. For human existence the implications are clear, if full conformity to the way things are is to take place. Human existence is already a positive existence, a particular, a some-thing, a protrusion, so to speak, and as such rides upon the movement of the Tao in its productivity. By this very fact, however, human conformity to the Tao requires reversion, not greater productivity, not further intensification. There can be no secondary production, as if the action of the Tao were not sufficient.

There can be only reversion, like the flow of water to the valley, like the stillness of the female, like the supple weakness of living grass.

This Taoist naturalism has spun itself out in a heterogeneous array of movements, some of which at first blush seem to share little in common with this philosophic-religious stance. Agreeing with Girardo that "the idea of a historical tradition is . . . that there is always a constantly changing series of interpretations and forms relative to a nuclear set of a few basic, and open-ended, religious convictions,"[18] we should not be surprised at this rich difference. There are traditions of exoteric and esoteric alchemy, revolutionary movements with an elaborate confessional piety, a priestly movement of unnumbered deities joined in an unwieldy hierarchy serviced by elaborate ritual display and, of course, the various forms and shapes that Taoist-related philosophical movements took.[19]

C. Two Visions for Human Community

As already indicated, the Confucian and Taoist from an early time seem to share some common family traits. For example, they early on share the basic *yin-yang* cosmological perspective.[20] The cosmic-egg mythology—the splitting of a primal unity into two countervailing forces—fits with the philosophical speculation of Taoism as well as the social speculation of Confucianism. The famous *t'ai-chi-t'u*[21] of the neo-Confucians is the most notable demonstration of this.

How they came by this congeniality, though agreeing on little else, is probably not to be known. It seems clear enough from the study of Girardo that Taoism has a close and almost direct rootage in the cosmic-egg type of mythology. There is no evidence that it is also so for the Confucian tradition. The two traditions, Taoism and Confucianism, developed out of distinct cultural matrices; to some degree it was southern and northern cultural influences, respectively.[22] Indeed, there is little evidence that cosmogony, as contrasted with cosmology, played any role in the early Confucian tradition. There was simply no interest in the question of an absolute beginning[23] that was prior to historical existence.

Nevertheless, there is a clear resonance of the Confucian cosmology with the Taoist cosmogony. The early shift in Chinese social thought to anthropocentricity is probably part of the answer. An "anthropocentric shift" occurred during the passage from the Shang (ca. 1500–1066 B.C.E.) to the Chou (ca. 1066–221 B.C.E.) in which the realm of the gods was gradually separated from the realm of the human. Together with this the gods lost their specificity, more or less collapsing into a generic idea of heaven (*t'ien*) or transcendence, this reconstructed idea of heaven then becoming a transcendent moral principle immanent within existence. Integral to this development was a progressive emphasis upon the socio-moral nature of human affairs. Of course, this development was a slow and complex process closely related to social, political, and intellectual developments of the time.

Accordingly, we read in the *Tso-chuan,* a pre-Confucian text, that "the way of heaven is far away from us, only the way of man is close."[24] Where such a way of thinking is accepted, in which heaven is distanced from the human, which in its turn takes on central importance, transcendence can be experienced in an immanental way only. If such is the case, then the immanentalizing of transcendence on this basis would in principle have no objection to a Taoist type of cosmogony. Both Confucianism and Taoism thus adopted a cosmology of dual cosmic forces, the *yin-yang* cosmology, which also serves as a cosmogony.

In fact, the Taoist and Confucian traditions are congenial in a number of ways. Both affirm mundane existence (nature/society) in a positive way; both perceive transcendence immanentally; both have an optimistic anthropology; both share the ethical structure of replication in which each seeks in its own way to realize on the human plane the more primordial dynamics of Tao. These congenialities are not small.

Yet, for all that, these congenialities by no means yield a common social vision, being rather near polar opposites. We will perhaps not be unduly surprised when it turns out that the one reads nature into society, while the other reads society into nature.[25]

In the *Tao-te-ching* we find this social vision:

Let there be a small country with few people.
Let there be ten times and a hundred times as many utensils but let them not be used.
Let the people value their lives highly and not migrate far.

Even if there are ships and carriages, none will ride in them.
Even if there are arrows and weapons, none will display them.
Let the people again knot cords and use them (in place of writing).
Let them relish their food, beautify their clothing, be content with their
  homes, and delight in their customs.
Though neighboring communities overlook one another and the crowing
  of cocks and barking of dogs can be heard,   .
Yet the people there may grow old and die without ever visiting one
  another.[26]

Both the *Tao-te-ching* and the *Analects* were fundamentally political documents.[27] Obviously, the agreement on the nature of human community is practically nil. In an encounter with a couple of recluses, predecessors of the Taoist school of thought, a disciple of Confucius is rebuffed when he makes a simple inquiry about directions. One tells him that Confucius ought to know where the bridge is, and the other chides him for his desire to change the world, advises him to shun "this whole generation of men," and returns to his hoeing. When told of this, Confucius ruefully responds: "One cannot herd with birds and beasts. If I am not to be a man among other men, then what am I to be? If the Way [*tao*] prevailed under Heaven, I should not be trying to alter things."[28]

Perhaps, as we might already suspect, the real argument is not concerning alternative social visions as such. Behind the alternative social visions lies the question of the priority of the individual over the social, of nature over culture. For the Confucian, "the time of the sage kings constituted an absolute limit." Culture was primordially human. It was the culture heroes who enabled people to distinguish themselves from "four-legged creatures and birds,"[29] and marked the beginning of history, of genuinely human being in the world.

It is precisely this cultural idea of the "absolute limit" posited by the "sage kings" that the Taoist finds fundamentally objectionable, positing nature instead as absolute limit. The list of terms and phrases deriding cultural activity is almost without limit. As striking a statement of this rejection as any can be found in a curious anticreation myth of Chuang-tzu, an inventive tale that utilizes ancient cosmogonic material:

The Emperor of the South was called Shu. The Emperor of the North was called Hu. And the Emperor of the Center was called Hun-tun. Shu and Hu at times mutually came together and met in Hun-tun's territory. Hun-tun treated them very generously. Shu and Hu, then, discussed how they could reciprocate Hun-tun's virtue, saying: "Men all have seven openings in order to see, hear, eat, and breathe. He alone doesn't have any. Let's try boring him some." Each day they bored one hole, and on the seventh day Hun-tun died.[30]

Hun-tun means "undifferentiated mass," and can be thought of as a sack, or shapeless lump of flesh. Lacking the differentiating marks of eyes, ears, nose, and mouth—he (or she) was without face or social character—he (or she) was not yet human. Consequently, the benevolent and humane act of providing that which was lacking was gratuitously donated by Hun-tun's erstwhile friends. Tampering with nature led, of course, to disaster. Taoist scorn for Confucian tampering knows few bounds.

The Taoist social vision is, without question, a thoroughly impractical one. Yet, this vision has had a persistence throughout Chinese history that demonstrates its inherent strength and efficacy. Its strength, first of all, is a negative one, and lies in the fact that it acts as a counterpoint, as a protest, to the actual social situation. It is, so to speak, the perpetual shadow of society's ills. As long as society continues to spawn injustice, inequality, constriction of human possibilities, so long will this vision display a certain potency. As indicated, this vision of a return to primitive naturalism is one that followed Chinese social thought right up to and into the present.[31] Its negative strength arises from the positive evils of actual social existence. There is, one should note, a critique only of society, but no critique of nature, for nature is revelatory of the Tao. Its strength, second, is a positive one that lies in its appeal to the priority of the individual, or at least of the smallest possible social grouping, in which a pristine harmony with nature is realized without effort, and devoid of all dissonance and conflict. In the *Tao-te-ching,* as we have seen, this unity of individual with nature is experienced in the perpetual rhythm or oscillation between reversion and production or, somewhat differently in the Chuang-tzu, as a perpetual flow with the natural metamorphoses of nature.[32] Both of these view nature as the *tzu-jan* (self-so-ness) that it is. And whether it is by reversion or by metamorphosis, the proper human destiny is a participation in the vitality of this self-so cosmos.

This Taoist vision of life, adumbrated only in the *Tao-te-ching*, eventually refracted into many disparate developments, as already noted. Whether all this disparity derived from a common Taoist premise (hardly likely), or whether a common premise attracted divergent movements (more likely), is a question we need not address here, other than to be aware of it. Whatever the case, all these developments shared a common emphasis upon the Tao as the locus of true and eternal vitality.

The way this vitality was affirmed could be as different as the ways advocated by Chuang-tzu and Yang Chu, some of whose views may in fact have been current even prior to the *Tao-te-ching*. Yang Chu, known only through reference to him by others, was traditionally known as an "individualist," "hedonist," and "anarchist."[33] Whether in fact he was so, it does seem clear that he placed the highest value upon life and its all-pervasive vital force. "Would you give a single hair of your body if you could thereby save the entire world?" he was asked. He would not do so, not so much because the state was unimportant as because life itself was the higher value, and the destruction of a hair was in fact the destruction of life, even if "merely the ten-thousandth part of the body."[34] The implications of this for the importance of individualism and self-expression seem obvious.

This kind of vitalism was radically different from the sometimes macabre antics and detached vitalism of Chuang-tzu. Chuang-tzu scandalized the Confucian by the mirthful singing and beating of drums at the death of his beloved wife. Death we learn was no more, and no less, than a renewed entrance into the great transformations of nature, in which every entity experiences a vital dispersal throughout the organic and inorganic universe.[35] Death and life are thus equally celebrated as part of a single, transformative reality. "One day," so it is said, "Chuang-tzu saw a skull, whitened by the sun." He poked at it with his riding whip, asked it questions about its late existence, and then proceeded to pick up the still silent object and take it home. Placing it under his pillow, he fell asleep. That night it appeared to him in his dreams, discoursing about the pleasantness of death. So Chuang-tzu put a question: "'If, with the help of the creator [or, creative force], I could restore your body to you, renew your bones and your flesh, and take you back to your parents, your wife and children and old friends, would you not gladly accept my offer?' The skull opened its eyes wide, furrowed its brows, and said: 'Why should I throw away a happiness greater than a king's once again to thrust myself into the troubles and anxieties of humankind?' "[36]

These two, Yang Chu and Chuang-tzu, mark off the limits of Taoist vitalism. But between these limits a truly unmanageable diversity existed. There was the alchemic tradition, both interior and exterior. By interior meditation it was hoped that the vital forces in the body could be so manipulated that immortality would be assured. Parallel to this was the development of the manipulation of various substances and chemicals to develop an elixir of immortality. There was, again, the specifically religious tradition. This led eventually to the growth of an elaborate priestly and monastic tradition, complex ceremonies, a thoroughly unmanageable hierarchy of gods and other spirits, a massive textual recension of divine revelation, and all the other accoutrements of religious institutionalism. This religious tradition absorbed local religious practices, thus taking on many forms of local color, as it sought to serve the vital, this-worldly needs of individuals and groups. Then there were the movements of religious rebellion, which sought to establish a kingdom on earth of universal peace (t'ai-p'ing) or its equivalent. And, of course, there were the philosophical movements that splintered off into many directions. Even the apparent political quietism we have noticed above provided a metaphysic for some of China's worst despotisms.[37] Thus, religious rite, the cultivation of meditation or the alchemic arts, revolutionary action, philosophical profundity, and political proposal—all these movements affirmed the intrinsic vitality of the cosmos as more primary than culture and society.

If the Taoist social vision was impossible to implement, the Confucian vision also, while seemingly more practical, was one which ever failed to be accomplished, proving to be almost as elusive as the Taoist. Indeed, we saw how Confucius was rejected, and as it turned out it was the harsh and bureaucratic practices of the later-arising legalist (fa) school that set the political directions for China's future.[38] Nevertheless, the Confucian social proposal lived on, in part being absorbed into the ethos of the Chinese bureaucratic system, and in part being a humane critique and modifier of it, eventually—in one of those profound ironies in which history delights—becoming the ideology espoused by the often despotic state.

D. Critical Breaks in Chinese Religious History

Before relating the above section to our study as a whole it will be helpful briefly to survey Chinese religious history.

Three breaks in this history far overshadow all others in their historical and religious significance. The first break was that immensely creative period during the 5th to the 2nd century B.C.E., which is often referred to in Chinese history as the period of "the hundred schools." The Confucian and Taoist traditions we have briefly looked at were only two of an immensely rich offering made available at that time. In terms of the ongoing development of Chinese religion, however, the two we have looked at were the most decisive.

This epoch marked a break between the failed political synthesis of the Patriarchal Empire of the Chou (1122–722 B.C.E.) and the aborted bureaucratic synthesis of the Ch'in (221–206 B.C.E.)—but shortly resurrected in a definitive form with the bureaucratic empire of the Han (206 B.C.E.–220 C.E.).[39] It was in this sociopolitical passage of several centuries that all the principal indigenous Chinese philosophical and religious proposals were generated. The essential religious character of this break was the sense of an immanental transcendence[40] experienced either through the natural or the social realm.

The second break was the introduction of Buddhism into China during the 2nd through the 6th centuries C.E. While the earlier break was in part brought about by the wider cultural involvements that the Chou synthesis had made possible, the cultures had to meet each other on pretty much equal sociopolitical terms. The entrance of Buddhism was the first significant incursion from a major cultural center not contiguous with the Chinese heartland. It was, however, a cultural incursion and not a political one.

Buddhism brought some entirely new conceptions into the Chinese universe. Perhaps the single most important of these was the fundamental pessimism with respect to both organic and social existence, and the quest for a radical, transcending liberation. Thus, a new experience of the tragic and of liberation from the circumstances of tragedy was introduced.[41] It entered China, moreover, at an exceedingly propitious time for Buddhism. The Han synthesis had fallen apart, Confucianism had been discredited as being inadequate to the tragic circumstances of life, Taoist rebellion had been suppressed, and the quietist options of Taoism now offered were inadequate to the situation. During the following centuries of political disunion it gained immense influence, and provided the integrating ideology for a renewed unification of China under the short-lived Sui (589–618 C.E.) dynasty. But the T'ang (618–907 C.E.) immediately picked up the fragments and produced one of the most long-lived and remarkable dynastic rules in China.

As Buddhism sank deeper roots into the Chinese soil, an indigenous response gradually took shape. Buddhism itself was modified, both in the area of religious practice, of which Pure Land and Ch'an (Japanese Zen) were the main response, and in the area of philosophical reconstruction, most notably T'ien-t'ai and Hua-yen. Taoism too was modified, most notably in patterning itself after the Buddhist *samgha,* with a rich development of religious institutional forms. The neo-Confucian movement was a response that integrated both Buddhist and Taoist philosophy and practice into its own self-construction, while yet remaining definably Confucian.

The third break was the incursion of the West, the most important incursion being that which began in the 19th century. This too came at a fairly auspicious time, for the Ch'ing dynasty had been fairly long-lived (established in 1644), and was now entering a period of weakness and decline. The encounter with the West hurried this process of decline along. This incursion was, however, fundamentally different from the Buddhist one, for it was a political incursion, not merely cultural. Buddhism was appropriated by China; the West foisted itself upon China.

But the very dynamics of this last incursion serve as a boisterous witness to the essential religious import of it. The West, no matter what religiocultural form its incursion took—whether Christian, social Darwinist, Marxist, or other secular form—introduced a significantly new set of temporal categories: the idea of advance through time, progress, temporal development.

The indigenous Chinese response was at first fitful: the T'ai-p'ing Rebellion of the mid-19th century, the failed reform movement of the late 19th, the fall of empire, and the Republican Era. In the end, the response was a massively political one, as China appropriated Marxism as its guiding ideology for revolution and for social reconstruction—modifying it in the process.

There is one important religious tradition absent from this account—Islam. Islam, too, entered China, and even though it continues as a major faith with followers in all parts of China, it never interacted with the Chinese social, cultural, political, and religious reality so as to constitute a major agent for change. This was not the case in Islam's penetration into India. Perhaps a major reason for this curious fact is that Islam was originally invited in as an aid to put down rebellion, and then subsequently largely appropriated by ethnic groups marginal to the dominant Han (Chinese) population. Certainly, a contributing factor for this lack of cultural impact was the close association of Islamic institutions with an Arabic revelation. Had Islam early become linguistically Chinese, as had Buddhism, the cultural and religious impact might have been quite different.[42]

This cursory historical review directs us to three matters for theological reflection. Endemic to the indigenous Chinese traditions was the tension between granting priority to nature or to culture. The subsequent entry of Buddhism disclosed a new dichotomy which had not really been previously present within the Chinese setting. This was a sense of discontinuity between the phenomenal world and final reality. This alternative of an absolute contrast lived in tension with the Chinese bias for continuity and harmony. Finally, the entry of the West introduced a further issue, that of time as advance, not simply as change, thus introducing a largely absent directional eschatology (teleology). These three issues simply outline major points at which the three families differ from each other.

In a sense it seems that the Confucian/Taoist controversy is the most basic and most universal. Wherever there has been an awakening to the distinctive cultural role the human plays in the cosmos, wherever this anthropocentric shift has taken place,[43] there there is also an awakening to a fundamental instability inherent in human existence. This instability is experienced as a tension between nature and culture, and ultimately also between the individual and the society.

It is a nature/culture tension, for if the cultural identity is posited with excessive vigor, then there is the threat that the human, free of all the constraints of nature, will experience loss of a metaphysical grounding. Perhaps a purely cultural humanity would be a contradiction in terms. No specifically religious worldview affirms culture without ambiguity, not even the Confucian. Nature places a constraint, one that is creative, upon culture. First of all, nature unites the human species in an integral way with the whole of the cosmos. Culture does not do this, but rather makes nature in the image of its human self. Culture lives by making distinctions (so as to make new syntheses, of course), and in that always lies danger of arrogance. A fundamental danger of the Confucian proposal was a cultural elitism, exemplified in the contrast between the civilized (*wen*) and the barbarian, between the "small persons" (*hsiao-jen*) and the morally "cultured person" (*chün-jen*). The Taoist summons culture back to its primordial ties with nature, undermines this overbloated effort at the making of distinctions, and summons to a radical, yet only natural, equality. On its part, the Taoist emphasis upon nature had its own dangers to face. Most especially these were the dangers of passivity (a loss of real vitality), on the one hand, or self-indulgence (excessive vitality), on the other. In this situation, culture is a summons to moral responsibility.

The Buddhist incursion demonstrated that the Chinese religious experience needed a deepening. With transcendence being so immanently available, so to speak, even if still beyond absolute reach, there was a danger that the sublime would become the prosaic. This was certainly the danger with the Confucian tradition which, always subject to a certain cultural naivete, lacked the ability to critique its own norms, assuming experience, whether cultural or individual, conveyed its own norms directly.[44] The Taoist tradition, far less naive in this respect, fell into the opposite danger of dispensing with norms, devoid of genuine care.

The Buddhist proposal introduced a new sense of disquiet, and with it a new sense of hope. This disquiet is both more basic and less basic than that disclosed in the nature/culture tension. It is less basic, for the very act of positing culture (that is, the act of becoming human) creates a tension with nature—a distancing, a transforming. At the same time, however, the Buddhist disquiet presupposes this more simple tension between nature and culture. But the Buddhist disquiet is more basic, for it goes beyond this nature/culture tension, not accepting either as the solution, and locates the root of human disquiet as an internal disquiet—a primordial *tanha* (thirsting).

In many ways the Buddhist proposal is more akin to Taoist naturalism. Perhaps this is so because culture is a higher level of discrimination than that experienced in a natural sort of way. But it would be a mistake to equate the two, for Buddhism also undermines or, if that is too strong a word, transforms the Taoist conviction. The phenomenal realm—whether nature or culture—as the product of a phenomenalizing mind is the consequence of an existential (*tanha*) or epistemological (*avidya*) error. For the Buddhist, the endless transformation of a Chuang-tzu would be simply endless bondage, unless it were accompanied by, or the product of, an even more primordial insight. The Taoist affirmations did not come out of a radical enough questioning of appearance.

E. A Question of Time

The Western ethos, incarnate in Christianity and Marxism, introduced a new and momentous experience of time.

In both the Confucian and Taoist worldviews, save for some abortive examples that became important only with the Western incursion,[45] there was no developmental concept of time. The *Book of Changes* (*I-ching*), for instance, a Confucian classic, was in its origins a prognosticatory text devoted to analyzing the manifold changes (*yi*) within time. But, even here, past and future played no fundamental role. "They collapse in the present since every actualized situation contains all others in a state of latency."[46] Indeed, "the very premise that everything is change endows change with a curiously static quality, something suspiciously homogeneous which precludes development properly so-called."[47] It was for this reason that we had to speak of the Chinese axiological framework as replication. The past, or the primordial, serves as model, and the task is moment by moment to replicate that model in the present. The passage from past, through present to the future has no independent value, and therefore no development. All this is so, despite the fact that within Confucian historiography there was a very sophisticated understanding of chronology and temporal sequence, as well as of temporal cycles.

Buddhism deepened the atemporal quality of existence. We have already seen that within the Mahayana Buddhist conceptions movement and change are illusory. Seng-chao, one of the first Chinese truly to appropriate Buddhist concepts and categories, came to the following insights about time:

> It is generally considered a self-evident premise that birth and life alternate, that winter and summer follow each other, that some things flow along and move [in our world]. For me, things are wholly different. Why? In the *Fang-kuang* it says: "There is no *Dharma* that comes or goes, there is no *Dharma* that changes its position." When we look more closely, we find that the act of "nonmovement" does not mean "the giving up of movement in the striving for rest," but undoubtedly "rest within all movement." Therefore [one can say]: Even if [things] move, they are yet always at rest. They do not stop moving to come to rest. And even when they are at rest, they do not abandon motion. It follows that movement and rest have never been fundamentally different forms of existence, but that they merely appear different because we are deluded. . . . In the *Chung-kuan,* it says: "[When people] look at a place and know of a man [getting ready to] walk there, this man is [in reality] no longer the same when he gets to that place. . . . The reason people talk of movement is that past [things] do not enter the present. They infer that movement [exists], but not rest. . . . But if past things do not come, how can present things go away? What follows? When we look in the past for things past, [we observe] that they are [there] forever. But when we look for them in the present, [we observe] that they are never present. That they cannot be found in the Now makes clear that they do not come [into the present]. That they remain forever in the past shows that they do not leave [the past]. . . . Therefore it is evident that there are no connections between things [across periods of time]. Since such connections are totally impossible, how can there be things that move? This means that even storms that uproot mountains are really calm. . . .[48]

This is characteristic of Buddhist absolutism, as we have seen. To view totality as the sum of discreet moments or to view a discreet moment as the pinpoint of totality is one and the same thing.

In Confucian and Taoist concepts of time we seem to have something akin to an endless series of replicating moments; the destiny of actual life is to replicate at this moment in time and space the natural rhythms of primordial reality (Taoism), or the moral rhythms of social reality (Confucianism). Buddhism, in turn, tends to radicalize and absolutize the moment. No longer is there a meaningful past/present/future movement, for the present absorbs past and future into its own infinity.

Showing some affinity to the cosmogony of the *Tao-te-ching*, yet expressing a Buddhist point, Suzuki says:

> The very moment something begins to move even the slightest bit, it runs into two. So the question is how to grasp what is prior to this movement. When we refer to something prior to even the arising of this concern, it appears to make no sense at all. And yet this is in fact the ultimate reality.[49]

This still sounds rather too Taoist. But others (to refer to another Japanese Buddhist) speak of being "bottomlessly in time."[50] This seems to mean that "all time is revealed in every now." As Nishitani puts it:

> On the field of emptiness, all times enter into each moment. In this circuminsessional interpenetration of "Time," or in Time itself, which only originates as such in interpenetration. . . all times are phantom-like. . . . Or, it may be stated that, because in the field of emptiness each time is bottomlessly "Time," all times enter into each time. . . .
> As a bottomless thing wherein all times can enter, each time actually comes into being as this or that time as it really is. Like-reality and like-phantom have to be at one.[51]

This seems to be saying that each moment, because it is an occasion that occurs in the boundlessness of emptiness, is itself without bounds, so that what is spoken of as past or as future is really only an aspect of the moment. Taken by themselves, past and future are phantoms; both appear, nevertheless, as elements in the boundless moment, which alone is reality. This construct inflates the moment to infinity, but in so doing sacrifices any real "passage" of moments, and with that the possibility of anything new really occurring in and through that passage.

The Semitic view of time, and in this case we speak particularly of the Christian form, was fundamentally different. Rather than an endless series of replicating moments, and rather than the infinite inflation of the moment by all times, the moment becomes unique, irreducible, and nonrepeatable, because it is the concurrence of two infinities—the infinity of the past and the infinity of the future—by which it lives, but which are not reducible to it. The moment remains a finite moment, always between two infinities. The unique moment sums up the past and anticipates the future in a unique way, even while being related to all pasts and all futures of other occurrences.[52] The hourglass has often been used to describe this experience of time. The moment is creative, for it sums up the past in a freely chosen way—despite all the bondages that may also be present in that moment—and initiates a movement with incalculable implications for the future. Each moment, therefore, reconstructs a past and creates a future.

This view affirms a genuine advance through time, and continually posits new possibles. The Semitic import hit the Chinese intellectual world, so to speak, like a thunderclap. Particularly intriguing was the discovery that an analogous conception of time lay buried in Chinese texts of the past, which were will-nilly ignored throughout the centuries.

"Time itself remained inescapably real for the Chinese mind," writes Needham, so that the "metaphysical idealism" of Buddhism "never really occupied more than a subsidiary place."[53] This was in particular the case within the Confucian tradition. "Connected with their intense preoccupation with human affairs is the Chinese feeling for time—the feeling that human affairs should be fitted into a temporal framework. The result has been the accumulation of a tremendous and unbroken body of historical literature extending over more than three thousand years. This history has served a distinctly moral purpose, since by studying the past one might learn how to conduct oneself in the present and future. . . . This temporal-mindedness of the Chinese marks another sharp distinction between them and the Hindus."[54]

As Needham makes abundantly clear, Chinese tradition supported a vigorous sense of "linearity."[55] He raised the question of the concept of time in China in order to see whether it had any relationship to the failure of modern science to develop from indigenous dynamics, despite the exceedingly impressive premodern scientific tradition there. He concludes that the Chinese sense of time was not a contributing factor.

Nevertheless, he does admit that the Chinese sense of time differed from the Western. "It would be fair to call it 'homeostatic' or 'cybernetic'. For there was something in Chinese society which continually tended to restore it to its original character (that of a bureaucratic feudalism) after all disturbances, whether these were caused by civil wars, foreign invasions, or inventions and discoveries."[56] It is for the same reason that we have referred to the essentially "replicative" nature of the Chinese moral consciousness. On the part of the Confucian tradition of historiography, while there was, in the passage of time, social and cultural development, or at least change, the task of the present was to activate the same moral ethos as that of the culture heroes of the past. On the part of the Taoist tradition of naturalism, the outlook tended to be much more cyclical in nature, for the inherent tendency of the Tao was reversion.

Nevertheless, there were some genuine ideas of historical development in Chinese thought. Two notions are of particular importance: that of the *t'ai-p'ing* (great peace/equality), and that of the *ta-t'ung* (great togetherness). Both of these concepts were at an early time incorporated into a temporal sequence that had potentially explosive implications for Chinese society and thought. While seemingly not derived from Confucian ideas, both were embedded eventually in Confucian texts. The key texts are worthy of citation:

When the Great Tao prevailed, the whole world was one Community [*t'ien-hsia wei kung*]. Men of talents and virtue were chosen (to lead the people); their words were sincere and they cultivated harmony. Men treated the parents of others as their own, and cherished the children of others as their own. Competent provision was made for the aged until their death, work was provided for the able-bodied, and education for the young. Kindness and compassion were shown to widows, orphans, childless men and those disabled by disease, so that all were looked after. Each man had his allotted work and every woman a home to go to. They disliked to throw valuable things away, but that did not mean that they treasured them up in private storehouses. They liked to exert their strength in labour, but that did not mean that they worked for private advantage. In this way selfish schemings were repressed and found no way to arise. Thieves, robbers and traitors did not show themselves, so the outer doors of the houses remained open and were never shut. This was the period of the Great Togetherness [*ta-t'ung*].

179

But now the Great Tao is disused and eclipsed. The world has become a family inheritance. Men love only their own parents and their own children. Valuable things and labour are used only for private advantage. Powerful men, imagining that inheritance of estates has always been the rule, fortify the walls of towns and villages, and strengthen them with ditches and moats. "Rites" and "righteousness" are the threads upon which they hang the relations between ruler and minister, father and son, elder and younger brother, and husband and wife. In accordance with them they regulate consumption, distribute land and dwellings, raise up men of war and "knowledge"; achieving all for their own advantage. Thus selfish schemings are constantly arising, and recourse is had to arms; thus it was that the Six Lords obtained their distinction. . . . This is the period which is called the Lesser Tranquillity [Hsiao-k'ang].[57]

This almost socialist program, probably of Mohist[58] origin, places the idea of the *ta-t'ung* in the immediate past, but implies it can be reconstituted. Another text places the parallel concept of *t'ai-p'ing* in a forthright temporal sequence of progress where *t'ai-p'ing* comes as the culmination. This passage reads:

In the age of which he heard through transmitted records, Confucius saw (and made evident) that there was an order arising from Weakness and Disorder [shuai-luan], and so directed his mind primarily towards the general (scheme of things). He therefore considered his own State (of Lu) as the centre, and treated the rest of the Chinese oikoumene as something outside (his scheme). He gave detailed treatment to what was close at hand, and only then paid attention to what was further away. . . .

In the age of which he heard through oral testimony he saw (and made evident) that there was an order arising of Approaching Peace [sheng-p'ing]. He therefore considered the Chinese oikoumene as the centre, and treated the peripheral barbarian tribes as something outside (his scheme). Thus he recorded even those assemblies outside (his own State) which failed to reach agreement, and mentioned the great officials even of small States. . . .

Coming to the age which he (personally) witnessed, he made evident that there was an order (arising) of Great Peace [T'ai-p'ing]. At this time the barbarian tribes became part of the feudal hierarchy, and the whole (known) world, far and near, large and small, was like one. Hence he directed his mind still more profoundly to making a detailed record (of the events of the age), and therefore exalted (acts of) love and righteousness. . . .[59]

Here the concept of development through time is clearly articulated. These two ideas, *ta-t'ung* and *t'ai-p'ing,* obviously had an attraction to each other. It was, therefore, not by chance that they became part and parcel of periodic movements of rebellion within the Chinese ecumene. However, even though the concept of the *ta-t'ung* and *t'ai-p'ing* were integral to both Confucian and Taoist social hopes, the evolutionary context within which they were enunciated did not enjoy the same prestige, being largely forgotten by all but periodic rebel ideologies. Perhaps it was in part because of the threat such a temporal scheme might pose to the stability of an imperial reign that these ideas never took solid root. The pattern of replication fit the status quo in a much less threatening way.

Christianity gave a new basis for a more dynamic temporal sense. We can hardly do better than to quote Needham's summary of what Christianity brought:

Unlike some other great religions, Christianity was indissolubly tied to time, for the incarnation, which gave meaning and a pattern to the whole of history, occurred at a definite point in time. Moreover Christianity was rooted in Israel, a culture which, with its great prophetic tradition, had always been one for which time was real, and the medium of real change. The Hebrews were the first Westerners to give a value to time, the first to see a theophany, an epiphany, in time's record of events. For Christian thought the whole of history was structured around a centre, a temporal mid-point, the historicity of the life of Christ, and extended from the creation through the *berith* or covenant of Abraham to the *parousia* . . . , the messianic millenium and the end of the world. Primitive Christianity knew nothing of a timeless God; the eternal is, was, and will be . . . "unto ages of ages" . . . ; its manifestation the continuous linear redemptive time-process, the plan (*oikonomia*) of redemption. In this world-outlook the recurring present was always unique, unrepeatable, decisive, with an open future before it, which could and would be affected by the action of the individual who might assist or hinder the irreversible meaningful directedness of the whole. A moral purpose in history, the deification of man, was thus affirmed, significance and value were incarnate in it, just as God himself had taken man's nature

181

upon him and died as a symbol of all sacrifice. The world process, in sum, was a divine drama enacted on a single stage, with no repeat performances.[60]

This new conceptuality of time influenced all the major movements for social change that postdated the 19th-century Western impact, awakening elements already latent, as we have seen, within the Chinese tradition: the T'ai-p'ings of the mid-19th century, propelled by millenary zeal and bringing about the death of some 20 million; the Reform Movement of which K'ang Yu-wei, the principal reinterpreter of Chinese social thought from this new perspective, was mentor; the Republican Era and Sun Yat-sen's social proposals; the iconoclastic May 4th movement; and, finally and most dramatically, Chinese appropriation of Marxism.

Yet, it was not the Christian transmission but the Marxist transmission of the Semitic concept of time that finally became decisive. Time was "the medium of real change." But the Marxist understanding of change through time brought this Semitic notion, stripped it of all overt transcendence, and offered an immanental, secular version. This bias towards immanence fit well with Chinese predispositions, as we have seen, but gave to that experience of immanence a new sense of direction and possibility, an experience most radically and forcefully articulated by Mao Tse-tung.

F. The Spirit

If there is any category available to Christian reflection that can aid in bringing the rich diversity of the world's religious heritage together in responsible and Christian theological discourse, it would seem to be the category of spirit.

The concept of spirit seems to be universal. Thus, for instance, the translators of the Hebrew Scriptures found a nearly perfect counterpart to the term *ruach* in the Greek *pneuma,* which in both meaning and derivation could hardly be a better fit. In China the choice was perhaps not quite so easy, but in the end the translators happily landed upon the term *ling.* In fact, it would be hard to find a better alternative, even though the overlap with the Hebrew and Greek terms is not so immediately clear.

The term *ling* has its origins in ancient Chinese ritual. It is composed of two parts, one part being the symbol for rain, the other part being the symbol for shaman, magician, or sorceress or, in an alternative written form, a symbol for jade. As such it means the making of offering through dance to heaven so as to secure rain. By extension it then means a marvelous power or energy, spirit. It is, thus, a term associated with the power of dance and the atmospheric element of rain or moisture and its power to give vitality and life.

What is important for us here is the primary thrust of the term *spirit* as a theological category. Several things can be said by way of introduction. First, the term bespeaks liveliness, vitality, dynamism. In the biblical tradition it is associated with wind and breath. In creation it is the Spirit that moves over the face of the waters of chaos. In the creation of humans God breathes into them and so gives them life. The Spirit is breath and wind, which is a movement that comes and goes as it will, without us knowing a whither or a whence. Flesh is contrasted to the creative spirit by the lack of its own vitality, utterly dependent upon spirit—God's Spirit is removed and all flesh decays.

A second thing to be said about spirit is that it identifies that by which an entity transcends itself. Just as we live from beyond ourselves by breathing—we live by the breath we inhale and necessarily exhale again upon the world—so, as spirit, we live from beyond ourselves. Our life is given from beyond, and is returned to that beyond. "Thus spirit is self-transcendence; the liveliness of each life is precisely its origin and end beyond itself."[61] Thus, "God. . . breathed into his nostrils the breath of life; and man became a living being."[62]

But this self-transcendence is both of an external kind, or towards our outside, so to speak, as well as of an endlessly interior kind. The spirit is the self-transcendence which is also self-knowledge. "What person knows a man's thoughts except the spirit of the man which is in him?" The conclusion with respect to God is that "no one comprehends the thoughts of God except the Spirit of God." The premise for both of these assertions about human self-knowledge and divine self-knowledge is that "the Spirit searches everything, even the depths of God."[63] This is a searching and a self-transcending that is inherently without limit, without exhaustion.

A third thing to be said is that *spirit* describes personhood, the essential quality of relationship one to another that inheres in the fact that we are speakers, communicators. That is to say, not only is spirit self-knowledge, it is also the quality of self-expression and the basis for other-interpretation; therefore, to be spirit is to experience the reality of speech. Appropriate to this, spirit is integrally associated with the category of word: "We impart this in words not taught by human wisdom but taught by the Spirit."[64] So also the long biblical association of the concept of prophecy and wisdom with spirit.[65] In this regard it should be noted that spirit is not an independent someone or something, but is always only descriptive of someone or something. Thus, we speak of the Spirit of God, the spirit of a person, the spirit of a group, the spirit of a nation. Not only is it so that "spirit is precisely the person or group as not immediately identical with itself; the genitive phrase marks the nonidentity,"[66] but it is also the case that it marks that which is perceptible to others of the true self of things.

A fourth thing that must be said is that the spirit is not merely associated with the beginning of things but, almost more importantly, with the end of things. It is thus inevitably associated with death ("All flesh is grass. . . . The grass withers . . . when the spirit of Yahweh blows upon it . . ."[67]); but also with judgment ("a spirit of judgment and . . . a spirit of burning"[68]); and especially in the biblical perspective with new creation both in the idea of resurrection and in the idea of consummation.[69] The spirit is thus a thoroughly eschatological category and uniquely belongs to the future.

In this regard we find a rather peculiar situation with the category of spirit. Associated as it is with the end of things, spirit has almost universally been associated with the dead and with disembodied realities. In many cases this introduces a certain fragmentation to the idea of spirit, which renders it in the end an ineffectual eschatological category.[70] Yet, in precisely the opposite way, it is because of the connection of spirit with future realities that the biblical reality of spirit is always of a transformative kind. It is because it moves reality from the status quo to a new situation—chaos to creation, ignorance to insight, sin to salvation, death to resurrection, end to new creation—

that spirit becomes the premier term for transforming creativity. It is the eschatological thrust of the concept that imbues all the other aspects with genuine significance.

All of the above, except perhaps for the specifically biblical eschatological function of the term, identify aspects in the idea of spirit which may be considered more or less universal. Yet, it would not serve Christian theological reflection on the relations among different religious Ways simply to extrapolate from these general statements. An essential feature of the biblical tradition is the specific association of the idea of spirit with God, specifically the God of covenant, Yahweh—both the Hebrew and Christian Scriptures—and, in the New Testament, with the historical individual Jesus. Does this specificity of the category of spirit in the biblical tradition vitiate any attempt to see the spirit in a broader cosmic function? One would rather say that it alone has the power to give cosmic significance to the particularity of historical event.

It is not our purpose here to exegete the specifically biblical witness to the understanding of spirit as supremely the Spirit of God and the Spirit of Jesus. The exegesis can be assumed. It is our purpose, however, to inquire as to how the category of spirit, assuming its specific tie with Jesus, might help us in attempting to make more "cosmic" statements, and so bring our discussion together in a Christian sort of way. We have noted a great deal of difference among the diverse religious Ways throughout our discussion, while at the same time always aware of certain common problematics. Must we simply leave difference lie unattended, or might that difference invite us to a further attentiveness? The latter is our conviction.

We shall proceed, then, in fairly orderly fashion, commenting first upon the Sinic contribution, then the Indic, represented specifically by Buddhism—realizing that Hinduism does not receive its due—and finally the Semitic tradition. This should lead us to some concluding comments.

We have stressed the Sinic bias towards taking present experienced reality more or less on its own terms—natural or social. While there may be a certain naivete that shows in this, perhaps it is a profound naivete. The Taoist adverts to nature almost by instinct, so it seems. Human being in the world is understood and interpreted in terms of natural categories. This is distinctly different from Western materialism which might argue that reality is reducible to matter, and is ultimately quantifiable. Nature for the Taoist is real precisely in that it is not quantifiable; nature in its own reality is mysterious, elusive of every effort at specification. This would seem to be much closer to the modern apprehension of nature, in which our scientific knowledge is fundamentally statistical, leaving a necessary, not merely optional, space to freedom and spontaneity.[71] "The Tao that can be named [or said] is not the eternal Tao." While nature as ultimate subject cannot be defined, its predication, its functioning, can be and is experienced. The human way of *being in* the world is to conform to nature's way of *being* the world. In the *Tao-te-ching* this way of being in the world was by continual reversion; in Chuang-tzu (not discussed above) this way of being in the world was by endless transformation. In either case, that which is the more primordial qualitatively, probably also temporally, has the greater prestige, for one is then closer to the origins and springs of cosmic vitality. In the *Tao-te-ching,* as we saw, the idea of reversion as conformity to Tao ultimately traced natural reality back to its roots as pure spontaneity—Tao conforms to self-so-ness.

The Taoist, perhaps somewhat peculiarly from our Western perspective, is not oppressed by the idea of necessity as adhering to the idea of nature. Rather, the Taoist is impressed by the idea of nature as rhythm, which ultimately derives from its own spontaneity. Thus, to experience nature is to experience freedom in its purest form. Perhaps here the Taoist is on to something that would be of great value for us. The aesthetic richness of the Taoist tradition, which—in painting, for instance—figures forth the mysterious spontaneity of nature into which the human form quietly, subtly, and imperceptibly disappears, surely conveys this sense of freedom. Its social vision articulated it in another sphere. And the ecological implications of this would seem to be great.

Does this illumine our understanding of spirit, or does our understanding of spirit illumine this? Perhaps it goes both ways.

We might speak of at least a fourfold insistence in the Taoist view of the world. This fourfold insistence is an insistence that nature is spontaneity, that human vitality is interdependent with the ecological rhythms of nature, that the physical is essential, and that nature is ultimately beneficent. A word about each.

Nature is spontaneity. This equation is not idle, for the term used for both is the same—*tzu-jan*. In fact, there was originally no abstract category in Chinese thought to correspond to the western category of "nature." When it became necessary to translate "nature" into Chinese, the category chosen was precisely this term. It was found fitting, for it conveys the idea of that which has not been altered by human labor.

Can we relate the biblical view of spirit to this Taoist insight? At the natural level we might just simply say that the Spirit of God is the spontaneity (or self-so-ness) of nature.[72] Ultimately, nature is grounded in freedom: "The earth was without form and void, and darkness was upon the face of the deep; and the Spirit of God was moving over the face of the waters."[73] This "movement" is the spontaneity which is nature.

If this Taoist insistence can be granted, then the succeeding points seem to follow quite naturally. The cosmogonic question—Why is there something rather than nothing?—is answered with the statement on spontaneity. The cosmological concerns—In what way is it that things are?—come next. The Taoist insistence, in answer to the cosmologic questions, is that there is a logic of interdependence between human vitality and natural rhythms, and that this logic can be discerned, and indeed ought to be discerned. It was this insistence that led to the scientific impulse emanating from Taoist thought.[74] A corollary of this insight is the insistence that the physical is not optional to reality but essential—it therefore pays to learn its rhythms; and in the end its movements are of a beneficent order.

It has often been observed that in Taoism the only kind of immortality looked for was some sort of physical immortality. This is so, surely, because it was precisely the physical that could not be given up. In some cases this led to crude efforts to sustain physical continuity leading, among other things, to the pursuit of very material alchemic arts. As time went on no claimant to Taoist immortality was ever undisputably present. Like "flying saucers," like the "snowman" of the Himalayas, the claimants were always shrouded in puzzling mystery. As a result, various secondary theories on physical immortality arose— immortals dwelt on an isle far off to the East; immortals assumed the appearance of death, but once buried dissolved into some kind of ethereal material existence; and so on. On the other hand, it led to sublime visions of identity with the rhythms of nature, and ultimately also with its spontaneity. To be spontaneous was to be immortal, an idea perhaps expressed best in Chuang-tzu.

For all the value that we might attribute to these Taoist insistencies, they were essentially fragmentary and unworkable as a comprehensive solution to the human predicament. To have followed Taoist counsels, whether the sublime or the magical, to the bitter end would have guaranteed the disappearance of any kind of discernable human community. Fortunately, the Taoist stance was never alone, but was essentially a protest and alternative to another vision, the Confucian.[75]

Confucian assumptions, as we have already noted, are in content different from Taoist assumptions, and so also are the concrete insistencies. If the Confucian is insistent about anything, this insistence will include at least two things: the insistence that human being in the world is essentially historical, that is, that human being is constituted in and through social and moral action; a corollary insistence that the doing of the good is a genuine human possibility.

Early Confucian thought completely elided the cosmogonic concern; thus the absence of any cosmogonic myth in early Confucian materials, or writings influenced by Confucian predilections. It was only later, under the pressure of Taoist and Buddhist questioning, that a metaphysic was incorporated into Confucian thought. In itself, the Confucian concern is entirely cosmologic—right moral being in the world. If there was any left over, not incorporated fully into the cosmologic concerns of early Confucianism, this would probably have to be sought as implicit in two places—in Confucian revalorization of the ancestral cult, in Confucian appropriation of the concept of heavenly mandate (*t'ien-ming*). In the ancestral cult, the issue of origins remained central, but only in a moral sense—gratitude towards the ancestors. Thus, the question of ultimate origins was foreshortened into the issue of immediate origins (parents) and one's moral response. The concept of *t'ien-ming* accentuated the moral ordering of the cosmos as an immanental reality—the cosmos was spontaneously (one could just as well say necessarily) moral in its ultimate character, not made so.[76]

Throughout both its success and failure, the Confucian vision was insistently optimistic with respect to human moral possibility.[77] It is, one might venture, a Confucian dogma. The human is capable of a full and complete morality on only human grounds. Unless righteousness is a human achievement, it is not righteousness. By definition, moral action is a free act proceeding from the self, that is, it directly expresses one's essence (*hsing*) or species character, to borrow a term.[78] The good is always self-predicated, *tzu-yu*.

Taoist insight invites us to understand the spirit in relation to nature; Confucian insight invites us to understand the spirit in relation to history. It is important that the Confucian understanding of human nature lays emphasis upon the acting, doing, willing side of things rather than upon knowing, contemplating, understanding. Human nature is stamped by a certain mode of being, a being that is known in the doing. If we are to harvest these considerations for our understanding of spirit we might put it this way: the Confucian invites us to understand spirit as the freedom for moral action, the kind of action that constitutes viable human community. Included in this statement is the Confucian insistence that moral action be human action. If the intent and acting have their source external to the self, then it falls short of a Confucian definition. Moral action must by definition be a free expression of one's own being (*hsing*).

To be sure, there is a great deal of the Confucian vision that is not included in this statement. The Confucian view of social relations almost always tended towards an unexamined acceptance of hierarchy in relationships. Nevertheless, this hierarchical structuring of human relationships would seem to be a secondary feature, and the easy acceptance of cultural givens as though they were cultural norms can be attributed to unexamined Confucian assumptions, the cultural naivete of which we have spoken. Throughout the Confucian tradition there were also impulses toward a more egalitarian understanding of community. The Mencian dictum on the four fonts and the vision of a great togetherness (*ta-t'ung*), as well as the understanding of heavenly mandate and the universal possibility of moral action by humans, and, finally, the essentially egalitarian social dyad of friend-friend (or universal brotherhood) are evidences of this. But, for all that, the limitations of a closed immanence inhibited openness, to criteria and norms transcending that which was already socially evident.

This Confucian naivete, however profound, is surely not adequate.

Buddhist insight radically challenged this naivete. Here was an insight that sought to cut the underpinnings from the unexamined acceptance of both nature and society with an equal forthrightness. Existence, whether natural or social, was suffering. Both history and nature were to be transcended. If the monk was called to forsake family—thus leveling out moral hierarchy—the monk was also called to contemplate the putrefaction and decay of the body—thus dispensing with any notion of inherent physical vitality.

It took a long time for the Buddhist challenge to be understood and appropriated.[79] Of interest here is that the Buddhist challenge invites us to a yet further consideration of what *spirit* means.

The Buddhist invitation seems clear enough. It is the invitation to perceive the inexhaustible reality of what we confusedly refer to as "the self." The Taoist and Confucian direct our attention horizontally, to the breathless vista and the constancy of change in nature, on the one hand, and the endless project to define the constant in change of history, on the other. The Buddhist invites us away from body and society, to a dissolution of the self-definable entity—whether past, present or future—and to a liberation which will be achieved only by the experience of totality. Is this not the Spirit? Does not the Spirit, the reality of the eternal, not simultaneously reach between God as primordial and God as end, achieving a totality unbound by time and space? And is not God's final self in fact constituted by this totality achieved by the Spirit?

But at the same time this Buddhist wisdom, as we have already pointed out, is coterminous with compassion. The way of discovery of the totality for the Buddhist is through the experience of the inexhaustible sorrow that impregnates all phenomena, natural and historical. By penetrating through the inexhaustibility of sorrow that attaches to all finite entities, the Buddhist arrives at reality as an unlimited totality that is without sorrow.

Surely no religious Way has given more compelling attention to cosmic sorrow than has Buddhism. This insight too we can garner for our understanding of the spirit, but it will now modify the Buddhist insight in a temporal direction. The inexhaustible sorrow that permeates our experience of the cosmos, natural and social—and perhaps even the cosmos itself—is the unfulfilled urge of reality towards a fulfillment that transcends present limits. The Spirit is the urge of the cosmos towards its not-yet-completed future or, put more bluntly, it is the urge of God's sorrowing love.

We now come to consider the Semitic contribution. The first thing we will have to say here is that the difference introduced, the difference we have found particularly compelling, is the difference in the experience of time. All the religious Ways deal in some fundamental way with time, with change, with becoming. In Taoism, time is, so to say, tamed by interpreting nature as endlessly recurring vitality. Time is the flow of nature and its rhythms. With the Confucian, time is treated as endless occasions for timely action. Each present is an occasion once more, under changed circumstances, to give expression to the moral constancy of the cosmos. Timeliness is unending. In Buddhism, time is sublated. All moments, whether past or future, collapse into the eternal now. Reality experienced by wisdom is an eternal stasis, without movement, bliss; as experienced by compassion it is eternal movement, restlessness, sorrow. The former is the transcending truth, the latter a seeming truth.

The Spirit, as already suggested, is transforming creativity, always directed towards the future. This is to say that reality is constituted temporally—there is a last which is more than the first. Time is "the medium for real change."

It is precisely at this point that Christian theology must begin to talk about the particularity of Jesus and the importance of this for God.[80] We may speak of importance in this way because if time is taken seriously we must ask whether time means anything for God. If not, then we deal with a changeless reality unrelated to temporal passage. This is hardly the biblical perspective.

We cannot, thus, simply speak of the God of history, of a God who is above and beyond history even if influencing it, unless we also speak of the history of God. To speak of our experience of God only, leaves God untouched, unless we also speak of the experience of God with us.[81] In Christian theology Jesus is God's temporal particularity, the space-time reference point for speaking of the history of God. But this particularity, inasmuch as it is a part of the movement of history, is not an end in itself, but ends beyond itself; it has a future reference— the point made by resurrection. In fact, God's particularity makes sense

191

only in the light of God's future, which includes our future and that of the cosmos as well.

What then are the consequences of this for our further discourse? Is it overmuch to propose that important Taoist, Confucian, and Buddhist insights begin to cohere when we interface them with a Christian proposal concerning the history of God? Let us see what happens if we so propose.

In the Taoist insight into nature and the Confucian insight into history there is little attention directed towards the future of things, though that directedness is not in principle excluded. The quest of some Taoists for physical immortality and the quiet hope for the Great Togetherness in Confucian tradition illustrate that openness. While open to the future, the future is not central to their convictions. This is so because no fundamental transformation within present reality is to be expected. All the conditions for change are already present within the world; it is simply a matter of sufficient activation of the conditions. To put it in different words, nature, full of wonders as it is, has no history, since it is entirely immanent to itself—the principle of Tao is reversion. The same limiting principle of immanence holds in the Confucian case as well. *T'ien-ming* is just so *t'ien-ming*. It always was and always will be the same. Replication, with profound social consequences to be sure, is still just that, replication. What future there is, is simply the realization of current possibility.

To affirm Jesus as the temporal particularity of God breaks open past and present to the future in a new way. Now the spontaneity which is nature reflects a freedom that is going somewhere. The human freedom to act that constitutes history is now not merely a history of present possibility but a history open to the utterly and transformingly creative action of God in whom, with whom, and for whom history occurs. Human events and natural events become not simply the expression of an immanence already to hand, but become events in and through which something new and unprecedented comes about. Events not only impact us, events impact nature and heaven, bringing transformation into both. Neither Taoist nor Confucian anticipated so great a transformation possible—for them transformation was limited to us, but was not a predicate of nature or heaven themselves.

As for the Buddhist plunge into the depths of cosmic sorrow, and so beyond it into blissful totality, the orientation within time gives this plunge a new significance. Perhaps it is best said in Romans 8. There we read that "the whole creation has been groaning in travail together until now," the background cause for this being that "the creation was subjected to futility." "Not only" is it "the creation, but we ourselves [who] groan inwardly." This groan of ours is made possible by our participation in the Spirit, "and he who searches the hearts of men knows what is the mind of the Spirit." We have thus a magnificent, but terrible, scenario in which nature, humanity, and God, interpenetrated by the Spirit, are caught up in a cosmic spasm of agony.

But this is where the whole notion of cosmic compassion is transformed by the introduction of temporal categories. Thus we read:

> I consider that the sufferings of this present time are not worth comparing with the glory that is to be revealed. The creation waits with eager longing for the revealing. . . . The creation was subject to futility . . . by the will of him who subjected it in hope. The creation itself will be set free from its bondage to decay and obtain the glorious liberty of the children of God. The whole creation . . . and we ourselves . . . groan inwardly as we wait for . . . the redemption of our bodies.[82]

This thoroughly transforms the scenario of cosmic agony into one of cosmic eagerness and hope for something new and something greater. The Spirit reaches between God as past and God as future, the between within which we live, penetrating nature and history in the process. It is, however, not an abstract penetration, for the cry that we shall learn, that of "Abba! Father!"[83] was the cry of utter trust unique to Jesus, who also uttered the abysmal groan, "My God, My God, why hast thou forsaken me?[84] The plunge beyond agony is to the freedom of all in the totality of the end, which is God's future.

It is because our time was taken up by Jesus into God's time that God with us has a history, a history that leads through agony to final transformation.

But perhaps we have moved too quickly. We left Mao hanging in midair, so to speak, some pages back. What about Marxism in particular? What about the modern agony and triumph of China? Can we move so quickly to talk of an untroubled future while still living in a troubled present?

It is true that the Western impact upon China from the 19th century to the present was most powerfully felt in the political sphere. We need not wax eloquent about China's century of shame at the hands of Western political, economic, and religious encroachment. It is sufficient to make the point that the dynamic concept of time that has been a big part of energizing the West has not been an unmixed blessing for China, to say the least.

We do not intend here to enter upon an analysis of Chinese Marxism, of whatever ideological brand. But one thing must be noted. Marxism introduced a radical concept of struggle into the Chinese scene, a concept in some ways more radical than any known before to the Chinese ecumene. We have already discussed this and other aspects of Marxism. Here we make only these points.

Marxism introduced into China a particularly potent form of the Semitic experience of time. For one thing, it stripped the Semitic understanding of any explicit category of transcendence, returning transcendence to pure immanence.[85] Both this and the Promethean vision of human being in the world,[86] insofar as this latter affirmed the achieving of the future community of mutuality and freedom as the product of truly human action, fit with many prior Sinic assumptions. Nor was the concept of dialectic uncongenial to the rhythms of the Tao perceived in the many Chinese cosmological speculations, most notably the Taoist, *Yi-ching,* five elements, and *yin-yang* speculations. Moreover, the Marxist vision of a future of freedom, spontaneity, and mutuality brought about by human achievement appealed to many elements in the traditional Chinese social visions. Nevertheless, the concept of struggle, so radically implemented, above all by Mao, had important new features in tension with the Sinic predilection for harmonious rhythms.

However we may wish to assess Marxism as a whole, or the Marxist event of modern China, this we must say. The Marxist concept of struggle was a radical application of certain elements in the Semitic understanding of time and history. The past is prelude, the present is possibility, the future is gained only through struggle. Something must die as the new arises. There is an inherently tragic dimension, as we earlier saw, to this vision of history.

Can we appropriate this concern for our understanding of the spirit as the Spirit of Jesus? We have, after all, not really dealt with the Marxist experience of evil, an experience deeply intertwined with the Marxist experience of history.

China has had a long history of so-called peasant rebellions and dynastic changes. The Marxist event of modern China is but the most recent demonstration of the painful truth that history moves forward only through conflict. There never has been a national history anywhere that has been a history of unhindered, continuous progress.

These matters lead to this reflection: not only nature (whose spontaneity is the Spirit) and history (whose moral freedom is the Spirit) are at root personal realities, but reality at its deepest is personal.[87]

What is the alternative? That reality is impersonal, but happens to have persons in it. If this is the case, then we will have to turn to a non-Semitic religious Way to learn how rightly to experience human being in the world. That the founding Semitic intuition with respect to transcendence is that the world is given is not an intuition of a static something which one may or may not respond to, but an assertion that the world is experienced only in a personal way, as an address to me as a bundle of willing, feeling, and thinking. The world in being already given is by that fact already a part of my willing and feeling and thinking. The logic of this argument is that reality is at bottom personal. The Spirit is this deep personal subjectivity. If so, human reality as personal is congruent with reality as it is in itself. We are made "in the image of God."

This relates directly to our consideration of the Marxist vision that triumphs through struggle. This Marxist vision is profoundly indebted to Hegel. Just as we cannot approach modern China theologically without taking into account her modern revolutionary convulsions—whether we see them for good or for ill—just so Hegel was forced to his interpretation of history as the history of consciousness. "It was exactly the sheer reality of historical change—the French Revolution—that burdened Hegel that he needed to explain, not explain away, and therefore he instead interpreted universal Consciousness by the biblical intuition of consciousness as primarily spirit."[88]

Marx, as we have seen, followed Feuerbach in applying a transformative critique which inverted the order of subject and predicate. In doing so, however, Marx did not eliminate a personal reading of history, but transformed it from an abstract reading of the personal in historical process to an intensified concrete reading. The historical transformation of nature, economics, politics, and religion in a way that makes the human individual and the human community a true subject rather than an object was the Marxian project.[89] To put both Hegel and Marx into theological language, "the world subsists in that it is transformed, by a God who is—far from static Mind—lively Spirit."[90] Here we have the modern experience of China: an attempt at the personal transformation of a people and a nation.[91]

The point we are making should be clear. History is as much a story of alienation as it is of reconciliation. The human effort to become a subject in all spheres has consequence both for evil and for good. This is so because it is the story of persons, persons such as we are. Persons act in freedom. Nevertheless, the ambiguity internal to us plays itself out in the larger arena of the public world of history and economics, politics and art. That we are in God's image is not apart from our lapsed estate. We have already discussed what a theology of the Fall means to this. Our destiny is to anticipate the future of full mutuality and freedom. Nevertheless, each anticipation redefines our own internal ambiguity. We live between the times.

God, too, relates to the world only in a personal way, and supremely as Spirit in the human individual Jesus. He was rejected by people, but approved by God. Our future is anticipated in his life and his person. His is the reconciliation which will ultimately triumph over alienation. Such can come about only through the free act of persons, in fact, this person. For the Christian confession is that his freedom is itself the free action of God, who is love, and who will draw us creatively into God's freedom in mutuality with Jesus.

This theology of the Spirit cannot become untied from Jesus, as it did in Hegel—world process becomes in effect God's Son—and in Marx—the proletariat becomes the real heirs to the kingdom of (what was in fact) an illusory deity. The story of Jesus is the story of love that goes to the death to bring reconciliation out of alienation. His life, a personal triumph of trustful obedience before God, even if a communal tragedy, was confirmed to be not tragedy but anticipation of God's future for the world, for God raised Jesus in the power of the

Spirit. God's personal will for us is disclosed in the concrete love of Jesus, and it is that love which shall finally triumph. This is the shape in an anticipatory way of the Spirit, of the final future.

Thus it is:

> In all these things we are more than conquerors through him who loved us. For I am sure that neither death, nor life, nor angels, nor principalities, nor things present, nor things to come, nor powers, nor height, nor depth, nor anything else in all creation, will be able to separate us from the love of God in Christ Jesus our Lord.[92]

This is the Christian hope for the future of the world. It is for this hope that those who have faith in Jesus are called to a responsible action in history that conforms to the reconciling love of Jesus which suffers even as it triumphs through the tragic antinomies of history.

5

SPEAKING
THE TRUTH

Throughout this study we have attended to quite a number of congruities among differing faith traditions. We have repeatedly stressed the family characteristics shared by the Semitic, Indic, and Sinic traditions, respectively. These are genetic congruities, for each of these traditions grew up within a common history and the influences of one upon another, or of some third term upon both, were certainly profound.

We have also noted many cross-family congruities. Thus, for instance, in some ways the Buddhist and Christian traditions are more alike, while the Muslim and Confucian seem more similar, and the Marxist and Taoist seem more congruent. Taking a different set of characteristics we would surely come up with a different mix of compatibilities. These are structural congruities and at the least testify to certain human universals, or relative universals.

But what of all this? Are these congruities important? Or are the incongruities more important? Or are neither important?

One could leave this question aside, saying that no one can answer it. Some may be content with a smorgasbord of choices, but the seriousness with which each puts forward a claim ought to cause us to take pause. Those with no claim live by someone else's claim. That is to live at second hand.

Ultimately, we are faced with the question of truth. Subjectively put, it is the question, by what truth shall I live? Objectively put, it is the question, what truth may I affirm that most truly conforms to the final truth about things? The "order of love and hate" whereby we live will not let us unhinge the subjective and objective question for, as we cited from Scheler at the beginning of the study, "any sort of rightness or falseness and perversity in my life and activity are determined by whether there is an objectively correct order of these stirrings of my love and hate, my inclination and disclination."[1] Unfortunately, the fact that each of the religious visions we have examined puts forward a claim seems not to help. At the same time, we cannot be undecided, or we decide by default.

When we speak of *truth,* the term as used here means "to accord with reality in an integral way." *Truth* does not necessarily mean truth in a strictly cognitive sense, though that is not to be excluded either. *True* is rather to be construed in the sense that a line is true because it is straight, or a house has a true north-south axis because it is oriented towards the North Pole.[2] What then of the Muslim, Buddhist, Christian, and other claims to truth in this sense? Are they all true? Is any one of them true? We have been arguing from a Christian perspective in this study. Is that warranted?

There is clearly a pluralism of claim. Perhaps there is a hidden value in this plurality of claim. The question of truth is in the end an eschatological question; it is, so to say, open-ended towards the future, and has to do with final consequence. If the final consequence is that nothing matters—illogical though such a contradiction in terms might be—then that nothing matters is the truth that matters. If, however, something does in fact matter, then the question of truth—the truth about what matters—is a question that discloses the truth about me. We all, then, live at the point of eschatological risk.

A. Three Approaches

We do still live in the present, and the present is a continuous flow of events. It is now, amid our events, that the question raised here concerning truth comes upon us. Within the Christian community there seems to be anything but unanimity as to how to state the case. When all is said and done it seems that there are three basic tendencies with respect to dealing with the question of truth. A brief consideration of some aspects of what constitutes an event can lead us into this discussion.

An event has at least three features, without which there surely can be no event: it takes a concrete form, it occurs within a context, it embodies a content.

I now hear thunder as I write. This thunder has a form—a loud noise; it has a context—atmospheric movements and nearness of a sensate being, myself; it has a content—it evokes a wide range of experience whether sensory, emotional, cognitive, or volitional. None of these three features (form, context, content) can be abstracted from the event and retain any reality in itself. This is what we might call a first-order knowledge, or primary intention.

Now, what we call religion is a second-order matter, a secondary intention. It is not the event itself, which is always only concrete and bearing these three signs. It is a secondary construal of an event or concatenation of events, a construal that is public, having a cultural form. In the above case, thunder did not lead to religion; to be sure, had there been a particular kind of religious construal of the world the event of thunder might have evoked a religious experience. In any case, religion is not something that arises de novo with every new experience but, like a language or cultural system, it enables experience to be ordered and to appropriate events in a meaningful, if not always lucidly intellectual, way. Religion is not a private experience that is then given expression; religion is a particular kind of public construal of the world that enables a private experience to be religious. Religion is public; a religious experience is private.

Three approaches to the question of truth which will concern us here reflect a more or less undivided attention to one or the other of these features of an event—form, context, and content. We shall term them particularism, historicism, and ontologism, respectively. There are virtually endless permutations of each of these, some being relatively purer representatives of each, and others more or less mixed. A word about each is in order.

Particularism emphasizes the concrete form of the event, and typically captures it in a cognitive or propositional, institutional, or ritual way. Thus, for instance, the divinity of Jesus is given a definite propositional form. This propositional form purports to correspond to the truth of these events associated with Jesús, and whatever content there is in the events is represented in the proposition. Commenting on one form of this option, insofar as it is cognitive, Lindbeck writes that this theory "emphasizes the cognitive aspects of religion and stresses the ways in which church doctrines function as informative propositions or truth claims about objective realities."[3]

In its stronger forms, the desire is to make Christian truth—for we are here talking principally about the Christian conversation—"into the sole truth to which everything else stands opposed," and secures this unique status for Christianity by removing the Christian revelation from any contamination by or admixture of fallible human elements.[4] It traces Christian truth to miracle, to immediate divine causality, and its philosophical undergirdings are some form of occasionalism.[5] A model to illustrate this might be:

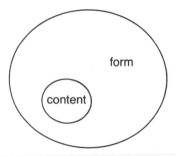

Historicism argues that one must begin with the data that are nearest to hand. These data are historical experience in a world of things and events. If we are to know anything of God it must be in the concrete, in the here and now. One cannot appeal to supernature, for that is to leap out of history. But history tells us that everything is unique. Everything is to be understood only in terms of its context. This is so because everything is conditioned, finite, contingent. While historicism does reckon with the individuality and uniqueness of every historical occurrence, it is far more attuned to the claim that this occurrence must be defined in terms of its context, and that whatever content there might be is to be taken primarily as a function of that context, of the structure of the whole. Historicism in this sense is thus a radical contextual understanding of life. A model to illustrate this might be:

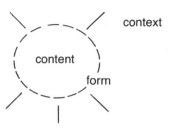

This contextual approach is denoted by Lindbeck as the cultural-linguistic. In place of context we could say the grammar, syntax, or structure of each event is primary. In this view the form of an event and its interpretation, as well as of the content evoked within it, are to be taken primarily as a function of that context, of the structure of the whole. By attending to the contextual character of an event one will then perceive how it is that an experience is evoked by the situation; since, moreover, no two contexts are entirely identical, every experience—of thunder, for instance—will be in some sense unique and sui generis. If there is anything religious in the experience, that will be because a grammar of meaning has already been brought with one into that event and indeed is part of that event's context. Every event, therefore, constructs its own reality. Truth is, so to say, always punctiliar, referable only to its context.

The ontologist approach is rather different. It is not concerned with the context, much less the form, but with the one content that is present in all historical contexts and that underlies all forms. It is thoroughly idealist in its stance. That which is evoked by the event, the experience itself, is taken to be its reality. Whatever expression interprets that experience remains no more than a secondary and imperfect reflection of that experience. In this view this experience, and not its expression, is the truth of religion. Lindbeck refers to this as the experiential-expressive way and suggests that it "interprets doctrines as noninformative and nondiscursive symbols of inner feelings, attitudes, or existential orientations."[6] It could be depicted as on page 204. There is one content that underlies a virtually limitless number of forms.

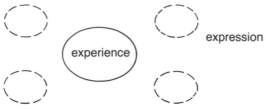

All of these are secondary appropriations, secondary intentions, of the original, first-order event. Each appropriation emphasizes one of the features of the event. To use a grammatical analogy, the first concentrates on the particular item, the vocabulary of the event; the second upon the syntax of the event; and the third upon the meaning or semantics of the event. Two are more cognitive in nature, and the other more emotive. All, however, whether cognitive or emotive, are secondary to the event itself in which the features are not separable or distinguished.

All this sounds rather abstract, and it is; so it might be well to illustrate each. We shall take the primary examples from within the Christian setting.

The particularist or propositional approach has a long history within Christian tradition. One form it has taken is Cyprian's assertion that "extra ecclesiam nulla salus" (outside the church there is no salvation). This institutional proposition is a claim that the church has captured, so to speak, the truth of the events connected with Jesus, and that any real connection with those ancient events is available through the mediation of the church alone. This church is the contemporary form of those events. Following out the logic of this statement, the Council of Florence (1442) declared that "no one, whatever almsgiving he has practiced, even if he has shed blood for the name of Christ, can be saved, unless he has remained in the bosom and unity of the Catholic Church."[7]

This strong Catholic view can be paralleled by typical, strong Protestant views. Here the issue is not the ecclesiastical form that truth has taken, but the scriptural form. Salvation is available only to those who have knowledge of this Scripture, "for there is no other name under heaven given among men by which we must be saved" than that of Jesus Christ. This propositional approach is typically stated in such fashion as the following: "I belong to the segment of the church which limits the ground of religious authority to the Bible: *the Scriptures are the Word of God written and have the force of law.*"[8]

There is no need to multiply illustrations of the tendency to isolate the form from the context. If pushed to its exclusive extreme, this approach not only abstracts from the context but draws the whole of the supposed content into its particular form, and then gives this form a hard and impenetrable surface so that the content is preserved from violation or contamination. Like a billiard ball it has a hard surface, and it encounters other claims much like other billiard balls.

The historicist emphasis upon context is another option. This is one that has been quite widely used in the descriptive studies of cultural and social anthropologists, as well as in historical studies.

As clear a theological affirmation of this context approach as any is the work of Troeltsch. To be sure, he had been profoundly influenced by the subjectivism of Schleiermacher; nevertheless, rather than appeal to the ineluctable inwardness of feeling, he wished to argue for the absoluteness of Christianity on the basis of empirical data. His quest historically to demonstrate this finally failed, for the logic of the historical-cultural context forced him to a thoroughly relativist or functional conclusion. This logic states: "The Christian religion is in every moment of its history a purely historical phenomenon, subject to all the limitations to which any individual historical phenomenon is exposed, just like the other great religions."[9] In the end each religion must be referred back to its cultural setting. This leads to at least two conclusions: all religions are relative to their culture, and thus revelation is not a logical possibility; all religions, historically viewed, are universes of truth unto themselves, cut off from the universes of each of the other culturally determined faiths.

The quiet logic of this approach, if pushed to its conclusion, would lock each particular into its own contextual box, for each particular is unique. There is no cross-cultural influence really possible, for the uniqueness of each culture forbids this possibility. Recognizing this logic, Troeltsch had to combine the experience-expression model with this cultural-linguistic model; indeed, in their pure forms they are the inverse of each other. He writes:

A truth which in the first instance is a truth for us [in our cultural or historical context] is nevertheless still truth and life. . . . If all of us in every group seek to develop what is highest and deepest, then we may hope to meet one another. . . . In our earthly experience the divine life is not one but many. To apprehend the one in the many—this is, however, the special character of love.[10]

This conclusion about the apprehension of the one was not the result of his historical studies, but a view appended to them.

The ontologist or experience-expression approach seems to have become the dominant theological model in the contemporary world, and certainly it is so in the area of interfaith questions.[11] It is the model of the one and the many. It can be expressed in the Tillichian dictum that "culture is the form of religion, and religion is the substance of culture."[12] Cultures, and empirical religions, are many; religion is subterranean, and finally one. While the roots of this "one and many" way of thinking are ancient, it is perhaps most of all the theology of Schleiermacher, with its emphasis upon experience as bearing a norming character, that has had the greatest theological influence, fitting best as it does with the mood of the postenlightenment age. As articulate an exponent of this perspective as any is John Hick.

Hick, who himself once experienced an evangelical, even fundamentalist, conversion, when encountering both philosophy and the concrete presence of so many others of different faith, eventually underwent a second conversion. He speaks of this in terms of a "Copernican revolution." No longer is Jesus Christ to be taken as the center of religious faith, but God. Jesus is only one of many manifestations of the reality we name *God*. This move to God as the center simultaneously places experience at the center. The supposed Incarnation becomes an idiomatic expression (in a day with different philosophical assumptions) for a profound experience. It "lacks any non-metaphorical meaning," for "the real point and value of the incarnational doctrine is not indicative but expressive, not to assert a metaphysical fact but to express a valuation and evoke an attitude."[13] As for Jesus, believers experienced him to be "so powerfully God-conscious that his life vibrated, as it were, to the divine life; and as a result his hands could heal the sick, and the 'poor in spirit' were kindled to new life in his presence. . . . He was so totally conscious of God that . . . [others] could catch something of the consciousness by spiritual contagion."[14] "His spirit was open to God and his life a continuous response to the divine love."[15]

Because of the contemporary importance of this approach it may be well briefly to expand upon it. Huston Smith, in heaping praises upon Frithjof Schuon's proposal concerning the "transcendent unity of religions,"[16] writes that this is "the most powerful statement of the grand, or better, primordial, tradition to appear in modern times." He draws a small diagram in the introduction that looks something like this:

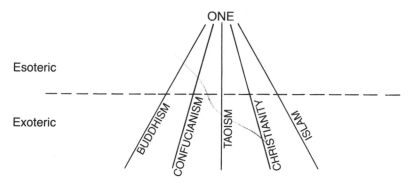

The fundamental distinction to make among religions is not that between religions but rather that between essence (esoteric) and form (exoteric). One compares vertically, so to speak, rather than horizontally. This is so, for everyone who understands truth primarily by reference to its givenness in a specific religion lives on the exoteric level; those who penetrate behind the forms to the essence and sense the primordial oneness of all religions live on the higher esoteric level. All forms are relatively false; the essence alone is true. It will eventually be discovered that what binds the religions together is far deeper and far more primordial than that which separates, for on the vertical axis all religions alike misrepresent the essence of things even while representing it.

Rhadhakrishnan, working out of an Indian Advaita Vendantic standpoint, summarizes the basic idea clearly:

> The different religions have now come together, and . . . they must develop a spirit of comprehension which will . . . bind them together as varied expressions of a single truth.

The Upanishads adopt the same view. The oneness of the Supreme is insisted on, but variety of description is permitted. The light of absolute truth is said to be refracted as it passes through the distorting medium of human nature. In the boundless being of Brahman are all the living powers that men have worshipped as gods, not as if they were standing side by side in space, but each a facet mirroring the whole. The different deities are symbols of the fathomless.[17]

Each of these three approaches has its point. If we think back to our analogy with an event it might appear that to emphasize any one of these in more or less isolation from the others is quite unsatisfactory, and the seamless totality that occurs in any and all events is torn. We might state the weakness of each approach taken in isolation in rather more forceful terms so as to make the point clear. The problem with a consistent particularism is that it finally excludes any significant continuities or relationships with the environment. Difference becomes so great that a "communication between" becomes highly problematic. As has been said, the absolutely unique is also the absolutely irrelevant. It is truth devoid of context and devoid of relation. Like a billiard ball, the truth and the symbol that conveys that truth are alike absolute and impermeable.

The problem with the ontologist option is the exact reverse. Here there is a claim to a common essence. However, no religion, no form has any clear edge on truth. The conditioned, the finite, the relative, the concrete is only a distorting fragment of that one truth. Whatever form religion finally takes is unimportant; it is the inner essence alone that is of value. No historical moment can have any intrinsic claim to be truer than any other, for they all simply clothe truth differently. The net result of this separation of content from form is that no revelation is possible, because everything is revelation. The truth is behind and beneath all forms, and ultimately not to be grasped. There is no decisive point of reference whereby to adjudicate among forms. It admits of no criterion.

Historicism seems to have the humbler claim, but if followed with consistency leads to equally irrational conclusions. The claim here is that every historical moment is a product of its context or environment. That is to say, the conditioned is relative to its context. In effect, the

context is absolutized so that the particular form is empty of content—
there is no self-being of the moment. No revelation, in short, is possible, for there is finally no content and there is finally nothing to
communicate, no "communication of."[18]

To sum up: Particularism says that a symbol is full of content, but
because there is no context there is finally no means whereby to communicate; historicism says there is finally only context and so the
symbol is empty of any intrinsic content, and there is nothing to communicate; ontologism says that every symbol is full of content, but all
symbols are in principle equally full, or equally empty, and since there
is no referent or principle of differentiation, there is no possibility of
communication. Content is appropriated by intuition alone.

Of course, those who work with some consistency within each approach instinctively realize the dead-end of such consistency and willy-
nilly appropriate something from elsewhere. Thus, the particularist
asserts propositions in human language, and translates into other languages, contradicting the very premise of particularism; the ontologist
grubs around for criteria and will generally find it in the moral or
emotional sphere; the historicist, like Troeltsch, will grasp for the hope
of some essential commonality beneath the infinity of contexts and
forms.

B. Our Approach

From the above discussion it would seem that to emphasize any one
of these in more or less isolation from the others is quite unsatisfactory,
and the seamless totality that occurs in any and all events is torn. The
final resort of Troeltsch, whose consistency in following out the logic
of the contextual emphasis led to an unwanted fragmentation of the
world of the many, prompted him to clutch after the oneness posited
in the experience-expression mode, and shows the need for a richer
approach that takes all three into account. How do we proceed?

Obviously, each approach has its problems. These problematics are
in a sense also their strengths. Historicism stresses context, for it wants
to say that relations are important. Contextual, relational, environmental considerations are absolutely essential if there is to be a com-

munication between. Particularism is concerned about a real, available, specifiable content. There is a truth content, and it can be known. If we are to communicate, there must be something to communicate, a communication of. Ontologism, finally, reminds us that this content is really transcendent and beyond confinement within the contingent and finite. There is always the element of mystery and the noncommunicable. This leads us, then, to a minimum set of test questions that need to be asked if there is to be a coherent presentation with respect to the truth question. We must ask, "Is the context taken seriously?" This is really a question about the theology of creation. We must ask, "Is the referent made clear?" Some principle of exclusion is required for coherence. This is really a question about norms, about Christology. We must also ask, "Is there openness here to the nonreducible character of this event?" This is certainly a question about one's understanding of Spirit, and leaves the door open for change and growth.

These are all different emphases. One could take one and run with it alone, but we have suggested that this leads to some kind of a deadend. What would seem to be more appropriate, if one considers the multivalent character of an event—form, context, content—would be to seek an effective way to relate the three emphases so that each has its appropriate role to play.

Let us begin with the two more objectively construed positions— the particularist and the historicist. Here we have the particular form of an event, which at the same time participates in a context. It is clear that one is not had without the other, and the relation between the two is reciprocal. In a certain sense the context, or the field, is logically prior to the particular, since it makes the arising of that particular possible. Nevertheless, the particular has a certain primacy in that it adds something, so to speak, to the context. Things are different now with this particular, compared to what they would have been without it. The particular precipitates change; there is a certain element of freedom attached to it, a certain creative role; it lends significance to a context that would otherwise be uninteresting and unimportant.

A similar reciprocity pertains to the relations between these two and the subjectivity of ontologism. Lindbeck argues that the primary difference between the cultural-linguistic and the experience-expression approaches is that the relation between form and content, outer and inner, is reversed. In the latter, it is experience that gives rise to the external features, while in the former it is the external features that give rise to experience.[19] Religion, as a cultural-linguistic system, makes possible the occasion for a religious experience.

Of course, as he also agrees, the relationship is reciprocal. Nevertheless, in the approach he proposes, "form has priority because experience, like matter, exists only insofar as it is informed."[20] By the same token, however, the experience is a response, an appropriation of the world out there, and, as appropriation, creates again a new situation. The full force of this feature of the total event must also be taken into account.

In the ordering of these emphases, it seems most adequate to interpret the contextual or structural character of the event as that feature of the whole which mediates between the particular form and the individual experience, between that which is most external and that which is most internal. We agree with Lindbeck in the general purport of this point: "part of the strength of a cultural-linguistic outlook is that it can accommodate and combine the distinctive and often competing emphases of the other two approaches."[21] We would stress, however, much more than he the creative or constitutive function that both the particular and the experiential play in bringing about an event that is eventful.

C. Speaking of Truth

We may now discuss some implications of this approach for our concern to speak the truth. *Truth,* as we have seen, is an ambiguous word. We have already offered a preliminary clarification of the term. Its meaning can range from something that is simply expressively meaningful ("I like it"), whether this is stated in an emphatic or desultory manner, to something that is true because it presumably corresponds with that which is really real ("the planets revolve around the sun")—and the more one clearly delineates the proposition, or whatever, the greater the degree of correspondence there is likely to be. For instance, when it is said that the Bible is the word of God, we get ever more precise theories of inspiration to specify ever more adequately (so it is thought) the assertion that it is indeed the word of God. The expressive/correspondence poles almost have an inverse relation to each other, the one implying that the more deeply interior the meaning is experienced, the more truthful it is, while the other implies that the more precisely the objective correspondence can be set forth the more true the proposition. In addition to these two understandings of truth as meaning and correspondence, Lindbeck speaks also of categorial truth, that is, what is said must have some discernible fit with the reality one thinks one is talking about. One might also wish to speak of a fourth understanding of truth, one that is important from the perspective of this study, and that is constitutive truth.

The underlying question of this whole study, as we have repeatedly indicated, concerns the order of our loving and hating, whether they are rightful, whether there is in fact a fit with the way things really are. Is that order, or any order, appropriate? With this in mind let us work through these approaches to truth.

Categorial truth is presupposed by all the others. Something must make sense, even if that sense be nonsense (supposing reality were itself nonsensical), before truth can be talked of in terms of expressiveness or correspondence. Our talk throughout the book about three religious families has been an effort to delineate the categorial truth of each of these religious ways of speaking. Buddhism must speak in a way that sets aside language about God as finally meaningful, for its fundamental informing category of without-self precludes any effective God-language. Similarly, the Confucian must work in moral categories, since its fundamental assertions require that. Faith in God for the Christian, in turn, requires certain kinds of speech and experience within the Semitic family of faiths. Whether in fact final reality is ultimately to be construed as God, or without-self, or moral relatedness, is another question. In any case, we have tried to argue that the categorial adequacy of each family seems to have some linkage with a facet of what we have referred to as the experience of transcendence. Now, the necessity of affirming categorial truth is not so much a matter to argue about but rather simply to be clear about. Each faith construes reality in a particular way, perhaps even construes its own reality. This construal is distinctive and proper to each, and to shift categories about in a slipshod way with the pretext of seeking after some unity that transcends the categories is not appropriate. Each sets forth a proposal. Let us be clear about that proposal. This, at least, categorial truth requires us to do. All the faith commitments with which we have dealt in this study are categorially true.

However, not quite enough has been said, for categorial truth cannot stand as a mere description of such and such a faith. All faiths, as we have argued, have a soteric thrust—they are lived, and true in the living. One will have to include within categorial truth some discussion also of truth as something that occurs in the performing. Truth as performance applies to all of the faiths we have discussed. Of course, the living of that faith will be appropriate to the categories or, the categories must be appropriate to that which is lived. Thus, the Christian category of love would remain false unless love is lived; the Buddhist category of insight would be falsehood unless there really is insight; and the Confucian category of humanity would be false without acting humanly. In this sense the performance is the truth of each faith.

Truth as performance might be seen as one form of religious expression—its moral form. This performance will always be accompanied by other ways of expressing as well—words, actions, social institutions. Such expressions are true to the degree that they conform to the truth of the performance.

The issue of truth as correspondence is also inescapable for a discussion of categorial truth, for the faiths concerned expect their proposals to have a genuine fit with the way things are, not just with the categories. Here, however, a clear and big divide opens up. For some it is part of their categorial truth that the inner has preeminence. This is, for instance, integral to Buddhist categories. Truth and falsehood have to do finally with a mental or perspectival transformation. For others, as for the Christian, the inner and the outer are correlative, and neither can yield to the other. To intensify one is to intensify the other. The failure to do so, or rather be so, is categorially false. In one sense the external has preeminence, for it is what one does with external realities—the poor, for example—that is finally decisive, not what one does with internal realities. The criteria whereby the truth of inwardness is put to the test reside in the external, public world. This is so because, at least in the Christian view presented here, reality has a social construction.

It is this divide that provides some of the greatest difficulties in all conversation about religious truth, even within the community that goes by the ancient name given to it by others, "Christians."[22] One here will decide whether or not one is willing to proceed to the further, and, in our judgment, decisive, way of talking about the truth of Jesus.

We refer to constitutive truth. By this we mean that reality is constituted by its events. Reality is not conceived of here as timely expressions of a timeless truth. Time is the medium of real change. This applies to us humans, indeed to the world. If the world had its beginnings in a big bang, the truth of that bang is not that it expresses something, it itself is the truth of the cosmos, at least insofar as it was its beginning. The post-bang cosmos is different from the at-bang cosmos, for time makes possible the real and the new. If Jesus who was in time is the truth, as Christians do confess, then time also applies to God. God is nothing but a specific mode of eventfulness, and Jesus is such an event. Jesus not only constitutes what it is to be human in some archetypal or paradigmatic way, which he does, but he is, though not all of God (*totum dei*), constitutive of what it is to be God (*totus dei*). To cite Heschel, not only must we speak of God in history, but even more radically of history in God. Uniqueness, moreover, is a characteristic of history. This will mean that the Jesus event is unique for our knowledge and experience of God. And since it is of God that we speak, this particular is also of universal currency. This will also mean that nowhere else in time and space is God so in history or is history so in God. This does not mean that God is therefore to be judged absent from all other history—far from it. But there will be no repeat. If there were such a repeat, if the significance of the Buddha is deep down no different from the significance of Jesus, than we would simply have a manifestation of the divine (or whatever), perhaps, but would also have surrendered a view of truth that takes historical event as serious, as constitutive of truth. Even here it is not possible to have two Lords. Nevertheless, this gives the Christian no excuse to ignore other human encounters with the reality we call God in other times and places. However, what those revealings are about will, if there is a fit with the way things really are, cohere with the Jesus event in decisive ways.

Reading back to the world from a Jesus event so construed, we will then conclude that God's history did not begin with Jesus. In creation, an other is established, and it is no longer possible to think of God apart from this other, this world, or to deny our own role in constituting God's reality. We should not, however, rejoice too quickly at our seemingly exalted role. The human rejection of Jesus may have something to say about our role in creating the suffering that is now in God's reality. Finally, God's history did not end with Jesus; it simply entered a new phase. The return of Christ is the symbol of the consummation of this phase. Then all things shall be turned over to God who, with us also so turned over, will be all in all.

D. The Particularity of Jesus and What It Means for Us and Others

How then does this lead one to deal with the question of the decisiveness of Jesus and the relation of this decisiveness to the people and the claims of other faiths? These two questions—concerning uniqueness and universality—are at the heart of the relation between the Christian faith and other faiths, and they need to be addressed.

What about the decisiveness and the universal relevance of Jesus? In looking at the New Testament a very basic discontinuity immediately shows itself. It is sometimes put this way: the faith of Jesus was theocentric; that of the church Christocentric. In fact, however, it would be more fitting to the New Testament data to say rather that the church was also theocentric, but with a difference.

What was this difference? It was simply this, that the church's theocentrism was nurtured in the light of the event of Jesus. Jesus had made a difference in their experience and understanding of God. But no less than that of Jesus, their faith was in God.

The event of Jesus gave them a whole new perspective on God's way of relating to the world. The basic thrust of the life and ministry of Jesus was a thrust towards universality. The issue of Jesus' relation to the Gentiles, which has been extensively argued this way and that, is not the most important matter. Far more important was his relation to the people of Israel. His ministry carried him around about the towns and villages of Palestine, always in the end gravitating towards Jerusalem. The consistent character of this ministry was the crossing of boundaries within Israel itself—the tax gatherers, the "fallen" women, the Samaritans, the sick and lepers—the list goes on. His words and deeds rocked the centripetalism of Israel. People from east and west, almost indiscriminately it seems, will sit at table with Abraham, the temple will be destroyed, Sabbath laws are flaunted, the horrible sinners of Sodom and Gomorrah will rise up in judgment, all nations will be judged on a single criterion. The relentless way Jesus pushed in the direction of universality in his teaching and deeds was shocking. God's compassion is extensive—directed towards all, and intensive—directed towards the least.

In contrast, the cross sharpened the thrust towards the particular that was inherent in Jesus' ministry. Suddenly it was apparent that this one who so taught and so acted was now silent and inert. "We had hoped that he was the one. . .," came the sorrowful complaint (Luke 24:21). The rejection of Jesus was of a particular person, at this time and in this place. But it was a particularizing that had no power beyond its own sad end. At most, this was the particularity of a martyr.

The Easter encounter transformed things. This was, first of all, a deepened particularizing. Suddenly life, death, and resurrection were focused upon this Jesus in a new and unprecedented manner. At the same time the particular took on a new kind of universal relevance. "This Jesus whom you crucified, God has made both Lord and Christ" (cf. Acts 2:36). This event is the shape of God's relation with the world. A faith quickened by this event was precisely a faith in God's way with the world, the kingdom of God. That kingdom is no abstraction, shrouded in mystery, but concrete and present, evoking response.

It is in the light of this theocentrism with a difference that the titles ascribed to Jesus (all being particular/universal in thrust) are to be understood. Lindbeck argues for a regulative theology as over against a doctrine-oriented theology. It is a view that takes the grammar of theology, rather than simply its vocabulary, as of primary importance. It is not a specific title or doctrine that is the basic issue, but rather the reasons for that title being used or that doctrine being articulated. Are there any fundamental regulating principles that account for the great variety of doctrines and titles related to the early church's interpretation of Jesus?

Lindbeck argues three regulative principles for understanding the

Christology of Nicea and Chalcedon. These same principles are clearly operative in the New Testament texts as well.

> First, there is the monotheistic principle: there is only one God, the God of Abraham, Isaac, Jacob, and Jesus. Second, there is the principle of historical specificity: the stories of Jesus refer to a genuine human being who was born, lived, and died in a particular time and place. Third, there is the principle of what may be infelicitously called Christological maximalism: every possible importance is to be ascribed to Jesus that is not inconsistent with the first rules.[23]

The principle of monotheism and the principle of Jesus as a real historical person are not principles under argument now, nor were they then. The real zone of controversy then and now, was the interpretation of the dynamic principle of maximalism. Presumably the Jewish community of Jesus' day could also affirm the principle of maximalism, but they might think that the principle of monotheism would require that they stop at the point of prophet or teacher. For Islam, to mention another case, the same three principles can apply to the estimation of Muhammad. And it is clear that the monotheistic principle as understood and applied by the Muslim would forbid any kind of maximalism that would find the idea of incarnation appropriate. Why did not the church stop at the same point?

Lindbeck himself seems to imply the need for a refinement of the third principle, for he goes on to add these words, which append a significant qualification: "This last rule, it may be noted, follows from the central Christian conviction that Jesus Christ is the highest possible clue (though an often dim and ambiguous one to creaturely and sinful eyes) within the space-time world of human experience to God, i.e., to what is of maximal importance." But it is still a question whether this modification is enough. It is only quantitative. Jesus, one might say, is the highest creature possible. Nicea struggled with this issue and found this formulation wanting. A qualitative amplification is also needed to describe the principles that informed the early church's theological decisions.

It would seem necessary to identify a fourth, decisive regulative principle in the early church's estimation of Jesus. That principle was that the human-divine boundary was permeable from the Godward side.

That is to say, God's freedom included the freedom to experience a real condescension.

In the New Testament, this principle in the end governed the other three principles. To be sure, there is a rich variety of Christologies, but none was deemed inconsistent with the high Christologies of divine condescension. This theological decision permeates the New Testament documents. One need only allude to the importance of this for the Johannine (e.g., John 1), the Pauline (e.g., Philippians 2 or Colossians 1), the Hebrews (e.g., Hebrews 1) traditions, to cite only the most obvious examples.

There are two corollaries to this kind of a theological decision. First, the once-for-all character of the event is integral to its being historical. History implies uniqueness, the unrepeatable. All ideas of repetition imply an idealistic hermeneutic in which history exemplifies or illustrates a transhistorical universal. The New Testament decision was for a materialist hermeneutic, one that refused to find God outside of the concrete, the actual, and the historical. That does not exclude the exemplary—there is much of that—but it refuses to be limited by, and decided by, that.

Constitutive truth does not "violate" the canons of historical relativism any more than does an idealist view of truth. Historicism, as we have already indicated, if consistent necessarily excludes the very idea of revelation, indeed, the very notion of coherence. To affirm revelation or disclosure of any kind is to refuse to be confined to a consistent historicism and all the problems that brings. If revelation is affirmed, the issue then becomes what the New Testament decision was for understanding that occurrence.

All the important New Testament Christologies are post-Easter phenomena. It is clear that the Christologies of eminence and ascent, which ascribe to the human Jesus titles of considerable exaltation—Lord, Christ, Son, and the like—are finally interactive with Christologies of condescension and descent, which ascribe to God the decisive freedom to be associated with matter. These latter Christologies are more ontologically responsive, and are frequently most under suspicion.[24]

It is this fourth principle, then, that accounts for the distinctive New

Testament assessment of Jesus and defines the decisiveness of the divine initiative that is encountered here—at least as the early church appropriated the impact of the Jesus event.

If we grant this sort of decisiveness, how does this relate us to the faith and the faith claims of those who do not now and perhaps never will acknowledge that same decisiveness? This is our final question.

It will be evident from this study that the relationship among the faiths involves a criss-cross of many lines. At many points there are elements of commonality, in some cases quite striking, even across family lines. In other points there is difference, sometimes of a very fundamental kind, even within a single family. Amidst this rich texture of continuities and discontinuities there is considerable possibility that interaction with one another will, or at least might, bring about significant change. That which is common, that which is different, and the ever-present possibility of change characterize the relationships among the faiths.

One way to try to get at the question of universal relevance is to draw once more upon an analogy from language. Every sentence is constructed around a subject and a predicate. The subject is that which acts, the predicate is that which sets forth this action.

Let us say that "the mule balked." Here *mule* is the subject and *balked* is the predicate. We could say that "the gray mule balked." Now we have two predicates—the mule is gray and it balked. The only way, in fact, that we know that the beast before us is a mule is because of the predicates—it balks, it makes a funny noise, its ears stick out, and so on. It is not a piece of wood, because it makes a noise, and it is not a bird, because it has four legs. The only subject we have is that made available in the predicate.

We may say the same in our knowledge, or presumed knowledge, of God. The only God we have is the God revealed, the God of the predicates. We have argued that all faith commitments are in some sense concerned with a common reality, or some facet of that reality, which Christians speak of as God. This takes seriously the proposition of the experience-expression approach, for this proposes that there is a fundamental coherence which lies hidden in a common ground of human experience, and that religious experience is an explicit response to reality experienced as an acting subject. It may go by the name

Buddha, Nature, or God, or something else, but it has to do with the experience of that reality—whatever it may be.

That reality, that subject, has been the topic of a great variety of predication throughout the course of human history. A number of the predicates that have concerned us in this study are the God of Abraham, Buddha, Jesus Christ, Allah as witnessed to by Muhammad, Heaven, Tao, and so on. The only subject we have, as a matter of fact, is that delivered in the predicates. Experience is entirely dependent. It is in fact not the case that we first experience some subject and then come up with a predicate, but the only subject experienced is the subject given in the predicate. This is the cultural-linguistic thesis.

Why the difference in predication? Many answers can be given to that. One set of solutions will argue from anthropology—we have different temperaments, we grow up in different cultures, we are somewhat ignorant and probably sinful, and so on. Another solution might argue from the subject. Perhaps the responses are not simply to a single subject, but to different subjects, or perhaps to varying features of an encompassing reality. The suggestion throughout this study has been this latter suggestion. We have spoken of religious families, each showing an openness to distinct features of reality.

How does such a proposal work out? One additional illustration here must suffice. Daisetz Suzuki, prior to his coming in the early part of this century to the West as a missionary of Zen, was in desperate straights—he had not experienced *satori*. How could one be unenlightened and presume to interpret Zen to others? In desperation he sat in intense practice. On the fifth day the breakthrough came, and his master confirmed it. He described *satori* as "just like ordinary everyday experience, except about two inches off the ground!"[25] Commenting later upon this experience, Suzuki remarked:

Satori is not seeing God as he is, as may be contended by some Christian mystics. Zen has from the very beginning made clear its principal thesis, which is to see into the work of creation and not interview the creator himself. The later may be found then busy moulding his universe, but Zen can go along with its own work even when he is not found there.

So far so good. That is what scientists do too. In this predication there is immense space for exploring a common experience. Ought the Christian not be prepared to grant that Zen does have an insight into the experience of reality—which Christians term creation—that is different from, and ought rightly to inform, Christian experience? But at this point the Zen claim seems to want to reach much farther, and include the space that Christians call God. Suzuki goes on: "Zen wants absolute freedom, even from God."[26] Here the predicate takes on a new dimension, and that which is potentially of common value, an experience of phenomenal reality (what Semitic faiths call creation), is suddenly threatened by the magnitude of difference.

This leads to a basic principle: in attending to our commonalities and differences, it is well to be generous with respect to the subject— we all finally have to do with one subject or with diverse features of that overarching subject—but attentive with respect to the predicate. If there is any controversy, and there is, it is a controversy of predicates, not of subject.

How then is this controversy of predicates to be handled? Is it a clear case of truth and falsehood? There are two assumptions that play their part here. One is that revelation or disclosure is finally possible. All religious perspectives assume this. This is why we must talk of a subject. Another is that the specific predicates are human articulations, whether cognitive, social, or emotive. The room for a partial human perception (whether for psychological or cultural reasons, or even other reasons) is always there.

Among these predicates there is both overlap and difference. It is first of all in the overlap that we have access into each other's worlds. Moreover, that which is distinctive is brought to this zone of our shared world. This was what we began to attempt in our discussion of the Spirit in the preceding chapter. The test of the adequacy of the predicates we or others affirm must occur within this zone of our common world. This means that two points of reference, two norms (the difference and the commonality into which it is brought) are interactive. As this interaction proceeds, it may well include a throwing of new and unexpected light upon our construal of that common world. It may also well be that predicates different from ours, the norms others appeal to, may also cast fresh light for us upon that world. In such a case it must be asked whether the predicate as we construe it, our norm, is open to that enrichment or not. It is in this situation of give and take that the testing takes place.[27]

Now this testing and continual reconceiving has both its temporal and eschatological aspects. By the temporal aspect we mean that all religious tradition is the product of a complex historical development. This development, to borrow language from Tillich, always involves a movement between the poles of verity and adaptation.[28] A religious tradition is a mix of many things, but not simply a mix, an endless and mindless adaptation to the environment. A religious tradition appropriates diverse elements from the culture on the basis of some underlying, regulative principles. Syncretism in this positive sense is as old as the faith of Abraham. Neither the Hebrew Scriptures nor the gospel of the New Testament would be conceivable without it.

There is no need for what we might term "title fundamentalism" in Christology, any more than there is room for "biblical fundamentalism" with regard to revelation. New Testament Christology drew upon the resources of its time in its interpretation of Jesus. It may well be that in other circumstances, such as ours today, a simple repetition of the New Testament Christology is not sufficient. It certainly was not for the church fathers. Now, as we live in an unprecedented religious and cultural interdependency, we must redo the work of the past. John Cobb has suggested that "Amida," the Buddha of compassion, is the Christ.[29] Perhaps so. Is it not time to begin to ask in a fundamental way who Jesus is for the world in terms that draw upon all relevant possibilities? This is the temporal aspect of the testing of which we speak. It has always been the task of the church to do this testing, and that task continues today. How we speak of Jesus in the future may well be very different from the way we speak of Jesus today. But not anything is possible. There are regulative principles. And these principles can only be derived from the earliest witness we have to Jesus, that of the Scriptures. In the end, to speak of Jesus today is nothing else than to speak of God, a continuance of the New Testament theocentrism with a difference.

But there is the eschatological test as well. There will always lurk the possibility—indeed probability, if not certainty—that the differences among the faiths will at their deepest be so vast as to be unbridgeable. There is, finally, no criterion outside that of the initial axioms, the faith out of which one speaks, that can decide the case in a public way. The decision is in the end an eschatological one. To expect the lines to come together is a foolish hope. To appeal to mystery and relativize the forms is to beg the question of history and its significance. Short of the eschaton, the real future, mutual respect amid continuing interaction and witness is the only appropriate stance. But the stance remains a dynamic one, for, short of the eschaton, the quest within each faith as it lives amid the others is for the most adequate articulation, the most ample presentation possible of the truth of the claim, in all the senses of truth identified above.

In the meantime, as far as the Christian stance is concerned, that which is distinctive should not be brought into that common experience so as to destroy, but so as to fulfill. Nevertheless, we cannot prejudge how it will fulfill. There is always discontinuity when God, as Christians would say, meets us in the actual world, the only place we encounter significant issues. The dialectical relationship between the "gospel of God" in the New Testament and the heritage of Israel is evidence of this unpredictable continuity in discontinuity. At least, so Christians see it. Nonetheless, the task at hand for the Christian, if the predicates are taken with seriousness, is continually to enter into and explore that continuity with the event of Jesus as the clue. Others also have their distinctives, and they too will explore, one might hope, that realm of our common experience in the light of their own particular clue. Short of the eschaton, one would expect that significant change will occur all around if this is in fact attended to. With that expectation we bear witness to the gospel of God.

NOTES

Chapter 1: Being In the World

1. Leszek Kolakowski, *Religion* (New York: Oxford University Press, 1982), p. 210, asks: "Does a phantom-God blur our vision of things or, on the contrary, does the world veil God from our sight?" See also p. 209, where he questions the adequacy of the Feuerbachian transformative critique of Hegel as the way to resolve the matter/mystery question.

2. As we shall see, some form of the question of reconciliation of these three underlies all the viewpoints we shall explore. As for Marx, Kolakowski comments: "Marx's point of departure is the eschatological question derived from Hegel: how is man to be reconciled with himself and with the world?" (*Main Currents of Marxism: Its Origins, Growth and Dissolution*, Vol. 1, *The Founders* [Oxford: Oxford University Press, 1981], p. 177).

3. *Selected Philosophical Essays* (Evanston: Northwestern University Press, 1973), p. 98.

4. For a detailed account of the life of the Buddha as represented in early texts and iconography see A. Foucher, *The Life of the Buddha: According to the Ancient Texts and Monuments of India* (Middletown: Wesleyan University Press, 1963). Summarizing the futile years of quest, Charles S. Prebish writes: "Seeking a teacher, he first studies with *Arada Kalama*. After mastering the system and experiencing the state of the sphere of nothingness (*akimcanyayatana*), he is offered status equal to Arada, but declines, realizing that this is not enlightenment. His second teacher, *Udraka Ramaputra*, teaches the attainment of the sphere of neither perception nor non-perception (*naivasamjnanasamjnayatana*), and here too Siddhartha finds the experience lacking and leaves. Shortly thereafter he begins to practice austerities with five other ascetics, each hoping that one of them breaks through to enlightenment, in order to teach it to the others. After six years of severe austerities, the Bodhisattva surveys his emaciated body and concludes that this path, like the luxurious pleasure seeking he experienced as a boy, also falls short of enlightenment" (in *Buddhism: A Modern Perspective*, ed. Charles S. Prebish [University Park: Pennsylvania State University Press, 1975], p. 12).

5. Prebish, ibid., 11f., observes that in early childhood "while watching the plough-ing festival, he inadvertently attained a meditational experience or *samadhi* as he was seated under a tree" and suggests it is this which provides the stimulus to forsake the way of austerities and yield rather to this way of spontaneity. For two traditional accounts of the Buddha's life see Henry Clarke Warren, *Buddhism: In Translations* (New York: Atheneum, 1963), pp. 1-110, and the *Mahapari-nibbanasuttanta*, trans. T. W. Rhys-Davids, *Sacred Books of the East, vol. 11*, ed. F. Max Muller (Oxford: Clarendon, 1881, pp. xxxi-xlviii, 1-136. The former comes from the collection of mythological tales of the previous lives of the Buddha, the Jataka tales. For a scholarly presentation which combines archae-ological evidence with textual see A. Foucher, *The Life of the Buddha.*

6. T'ang Chün-yi, in his *Chung-guo che-hsüeh yüan-tao lun, Yüan-tao p'ien yi* (Taipei: Taiwan hsüeh-sheng shu-chü, 1978), p. 6, writes: "Buddhism teaches the way to be liberated from this world and attain extinction [nirvana]. Therefore, it must have a theory to explain that the present world is thus and so. It must also have a theory that explains how it is that one can transcend this world. It must yet again have a theory as to how one can step by step do this. Finally, it must have a theory that speaks about the 'result' of so doing. Mahayana Buddhism refers to the first two of these as the 'phenomenal realm' (*jing*), and includes epistemology, cosmology, and metaphysics. The third is referred to as the 'action' (*hsing*), and includes morality, religion, and cultivation [of the individual]. The fourth is termed the 'result' (*guo*), and includes the Buddhist teaching on human nature, the Buddha nature or the absolute. However, the first two of the four truths of original Buddhism, on suffering and the aggregates, deal with the phe-nomenal realm, extinction [third] with the result and the pathway [fourth] with action, thus completing these three."

7. A helpful introduction to the subject is E. R. Sarathchandra, *Buddhist Psychology of Perception* (Colombo: Ceylon University Press, 1958). An elaborate analysis of consciousness is characteristic of both the Abhidharma schools of Theravada and the Yogacara (or Vijnanavadin) school of Mahayana Buddhism. For further introductions to these one might turn to Herbert V. Guenther, *Philosophy and Psychology in the Abhidharma* (Berkeley: Shambala Publications, 1976) and Seibun Fukaura, "Alaya-Vijnana," in the *Encyclopedia of Buddhism*, ed. G. P. Malalasekera, vol. 1, fasc. 3 (Colombo: Government of Ceylon, 1964), pp. 382-388. In a somewhat different way Zen has attracted the interest of Western psychological theory. See, for instance, *Zen Buddhism and Psychoanalysis*, ed. Erich Fromm (New York: Grove Press, 1963); Tomio Hirai, *Psychophysiology of Zen* (Tokyo: Igaku Shoin, 1974); William Johnston, *Silent Music: The Science of Meditation* (New York: Harper and Row, 1974); and especially Edward W. Maupin, "Zen Buddhism: A Psychological Review," *Journal of Consulting Psy-chology* 26 (1962): 362-378.

8. Quoted from de Silva, *The Problem of the Self in Buddhism and Christianity* (New York: Harper and Row, 1979), p. 38. See also H. Saddhatissa, *Buddhist Ethics: Essence of Buddhism* (New York: George Braziller, 1970), p. 37, or any discussion of the *paticcasamuppada* (or *pratityasamutpadda*) concept.

9. T. R. V. Murti, *The Central Philosophy of Buddhism* (London: George Allen and Unwin Ltd., 1960), p. 141, puts it thus: "The Absolute is not one reality set against another, the empirical. The Absolute looked at through thought-forms

NOTES

(vikalpa) is phenomenon *(samsara* or *samvrta,* literally, "covered"). The latter, freed of the superimposed thought-forms *(nirvikalpa, nisprapanca),* is the Absolute. The difference is epistemic (subjective), and not ontological."

10. Ibid., p. 19. For a further discussion of the relative stability of matter over mind in Buddhist thought and what this means see Sarathchandra, *Buddhist Psychology.* pp. 42ff.

11. De Silva, *Problem of the Self,* p. 24.

12. For the Pali terms see ibid., p. 39.

13. For further description of the Eightfold Path see, e.g., Har Dayal, *The Bodhisattva Doctrine in Buddhist Sanskrit Literature* (Delhi: Motilal Banarsidass, Reprint 1975), pp. 160-164.

14. By "psycho-mythological" I refer to the mental mythology that arises in certain forms of Buddhism, a phenomenon given full reign in Yogacara and in Tibetan tantrism.

15. This is commonly recognized. See, e.g., Kolakowski, *Main Currents of Marxism* 1:413.

16. Since the publication of the *Grundrisse* in the German original in 1953 it has become impossible to speak of an early and late Marx as if they were discontinuous. The *Grundrisse* demonstrates the transition from the dominant humanist emphasis in his earlier writings to the economic emphasis of *Capital.* For further discussion of the mediating position of the *Grundrisse* see Martin Nicolaus, "Foreword," in Karl Marx, *Grundrisse* (New York: Vintage Books, 1973). The unity of Marx's thought is now generally recognized. Kolakowski, *Main Currents of Marxism,* chap. 9, identifies 10 principles from which Marx never departed. W. A. Suchting sees it as a "unity not of a particular set of doctrines but of a political commitment" and the guiding role of certain leading ideas *(Marx: An Introduction* [New York: New York University Press, 1983], pp. xviii, xx).

17. Eugene Kamenka, *The Ethical Foundations of Marxism* (New York: Praeger, 1962), p. 2, observes that Marx's own ethical impulse stems from Rousseau and Kant and the ethic of German romanticism. This is a sustained argument for the ethical basis of Marx's thought. For other views also affirming this see Karl R. Popper, *The Open Society and Its Enemies* (New York: Harper and Row, 1962), chap. 22, "The Moral Theory of Historicism," and Jose Miranda, *Marx against the Marxists* (Maryknoll, N.Y.: Orbis, 1980).

18. The four points in italics can be compared with the fourfold structure of the Buddhist critique.

19. This is a common thesis by those who wish to make Marx's thought into a value-free science. Thus Hilferding asserted in 1910 that, "the theory of Marxism, as well as its practice, is free from judgments of value." Not uncommonly, the effort is made to derive an ought from the "is" of the Marxist description. Kamenka, *Ethical Foundations,* pp. 2-3. Popper, *Open Society,* notes how this historicism (descriptive pretense) and activism (subjective commitment) have a hard time being held together.

20. Thus Kamenka, *Ethical Foundations,* p. 1. On p. 9 Kamenka observes: "This ethic [commitment to human freedom] was reinforced by Marx's leading character trait—his tremendous concern (in reaction against his prudent father and the humiliations invited by his Jewish origin) with *dignity,* seen as independence and

227

mastery over obstacles. As late as 1873, asked to state the vice he detested most, Marx replied: 'Servility.' ''

21. Quoted by David McLellan, *Marx before Marxism* (New York: Harper and Row, 1970), p. 70, from K. Marx and F. Engels, *Historisch-kritische Gesamtausgabe,* ed. D. Rjazanov and V. Adoratskiu (Berlin, 1956 ff.), I, i (2)268f. (hereinafter: *MEGA*).

22. Jose Miranda, *Marx and the Bible* (Maryknoll: Orbis, 1974) pp. xvii and xxi, n. 7, makes this observation: "Various Christian authors have already pointed out that Karl Marx belonged to the category of the prophets of Israel and that both his messianism and his passion for justice originated in the Bible. But they point out this connection in order to diminish Marx's importance by saying that he is not original. This is an astonishing procedure."

23. Eugene Kamenka, *Marxism and Ethics* (London: MacMillan, 1969), p. 11 writes: "In the formative years of his life, between 1841 and 1845, Marx did emerge with a doctrine that represented as worked-out a position on ethical philosophy as he ever reached, and which remained—I believe—implicit in the rest of his work, shaping. . . his whole conception of human history, its problems and its destiny." See also Kamenka, *Ethical Foundations*.

24. *Writings of the Young Marx on Philosophy and Society*, ed. Loyd D. Easton, and Kurt H. Guddat (New York: Anchor, 1967), p. 39. This examination essay was written in 1835.

25. See, e.g., Kamenka, *Ethical Foundations*, pp. 21f. Marx never gave up this element of freedom, even in his later, seemingly more deterministic, moments. As late as April 17, 1871, he wrote in a letter to Kugelmann: "World history . . . would be of a very mystical nature if 'accidents' played no part in it. These accidents fall naturally into the general course of development and are compensated by other accidents. But acceleration and delay are very dependent upon such 'accidents,' including the 'accident' of the character of those who at first stand at the head of the movement" (cited from Kolakowski, *Main Currents,* p. 339). For the whole letter see Saul K. Padover, *The Letters of Karl Marx* (Englewood Cliffs: Prentice-Hall, 1979), p. 281.

26. *The Marx-Engels Reader,* ed. Robert C. Tucker, 2nd ed. (New York: Norton, 1978), p. 9.

27. Padover, *Letters,* p. 12. The rather long letter documents many factors that led to this inward discomfort, both philosophical and personal.

28. In 1837; see ibid., p. 515.

29. Easton and Guddat, *Writings of the Young Marx,* p. 78. This is from Marx's first published article, that of February 1843; quoted from *MEGA,* I,i(1)162f.

30. McLellan, *Marx before Marxism,* p. 85; quoted from *MEGA,* I,i(1)199.

31. Kolakowski, *Main Currents,* 1:408-416.

32. Ibid., 1:412.

33. Tucker, *Marx-Engels Reader,* p. 10.

34. Padover, *Letters,* pp. 29-32. Marx puts it this way in a letter to Ruge in 1843: "I asked. . . that religion be criticized through a criticism of the political situation, rather than that the political situation be criticized through religion" (Jose Miguez Bonino, *Christians and Marxists* [Grand Rapids: Eerdmans, 1976, p. 43; cited from Karl Marx and Frederick Engels, *Werke,* 39 vols. (Berlin, 1956), 27:412. For a brief introduction to Marx's critique of religion see Bonino. For a more

detailed presentation of the material on religion in Marx see Delos B. McKown, *The Classical Marxist Critiques of Religion: Marx, Engels, Lenin, Kautsky* (The Hague: Martinus Nijhoff, 1975). For a more profound theological discussion see Nicholas Lash, *A Matter of Hope: A Theologian's Reflections on the Thought of Karl Marx* (Notre Dame: University of Notre Dame Press, 1982), especially chap. 13, "The Criticism of Religion." This also has a partial but helpful bibliography. For very useful historical discussions of Christian-Marxist understandings see James Bentley, *Between Marx and Christ: The Dialogue in German-Speaking Europe 1870–1970* (London: Verso Editions, 1982), and Paul Mojzes, *Christian-Marxist Dialogue in Eastern Europe* (Minneapolis: Augsburg, 1981).

35. Quoted from James Bentley, *Between Marx and Christ* (London, 1982), p. 100, who quotes from David McLellan, *Marx before Marxism* (New York: Harper and Row, 1970), p. 82.

36. Karl Marx, *Early Writings,* trans. Rodney Livingstone and Gregor Benton, with introduction by Lucio Colletti (New York: Vintage Books, 1975), p. 251.

37. Ibid., pp. 244f. For the phrase "categorical imperative," see p. 251.

38. Karl Marx, "On the Jewish Question," in ibid., p. 229.

39. Ibid., p. 231.

40. Cf. Kamenka, *Ethical Foundations,* p. 70.

41. Karl Marx, "Preface" [to *A Contribution to the Critique of Political Economy*], in *Early Writings,* p. 425.

42. Karl Marx, "The German Ideology: Part I," in Tucker, *Marx-Engels Reader,* p. 163.

43. Kolakowski comments that Marx spent his whole life writing "one book": "It would, of course, be quite wrong to imagine that the Paris manuscripts contain the entire gist of *Capital;* yet they are in effect the first draft of the book that Marx went on writing all his life, and of which *Capital* is the final version" (see *Main Currents of Marxism,* 1:132).

44. Robert C. Tucker, *The Marxian Revolutionary Idea* (New York: W. W. Norton, 1970), p. 5. On history as man's "act of becoming," see. p. 9.

45. Cf. Donald J. Munro, "The Malleability of Man in Chinese Marxism," *China Quarterly* 48 (October/December, 1971): 609-640, for a helpful discussion of Marx's understanding of human nature. For a philosophical analysis see Carol C. Gould, *Marx's Social Ontology: Individuality and Community in Marx's Theory of Social Reality* (Cambridge, Mass.: MIT Press, 1978), especially the chapter on the "Ontology of Freedom." Though Gould does not use this language, these three aspects are accounted for in her analysis. "Marx's Aristotelian insistence on the ontological primacy of real individuals," which includes a subject's will or desires, and the importance of external conditions for self-realization correspond with the "already givens" (pp. 107-110); her discussion of "freedom as presupposition" and the philosophical problems this raises, and which she addresses, corresponds with our "teleological givens" (pp. 111-119); and her discussion of "the dialectic of freedom in the stages of social development" relates to the "changing nature" (pp. 119-128). One can hardly help thinking of formal (already given), efficient (changing nature) and final (teleologically given) causality.

46. On this see, for instance, Karl Marx, "The German Ideology: Part I," in Tucker,

Marx-Engels Reader, pp. 155-159, where Marx outlines the four premises of history.

47. Karl Marx, *Capital,* in ibid., pp. 344f.

48. Marx argues the material derivation of mind in this way: "The production of ideas, of conceptions, of consciousness, is at first directly interwoven with the material activity and the material intercourse of men, the language of real life. Conceiving, thinking, the mental intercourse of men, appear at this stage as the direct efflux of their material behavior" ("The German Ideology," in ibid., p. 154; cf. 158). We might note that the first intimations of consciousness are "interwoven," that is, integral in material activity, yet distinct. To obliterate the distinction would reduce the human to the animal, and then we are speaking no longer of humans. Some glimmer of "imagination" is implied everywhere Marx uses the word *human.*

49. Notice Jose Miguez Bonino's recognition of the first two of these: "In so far, then, as historical or even dialectical materialism would limit itself to asserting that human life must be seen as the history of man's involvement in the domination and transformation of the world (work), as the effort to respond to human needs, in the context of a net of interconnecting relationships which embraces the whole of society, the Christian faith need not feel scandalised or threatened by such a theory." He goes on: "But historical and dialectical materialism does not stop here: it presents itself as a total, all-embracing, self-sufficient and exclusive understanding of reality." This reflects the third given, the finality of the Marxist vision of reality (*Christians and Marxists,* p. 97).

50. Karl Marx, *Capital,* in Tucker, *Marx-Engels Reader,* p. 344. The externality of nature as objectivity is essential for Marx's understanding of labor, for the human being is indeed a passive being; but subjectivity is also necessary, for the human is at the same time "a being-for-himself, not merely a natural being." See the same themes earlier in "Economic and Philosophical Manuscripts," in Marx, *Early Writings,* pp. 390f. See also Kolakowski, *Main Currents,* 1:133.

51. But even this can be called into question. See, e.g., the much later theories of Marx on the development of language. Kolakowski, *Main Currents,* 3:141.

52. Karl Marx, "Concerning Feuerbach," in Marx, *Early Writings,* p. 423.

53. Karl Marx, "Economic and Philosophical Manuscripts," in ibid., p. 391.

54. His thinking in this regard is therefore really utopian despite his best efforts to avoid it. Kamenka, *Ethical Foundations,* pp. 20, 22f., observes that true understanding for Marx "can only be gained by looking at the concept, the motive power which is in things and yet outside them as their aim, the 'energizing principle' which determines their character and development, not by external compulsion, but as an inner self-realisation. . . [and thus] to grasp the concept working dialectically through things toward an ultimate harmony that represents the truly real come to empirical existence."

55. Gould, *Marx's Social Ontology,* pp. 119ff.

56. Our discussion here relies in part on Gould's fine analysis of the "ontology of freedom" in Marx; ibid., chap. 4.

57. Karl Marx, "The German Ideology," in Tucker, *Marx-Engels Reader,* p. 156.

58. Ibid., p. 157.

59. Meng-tzu (Mencius, fl. 372–289 b.c.e.), 4b.19. The Hsün-tzu (fl. 298–238 b.c.e.) quote is from *Hsün-tzu,* §23, cited from *Hsün-tzu: Basic Writings,* trans.

Burton Watson (New York: Columbia University Press, 1963), p. 159. Elsewhere (§9) Hsün-tzu says: "Fire and water possess energy but are without life. Grass and trees have life but no intelligence. Birds and beasts have intelligence but no sense of duty. Man possesses energy, life, intelligence, and, in addition, a sense of duty. Therefore he is the noblest being on earth" (cited from Watson, p. 45).

60. T'ang uses the term *wang-wo* (self-forgetting).

61. This discussion is based on T'ang Chün-yi, *Chung-kuo wen-hua chih ching-shen chia-chih*, rev. ed. (Taipei: Cheng-chung shu-chü, 1979), §7.2, pp. 186-187. This is an early writing of his. In his crowning work, *Sheng-ming ts'un-tsai yü hsin-ling ching-chieh*, 2 vols. (Taipei: Hsüeh-shen shu-chü, 1978), 2:855, he returns to this structure with its implications for him. See also Thomas A. Metzger, *Escape from Predicament: Neo-Confucianism and China's Evolving Political Culture* (New York: Columbia University Press, 1977), 2.b, "the exegesis of experience," where he describes and critiques this epistemology, pp. 33-37. It is evident that both Buddhism and phenomenalism have influenced his language.

62. Meng-tzu, 4b.19 (my translation); Shun, an ancient ideal Chinese ruler (2255?–2206? B.C.E.), is usually paired with Yao (2356?–2256?).

63. This phrase, *cheng–ming*, appears first in *Lun-yü (Analects)*. It is subsequently picked up and developed in a number of ways. Hsün-tzu entitles a chapter "Cheng-ming" and interprets it as normative social convention; in the *Tao-te-ching* (Lao-tzu) the counternotion of *wu-ming* (without naming) is developed; Kung Sun-lung distinguishes the term *ming*[1] (name) from *shih* (reality) and explores the logic of this problem.

64. *Lun-yü* 13.3 (*tzu-lu*), cited from Fung Yu-lan, *A History of Chinese Philosophy* (Princeton: Princeton University Press, 1952), 1:59f.

65. *Lun-yü* 12:11 (*Yen-huan*).

66. The distinction between necessary and sufficient reason is not only Aristotle's. It is implicit here, but is made explicit in Mo-tzu, who terms them the "lesser reason" (*hsiao-ku*) and "greater reason" (*ta-ku*). See the discussion of Cheng Chung-ying, "Conscience, Mind and Individual in Chinese Philosophy," *Journal of Chinese Philosophy* 2 (1974): 16-25. In this section we draw freely on his brief essay.

67. *Lun-yü* 13:3. This passage articulates the *yen/hsing* (word/act, theory/praxis) distinction that is so important throughout Chinese thought. On this see Cheng Chung-ying, "Conscience," pp. 45ff.

68. *Lun-yü* 7.33 (*Shu-erh*) (my translation).

69. Thus Fang Yi-ling, *Lun-yü Hsin-ch'üan* (A New Interpretation of the Analects) (Taipei: Taiwan Chung-hua shu-chü, 1978), pp. 26-27, on *Lun-yü* 2.4.

70. The following discussion will draw heavily upon T'ang Chün-yi, *Chung-kuo che-hsüeh yüan-lun*, vol. 1 (Taipei: Hsin-ya yen-chiu suo, 1976), pp. 71-109.

71. Donald J. Munro, *The Concept of Man in Early China* (Stanford: Stanford University Press, 1969), p. 23.

72. This, of course, is a lifelong venture, as this courtly translation of *Lun-yü* 8.7 by Arthur Waley makes clear: "The true Knight of the Way must perforce be both broad-shouldered and stout of heart; his burden is heavy and he has far to go. For Goodness [*jen*] is the burden he has taken upon himself; and must we

not grant that it is a heavy one to bear? Only with death does his journey end; then must we not grant that he has far to go?" (*The Analects of Confucius* [London: George Allen and Unwin Ltd., 1956], p. 134).

73. *Jen* has many translations including love, goodness, humanity, benevolence, and others. In its broadest sense it is the summation of all virtues, and bears an intrinsic humane and social character. For a discussion easy to access see Waley, ibid., pp. 27-29.

74. *Lun-yü* 1.2.

75. Ibid., 6.28.

76. Ibid., 1.2.

77. Ibid., 15.23.

78. Ibid., 4.15.

79. Ibid., 5.13.

80. Ibid., 17.2.

81. Julia Ching, *Confucianism and Christianity: A Comparative Study* (Tokyo: Kodansha International, 1977), p. 75.

82. *Meng-tzu* 7a.4.

83. Ibid., 6a.15.

84. See ibid., 2a.6.

85. *Hsün-tzu*, chap. 22; cited from Fung, *A History*, p. 289.

86. Chou Tun-yi's "Diagram of the Supreme Ultimate" is one of the more famous statements of this. See, e.g., Fung, *A History*, 2:435-438, for a translation of this. The word *ternion* translates a rather complex Chinese term, *ts'an*, which has important philosophical ramifications. The term means both "join" and "three," simultaneously. It should probably be taken in a dynamic, functional sense, rather than a static, descriptive sense. Pang Pu, characterizing its philosophical sense, writes: " 'Ts'an' is '3', '3' in large writing. As with the idea of 'supreme harmony' (*t'ai-ho*), 'ts'an' can also be spoken of as the 'supreme threesome' (*t'ai-san*), the Great Three. Three is a number, and whether here or elsewhere, in ancient times or the present, has always been recognized in philosophy as a completeness. '1' is the beginning of numbers, an odd number, singular; '2' is a differentiation, an opposition; whereas '3' is the unification of an opposition, the completion of numbers. It is a wholeness that embraces both that which is in opposition to the self and the self. This is what is termed 'ts'an.' " It would only be fair to point out also that Pang Pu questions whether the idea that heaven, earth, and humanity form a moral whole adequately interprets this idea in its dynamic sense. That is perhaps a matter for debate, but we do raise it to point to the inherent dynamic idea that this concept seeks to express. See Pang Pu, " 'Zhong-yong' ping-yi" (An Inquiry into the Doctrine of the Mean), *Zhongguo shehui kexue* 1 (1980): 94-96. We use *ternion* to express this idea since it is an archaic term and does not carry the numerous connotations that *triad* or *trinity* carry for us.

87. *Lun-yü* 14.28.

88. Ibid., 12:10.

89. Ibid., 9:29.

90. Ibid., 11:12.

91. Ibid., 4:6.

92. Ibid., 14:38.

93. Ibid., 14:35.
94. See, e.g., ibid., 9.5.
95. Ch'ien Mu, *Lun-yü hsin-chieh* (A New Explanation of the Analects), 2 vols. (Kowloon, Hong Kong: Hsin-ya yen-chiu suo, 1963), 1:34.
96. Cf. n. 86.
97. Our discussion in the following paragraphs on the three strands of Confucian tradition is based on Mou Tsung-san. See his *Chung-kuo che-hsüeh-ti t'e-chih* (The Uniqueness of Chinese Philosophy) (Taipei: Taiwan hsüeh-sheng shu-chü, 1963). See especially page 68. Compare his more extended discussion in *Hsin-t'i yü hsing-t'i* (The Moral Consciousness and Moral Nature of Man), vol. 1 (Taipei: Cheng-chung shu-chü, 1968).
98. The May 4th Movement of 1919 is universally recognized as a critical event in the political and cultural awakening of modern China. The event itself was sparked by student demonstrations in Peking and elsewhere protesting the agreement of the Western powers to give Japan Germany's rights in Shantung (a province of China) as the fruits of her participation in World War I. China's contribution to the Allied cause was ignored and she was not consulted in this action. This protest movement became the symbol for Chinese national self-consciousness. Integrally associated with it was a literary renaissance which gave rise to a wholly new kind of literary culture, of which the development of a colloquial (as contrasted to a classical) literature was a principal feature. A standard study of the movement is Chow Tse-tsung, *The May Fourth Movement: Intellectual Revolution in Modern China* (Stanford: Stanford University Press, 1960).
99. Of course, the number *three* greatly simplifies historical complexity. Speaking only of the neo-Confucian period, Metzger, *Escape from Predicament*, pp. 52ff., identifies eight divergent strands. For a helpful survey of Confucius and the Confucian tradition in history in English see D. Howard Smith, *Confucius* (New York: Scribner, 1973).
100. A guiding assumption throughout this chapter is the dictum that "religiously important claims. . .are empirically grounded" (Robert C. Neville, *The Tao and the Daimon* [Albany: State University of New York Press, 1982], p. 112).
101. "Every presentness, even presentness of the Divine, must be cast in the mould of the Absent" (J. G. Arapura, *Religion as Anxiety and Tranquillity: An Essay in Comparative Phenomenology of the Spirit* [The Hague: Mouton, 1972], p. 76, in his section on "The Absent").

Chapter 2: The Elusive Presence

1. A somewhat parallel idea is the notion of "thatness" that Robert C. Neville develops. See his *The Tao and the Daimon* (Albany: State University of New York Press, 1982), p. 44., and, for the distinction between ontology and cosmology on which the idea is grounded, see pp. 30f. On p. 31 he writes: "A tao of faith and practice. . . addresses the positivity of existence. . . . The symbolisms of divinity orient the responses we make to the ontological fact."
2. John Cobb Jr., in *Beyond Dialogue* (Philadelphia: Fortress, 1982), pp. 66f., reveals an awareness of this differentiation. While critiquing F. S. C. Northrop's theory of an East/West complementarity in *The Meeting of East and West*, he writes: "When viewed globally there appear to be three major forms of cultural

and religious life: Indian, Chinese, and Western. E. A. Burtt presents India as most interested in the self and its growth toward cosmic maturity, China as preoccupied with society and harmonious interpersonal relations, and the West as absorbed with individualism, analysis, and the external world. Yves Congar describes India as idealistic, China as naturalistic, and the West as dualistic. Huston Smith identifies India, China, and the West 'respectively as acosmic, cosmic, and theistic.' " While Neville's twofold distinction is subject to the same critique as that of Northrop, he still draws an interesting distinction between East and West religiously (*The Tao and the Daimon*, p. 120).

3. See Edward Schillebeeckx, *Interim Report on the Books Jesus and Christ* (New York: Crossroad, 1982), pp. 3ff., on two sources and "experience with experience," as well as p. 143, n. 2; see also his *Christ: The Experience of Jesus as Lord* (New York: Seabury, 1980), pp. 56f.

4. Abraham Heschel, *The Prophets: An Introduction*, 2 vols. (New York: Harper, 1962), 1:16. Robert C. Neville, *The Tao and the Daimon* (Albany: State University of New York Press, 1982), p. 133, puts it in philosophical language: "Positivity is ontologically prior."

5. John Bowker, *The Sense of God: Sociological, Anthropological and Psychological Approaches to the Origin of the Sense of God* (Oxford: Clarendon, 1973), p. x. He goes on to say: "It may even be reasonable to conclude that it is no longer so impossible or absurd as it has seemed in recent years to infer that a reality exists, external to ourselves, which creates differentiating effects in the construction of human lives, and which is (or has been, up to the present) characterized theistically." For the argumentation behind this see his book, *The Religious Imagination and the Sense of God* (Oxford: Clarendon, 1978).

6. Heb. 11:6.

7. John Wansbrough, *Quranic Studies: Sources and Methods of Scriptural Interpretation* (Oxford: Oxford University Press, 1977), p. 5. On "signs" generally see also Richard Bell, *Bell's Introduction to the Qu'ran*, rev. and enlarged W. Montgomery Watt (Edinburgh: Edinburgh University Press, 1970), pp. 121-127, and Ary A. Roest Crollius, *The Word in the Experience of Revelation in Quran and Hindu Scriptures* (Rome: Universita Gregoriana, 1974), p. 150f.

8. Sura 45:3-6, according to the Egyptian official numbering. Flügel's numbering, followed by most English works up till 1950, is indicated in parentheses. Arberry follows Flügel, and Ali and Pickthall the Egyptian numbering. We quote from Arberry unless otherwise indicated: A. J. Arberry, *The Koran Interpreted* (New York: Macmillan, 1964), 2:210. In Arberry the numbering is 45:2-5. The two most widely used translations, both by Muslims, are Abdullah Yusuf Ali, *The Meaning of the Glorious Qur'an*, 2 vols. (Cairo: Dar Al-Kitab Al-Masri, ca. 1934), and M. M. Pickthall, *The Meaning of the Glorious Koran* (New York: New American Library, n.d.). Arberry's language seems to best catch the rhythm of the Koran.

9. For these "stories of punishment" (*al-mathani*) see, e.g., *Bell's Introduction*, pp. 127-135.

10. Sura 12:2 (12:1).

11. Sura 17:90-93 (17:92-95).

12. Sura 17:88 (17:90).

13. Sura 112:1-4.

14. Sura 13:16.
15. Sura 42:49.
16. The concern in the Qur'an is not metaphysical but personal, divine will. Roest Crollius, *The Word,* p. 22, n. 7, observes that *kun* occurs eight times in the Qur'an and that "these texts are related either to the origin of Jesus or to the resurrection of the dead." The interest is in the concreteness of divine willing, not causality.
17. Sura 105:8.
18. On the Arab understanding of Allah before Islam see "Ilah," in *The Encyclopaedia of Islam,* New Edition, ed. H. A. R. Gibb, et al. (Leiden: E. J. Brill, 1960—).
19. This striking locution of Rudolf Otto is actually self-contradictory. If something were *wholly* other it could not be known that it were so; that it is *other* implies its counterpart in a subject/object schema and is therefore related. Cf. also Ninian Smart, *The Philosophy of Religion* (New York: Oxford University Press, 1979), pp. 45, 60.
20. Sura 2:2-3.
21. Sura 58:7.
22. Sura 24:35.
23. Sura 2:115 (2:109).
24. Sura 42:51, cited from Roest Crollius, *The Word,* p. 40.
25. Ibid., pp. 41f.
26. Ibn Ishaq, *The Life of Muhammad (Sirat Rasul Allah),* trans. A. Guillaume (Lahore, Pakistan: Oxford University Press Branch, 1974), p. 105.
27. See the argument as W. Montgomery Watt develops it in *Muhammad: Prophet and Statesman* (London: Oxford University Press, 1961), pp. 46-55.
28. Dirk Bakker, *Man in the Qur'an* (Amsterdam: Drukkerij Holland N. V., 1965), chap. 3.
29. Sura 53:1-18; 81:15-25.
30. Ishaq, *Life of Muhammed,* pp. 106f.
31. J. G. Arapura, *Religion as Anxiety and Tranquillity: An Essay in Comparative Phenomenology of the Spirit* (The Hague: Mouton, 1972), pp. 85, 88.
32. Ibid., p. 90.
33. Jürgen Moltman, *The Trinity and the Kingdom: The Doctrine of God* (San Francisco: Harper and Row, 1981), p. 105.
34. See, e.g., Julia Ching, *Confucianism and Christianity: A Comparative Study* (Tokyo: Kodansha International, 1977), chap. 4: "The Problem of God"; see also C. K. Yang, *Religion in Chinese Society* (Berkeley: University of California Press, 1967), chap. 10: "Religious Aspects of Confucianism in Its Doctrine and Practice."
35. On the state cult of Confucius see J. K. Shyrock, *The Origin and Development of the State Cult of Confucianism* (New York: Century, 1932).
36. *Lun-yü* (Analects) 3.12.
37. Ching, *Confucianism and Christianity,* p. 113.
38. Ibid., p. 127.
39. T'ang Chün-yi, *Sheng-ming ts'un-tsai yü hsin-ling ching-chieh,* 2 vols. (Taipei: Hsüeh-sheng shu-chü, 1978), p. 867.
40. Ibid., pp. 834f.

41. Ibid., p. 871.
42. The concept of *t'ien* (heaven) is a very complex one in Chinese. Its basic meaning is that which is eminent, over all; it also means the heavens or firmament, God as lord and creator, the natural order, destiny, and much else. See, for example, *Chung-wen ta-ts'u-tien* (The Encyclopedic Dictionary of the Chinese Language) (Taipei: Chung-guo wen-hua yen-chiu-suo, 1963), p. 3340. As for heaven signifying a category of immanence, Heschel, *The Prophets*, 2:16, is entirely correct when, speaking of the Chinese way, he says: "God is essentially the moral order of the universe, an order operating in the phenomena of nature as well as in the course of history and the destinies of individuals."
43. T'ang, *Sheng-ming*, p. 872.
44. *Chung-yung* (The Doctrine of the Mean), chap. 1. For an English translation see James Legge, *The Li Ki Books XI–XLVI*, in Sacred Books of the East, ed. F. Max Muller (London: Oxford University Press, 1885), 28:300. He translates the phrase "What Heaven has conferred is called the nature."
45. Ching, *Confucianism and Christianity*, p. 134.
46. *Wang Wen-ch'eng kung ch'üan-shu* (Complete Works of Wang Yang-ming), compiled by Hsieh T'ing-chieh, in the *Ssu-pu ts'ung-k'an* (Shanghai: Shang-wu yin-shu-kuan, 1922–1929, double leaves, photoreproduction), chüan 1:60b. See Ching, *Confucianism and Christianity*, p. 136, and Wing-tsit Chan, *Instructions for Practical Living* (New York: Columbia University Press, 1963), pp. 80-81. For a full discussion of Wang Yang-ming, see Julia Ching, *To Acquire Wisdom: The Way of Wang Yang-ming* (New York: Columbia University Press, 1976); for this passage see p. 144. I have slightly adapted the translation.
47. On *hsin* (heart-mind) see Ching, *To Acquire Wisdom*, p. 137, and *Confucianism and Christianity*, p. 135. See also Munro, *The Concept of Man in Early China* (Stanford: Stanford University Press, 1969), pp. 50f., as well as the whole of chap. 3.
48. Quoted from Julia Ching, *To Acquire Wisdom*, p. 29.
49. Quoted from Fung, *A History of Chinese Philosophy* (Princeton: Princeton University Press, 1952), 2:597.
50. Quoted from Ching, *To Acquire Wisdom*, p. 53.
51. Wang Yang-ming, *Wang Wen-ch'eng kung ch'üan-shu* [Complete Works of Wang Yang-ming], chuan 1.5b, quoted from Tu Wei-ming, *Neo-Confucian Thought in Action: Wang Yang-ming's Youth (1472-1509)* (Berkeley: University of California Press, 1976), p. 173.
52. Quoted from ibid., p. 176.
53. See Chan, *Instructions*, p. 243, and introductory discussion to the section, and Ching, *To Acquire Wisdom*, pp. 149f.
54. Ching, *To Acquire Wisdom*, p. 127.
55. Ibid., p. 139.
56. Ibid., p. 47.
57. See chap. 1, note 8.
58. Alfred North Whitehead, *Religion in the Making* (New York: Macmillan, 1926), p. 50.
59. The assumption in saying this, of course, is that Buddhism is not fundamentally a metaphysic, but a soteriology, and that whatever metaphysic attaches to it is derived or constructed on the basis of the soteriology. Arapura, *Religion as*

Anxiety, p. 79, states the case clearly but rather too strongly: "Buddhism . . . has gone about its philosophical business not only without commitment to any metaphysical view but without even interest in considering any, which is what is truly unique about it. Buddhism sought to bracket such inquiries and to divorce what to it appeared as the spurious metaphysical problem of being from a genuine existential ontology that has essentially to do with the state of tranquillity." Our point is not quite the same. This seeming "abandonment of metaphysical inquiry" in the service of a soteriology does, nevertheless, have its own metaphysical implications, which Buddhism repeatedly sought to address on the philosophical level. It is for this latter reason that Th. Stcherbatsky, for instance, is able to speak of the type of Buddhism he is analyzing as "a metaphysical theory developed out of one fundamental principle, *viz.,* the idea that existence is an interplay of a plurality of subtle, ultimate, not further analysable elements of Matter, Mind, and Forces" (*The Central Conception of Buddhism and the Meaning of the Word "Dharma"* [Calcutta: Susil Gupta 1961–1923], p. 22). Perhaps Leszek Kolakowski's characterization of Plotinus best states the relations here between metaphysics and soteriology: "Plotinus's work is not a metaphysical system, since language cannot express the most important truths; it is not a theory but a work of spiritual counsel, a guide for the use of those who wish to set about liberating themselves from temporal being" (*Main Currents of Marxism,* 2 vols. [Oxford: Oxford University Press, 1981], 1:16).

60. The two understandings of contingency within the Aristotelian and Platonic traditions, both of which influenced Christianity, are analogous to this. In the one case it "denoted the state of a finite being that might or might not exist but was not necessary." Such an entity existed simply because of a particular set of prior conditions that was not in the nature of things necessary. This was a description of fact. In the Platonic tradition contingency was the experience of one's empirical, temporal, and factual existence as a difference, and an unfortunate difference, from extratemporal Being as such. This was a fault that needed a remedy, a return to the One (Kolakowski, *Main Currents of Marxism,* p. 12).

61. T. R. V. Murti, *The Central Philosophy of Buddhism: A Study of the Madhyamika System* (London: George Allen and Unwin Ltd., 1960), p. 7.

62. Ibid., p. 25. In this regard he identifies the "well-defined stages of development" of "every Indian system": "A seer . . . gives utterance to his intimate vision of reality; this is the mulamantra, the original inspiration. . . . The second stage consists in systematising . . . in aphoristic form (sutra or karika) . . . . There is further elaboration, drawing of implications, application to details of experience, removing of discrepancies, etc. A further stage is reached when the systems indulge in criticism and refutation of other systems to strengthen their own position." All Buddhist systems are thus differing attempts to interpret this single vision. There is no point in contrasting the original vision from later interpretations as though they are mutually contradictory.

63. David J. Kalupahana, *Causality: The Central Philosophy of Buddhism* (Honolulu: The University Press of Hawaii, 1975), p. 185.

64. Ibid., p. 104.

65. Ibid., p. 141.

66. Ibid., pp. 116, 119. Cf. the discussion of Sarathchandra, *Buddhist Psychology,*

part three, on the theory of *bhavanga* both in relation to birth and death and in relation to *alaya vijnana*.

67. Kalupahana, *Causality,* p. 122.
68. Ibid., p. 139.
69. David J. Kalupahana, *Buddhist Philosophy: A Historical Analysis* (Honolulu: The University Press of Hawaii, 1976), pp. 81f. In his book *Causality: The Central Philosophy of Buddhism,* Kalupahana makes his empiricist position even clearer: "Thus, here, as with the question of the extent and duration of the universe, there appears to be an epistemological problem, the limitation of empiricism. That, we believe, is why the Buddha was silent on the status of the enlightened one after death. . . . The silence of the Buddha was thus due to his awareness of the limitation of empiricism, rather than of concepts" (p. 180).
70. Th. Stcherbatsky, *Central Conception,* pp. 37-38. See Kalupahana, *Causality,* pp. 69-70.
71. Murti, *Central Philosophy,* p. 86.
72. Ibid., p. 141.
73. Kaluphana, *Buddhist Philosophy,* p. 75.
74. Karl Marx, "Critique of Hegel's Philosophy of Right," in Marx, *Early Writings* (New York: Vintage, 1975), p. 251.
75. Saul K. Padover, *The Letters of Karl Marx* (Englewood Cliffs, N.J.: Prentice-Hall, 1979), p. 21.
76. F. Engels, "Ludwig Feuerbach and the End of Classical German Philosophy," in Marx, Engels, Lenin, *On Historical Materialism* (Moscow, 1972), p. 234; quoted in Nicholas Lash, *A Matter of Hope* (Notre Dame: University of Notre Dame Press, 1982), p. 167.
77. Vitezslav Gardavsky, *God Is Not Yet Dead* (Harmondsworth: Penguin Books, 1973), p. 169.
78. Cf. ibid., pp. 165ff.
79. Ludwig Feuerbach, *The Essence of Christianity,* trans. George Eliot (New York: Harper, 1957), p. 269.
80. Padover, *Letters,* p. 21.
81. Marx, *Early Writings,* p. 244.
82. Lash, *A Matter of Hope,* pp. 158ff., quoted from V. Lenin, "Socialism and Religion," in K. Marx, F. Engels, and V. Lenin, *On Historical Materialism,* ed. T. Borodulina (Moscow: Progress Publishers, 1972), p. 411.
83. Cited in Lash, *A Matter of Hope,* p. 163; quoted from L. Althusser, *For Marx* (New Left, 1977), p. 232.
84. Thus Lash, *A Matter of Hope,* p. 166.
85. Karl Kautsky, *Foundations of Christianity* (New York: Russell and Russell, 1953), p. 137.
86. Gardavsky, *God Is Not Yet Dead,* p. 201.
87. Ibid., pp. 204f.
88. Ibid., p. 210.
89. Ibid., p. 213.
90. Ibid., p. 204.
91. Ibid., p. 218.
92. Ibid., p. 211.
93. Ibid., p. 209.

94. Ibid., p. 208.
95. Ibid., p. 207.
96. Ibid., p. 211.
97. Ibid., p. 215.
98. Ibid., pp. 215f.
99. Ibid., p. 216.
100. Ibid., p. 217.
101. Ibid., p. 218.
102. Ibid., p. 210.
103. Lash, *A Matter of Hope*, p. 168.
104. Gardavsky, *God Is Not Yet Dead*, p. 205.

Chapter 3: The Suffering Presence

1. T'ang Chün-yi, *Sheng-ming ts'un-tsai yü hsin-ling ching-chieh* (Taipei: Hsüeh-shen shu-chü, 1978), p. 754.
2. On religious knowledge as a means of transformation see Frederick J. Streng, *Emptiness: A Study in Religious Meaning* (Nashville: Abingdon, 1967). On p. 175, for example, he identifies two elements in a religious apprehension: "awareness of the deficient character in human existence . . . plus . . . the means to transform the deficiency."
3. T. R. V. Murti, *The Central Philosophy of Buddhism: A Study of the Madhyamika System* (London: George Allen and Unwin, 1960), p. 141.
4. The *klesas* are all the distress and contaminations that arise from the passions and from ignorance. There are many subdivisions. One of the most common is into the three passions of greed, hatred, and delusion. See, e.g., William Edward Soothill and Lewis Hodous, *A Dictionary of Chinese Buddhist Terms* (London, 1937), p. 406, on *fan-nao*.
5. *Lun-yü* 2.23.
6. The theme of return, of course, is quite universal, and secular as well as religious in its forms. See Leszek Kolakowski, *Main Currents of Marxism: Its Origins, Growth, and Dissolution*, 2 vols. (Oxford: Oxford University Press, 1981), 1:39. See also Mircea Eliade: *Cosmos and History*, trans. W. R. Trask (New York: Harper and Row, 1959); the subtitle of Eliade's book is *The Myth of the Eternal Return*.
7. Soothill and Hodous, *Dictionary*, p. 265.
8. Ibid., p. 465.
9. Paul Ricoeur, *Fallible Man: A Philosophy of the Will* (Chicago: Henry Regnery, 1965), p. 71.
10. Ibid., p. 4.
11. We will not enter into the discussion as to whether this section is from the hand of Hsün-tzu or a later legalist insertion.
12. See Donald J. Munro, *The Concept of Man in Contemporary China* (Ann Arbor: University of Michigan Press, 1977), pp. 15-25; the book as a whole is an exegesis of this.
13. Thomas A. Metzger, *Escape from Predicament* (New York: Columbia University Press, 1977), p. 49.
14. See, e.g., his claim that "I have never seen any without the ability" (*Lun-yü* 4.6).

15. See the famous fonts passage, *Meng-tzu* 2a.6.
16. Julia Ching, *To Acquire Wisdom* (New York: Columbia University Press, 1976), p. 148. She is commenting here on Wang Yang-ming's use of the distinction between *t'i* (substance) and *yung* (activity).
17. Ibid., p. 18 (I have made some slight changes). Cf. Metzger, *Escape from Predicament*, p. 111, and his comment on *Shujing*.
18. Ching, *To Acquire Wisdom*, p. 18. Cf. the "elusive immanence" of Metzger, *Escape from Predicament*, p. 111.
19. There were in fact different ways of applying this distinction. It could be interpreted as dual metaphysical principles or as two integral aspects of human nature itself (Ching, *To Acquire Wisdom*, p. 18).
20. Note Metzger's comment on eight other viewpoints (*Escape from Predicament*, p. 5). Our comments are an oversimplification, useful for general discussion.
21. Cf. the Fang approach and Chu-hsi's instructions for daily living.
22. See Wm. Theodore de Bary, "Neo-Confucian Cultivation and the Seventeenth-Century 'Enlightenment,' " in *The Unfolding of Neo-Confucianism*, ed. de Bary (New York: Columbia University Press, 1975).
23. Metzger, *Escape from Predicament*, p. 110, quoting Chu-hsi.
24. Ibid., p. 87.
25. Ibid., pp. 87f. Wang Yang-ming asks precisely the same question. His formulation is: "Now the original substance of the mind is man's nature. Human nature being universally good, the original substance of the mind is correct. How is it that any effort is required to rectify the mind? The reason is that, while the original substance of the mind is originally correct, incorrectness enters when one's thoughts and will are in operation. Therefore he who wishes to rectify his mind must rectify it in connection with the operation of his thought and will." See his *Instructions for Practical Living and Other Neo-Confucian Writings*, trans. Wing-tsit Chan (New York: Columbia University Press, 1963), p. 277.
26. Metzger, *Escape from Predicament*, p. 115.
27. Ibid.
28. Ibid., p. 111.
29. Ibid.
30. Munro, *Early China*, p. 89.
31. Metzger, *Escape from Predicament*, p. 154.
32. Walpola Rahula, *What the Buddha Taught*, rev. ed. (New York: Grove, 1974), p. 93; from his translation of the "Dhammacakkappavattanasutta" of the *Samyutta-nikaya* lxv, 11.
33. Murti, *Central Philosophy*, p. 309.
34. Ibid. This has profound implications for the different perspectives of Buddhist and Christian with respect to suffering, as we shall see later.
35. Joaquin Perez-Remon, *Self and Non-self in Early Buddhism* (The Hague: Mouton, 1980), p. 67. The etymological meaning of the word *asmimana* is "the conceit (*mana*) of I am (*asmi*)" (from the *Salayatanasamyutta*). It should be noted that Perez-Remon has been severely criticized for his argument that early Buddhism, after all, was really an *atman* or soul theory.
36. See Murti, *Central Philosophy*, p. 310: "the Absolute is the reality of the appearances."
37. There are strong similarities with the Platonic tradition at this point: "The fact

that man as a finite, temporal being was different from the essence of humanity signified that 'man was other than himself', i.e. his empirical, temporal, factual existence was not identical with the ideal, perfect, extra-temporal Being of humanity as such. . . . The world in which we live as finite individuals, conscious of our own transience, is a place of exile" (Leszek Kolakowski, *Main Currents of Marxism* [Oxford: Oxford University Press, 1981], 1:12). One has to read this without a substance ontology.

38. Pannenberg's objection to myth as a term that adequately applies to Christian discourse about historical revelation (see *Jesus—God and Man* [Philadelphia: Westminster, 1968], pp. 186f.) is well taken if myth is understood in the narrow "Eliadian" sense of stories about gods and unearthly creatures which divulge the truth about a time of origins and which is endlessly reenacted in the telling and in the doing (ritual). We take myth in a broader sense, namely, the significant appropriation of an event in story form which speaks of the divine-human relationship. It so happens that in the Christian "myth" the linear character of story integral to myth is also integral to the event that is appropriated. But for this very reason it must be a myth shaped by history rather than a history created by myth. There seems to be no reason that the language of "absolute metaphor" might not apply here.

39. Cf. John Macquarrie, *Principles of Christian Theology* (New York: Scribner, 1966), p. 321 et passim, on creation-reconciliation-consummation as three phases of a single movement of Being. His formulation is more existentially cast than is ours.

40. See Ted Peters, "Cosmos and Creation," *Word and World,* 4/4 (Fall 1984), pp. 372-390.

41. On the fall see Paul Sponheim, "Sin and Evil," in *Christian Dogmatics,* ed. Carl E. Braaten and Robert W. Jenson, 2 vols. (Philadelphia: Fortress, 1984), 1:359-464; cf. his reference to the "new" act of the fall (p. 448).

42. See the comments on the implications of the doctrine of traducianism in Paul R. Sponheim, *Faith and Process* (Minneapolis: Augsburg, 1979), pp. 47, 336 (note 18).

43. Gal. 4:4-5.

44. On the importance of succession, the irreversibility of time, and novelty see Sponheim, *Faith and Process,* pp. 298 (note 63), 75, 84, et passim.

45. See, e.g., Jürgen Moltmann, *The Crucified God* (New York: Harper and Row, 1974), chap. 6, and *The Trinity and the Kingdom: The Doctrine of God* (San Francisco: Harper and Row, 1981).

46. 1 Cor. 15:24-26,28.

47. Abraham Heschel, *The Prophets,* 2 vols. (New York: Harper, 1962), 1:16.

48. Exod. 19:4-5; Gen. 12:1,4; and Deut. 26:5-9.

49. Heschel, *The Prophets,* 1:21.

50. Ibid., 1:26.

51. Ibid., 1:24.

52. Jer. 2:12-13.

53. Jer. 7:9-15.

54. Amos 5:24.

55. Amos 3:1-2.

56. Jer. 5:1,5.

57. Jer. 8:10.
58. Hos. 4:1.
59. Ps. 14:3.
60. Heschel, *The Prophets,* 1:13.
61. Ibid., 1:14.
62. For instance, Ezekiel 18.
63. Paul Ricoeur, *The Symbolism of Evil* (Boston: Beacon, 1969), p. 126.
64. Ibid., p. 121; the quote within the quote is from R. Travers Herford, *The Pharisees* (New York, 1924), p. 18.
65. Pannenberg, *Jesus—God and Man,* pp. 53ff.
66. Ricoeur, *Symbolism of Evil,* pp. 119f.
67. Ibid., p. 119.
68. Ibid., p. 123.
69. Ibid.
70. Ibid., p. 126.
71. See especially Psalms 19 and 119.
72. Ricouer, *Symbolism of Evil,* p. 127.
73. Matt. 5:48.
74. Matt. 15:11,18-19.
75. Mark 2:27.
76. Luke 10:26-27.
77. Matt. 5:18.
78. Pannenberg, *Jesus—God and Man,* p. 255.
79. Gal. 3:24.
80. E.g., Gal. 3:19.
81. Pannenberg, *Jesus—God and Man,* p. 256.
82. Rom. 2:14f.
83. Rom. 7:24.
84. Ricoeur, *Symbolism of Evil,* p. 233.
85. Ibid., p. 242.
86. On typical mythic patterns of this sort see Charles H. Long, *Alpha: The Myths of Creation* (New York: George Braziller, 1963).
87. Li Zehou, "Kongzi zai pingjia [A Reassessment of Confucius]," in *Zhongguo Shehui Kexüe* 2 (1980): 5-6.
88. Ibid. Li refers at this point to Hegel's "Aesthetics" and conception of tragedy. He no doubt means Hegel's treatment of the problematic of the antinomies of existence and art. See G. W. F. Hegel, *On Art, Religion, Philosophy* (New York: Harper, 1970), especially pp. 85ff.
89. Li Zehou, "Kongzi zai pingjia," pp. 5-6. It would be interesting to compare Metz's idea of the role of memory in redeeming past suffering. See Johannes Metz, *Faith in History and Society: Toward a Practical Fundamental Theology* (New York: Seabury, 1980).
90. For a straightforward study that discusses much of the relevant textual material see Har Dayal, *The Bodhisattva Doctrine in Buddhist Sanskrit Literature* (Delhi: Motilal Banarsidass, 1932 [reprinted 1975]). For a brief but competent introduction see Richard Robinson, *The Buddhist Religion: A Historical Introduction* (Belmont, Calif.: Dickenson, 1970), pp. 58-70. Perhaps the best short introduction is Louis de La Vallee Poussin, "Bodhisattvas," in *Encyclopaedia of Religion*

and Ethics, ed. J. Hastings, 13 vols. (Edinburgh, 1908-1926), 2:739-752. See also D. T. Suzuki, *Outlines of Mahayana Buddhism* (New York: Schocken, 1963), pp. 242-307.

91. Quoted from Michael Pye, *Skilful Means: A Concept in Mahayana Buddhism* (London: Gerald Duckworth, 1978), p. 107; translated from T XXV 262c.

92. Dayal, *Bodhisattva Doctrine,* p. 248. For a helpful introduction to the idea of *upaya (fang-pien* in Chinese) see Alicia and Daigan Matsunaga, "The Concept of Upaya *fang-pien* in Mahayana Buddhist Philosophy," *Japanese Journal of Religious Studies* 1/1 (1974): 51-72. Besides Pye the only other major treatment in English of this concept is Alicia Matsunaga, *The Buddhist Philosophy of Assimilation: The Historical Development of the Honji-Suijaku Theory* (Tokyo: Charles E. Tuttle, 1969).

93. Pye, *Skilful Means,* p. 1.

94. Ibid., p. 36.

95. Ibid., p. 131.

96. See the discussion in ibid., chap. 3, for this and the following sections.

97. Ibid., p. 65; cited from T IX 2c.

98. Ibid., p. 71.

99. Ibid., p. 73; cited from T IX 34a.

100. Ibid., p. 66; On the translation "present Buddha" see p. 62, note 11; cited from T IX 5b.

101. Ibid., pp. 94f.

102. Ibid., p. 92.

103. Ibid., p. 95.

104. Ibid., pp. 100f.

105. Ibid., pp. 55-56; cited from T IX 42b-c.

106. For a detailed treatment of this see Wilhelm Thüsing and Karl Rahner, *A New Christology* (New York: Seabury, 1980).

107. Gal. 3:6.

108. Heb. 5:8-9. On the paucity of such New Testament references, despite the importance of the sonship/obedience linkage for Christology, see Pannenberg, *Jesus—God and Man,* p. 159, note 99.

109. Heb. 12:2.

110. Hebrews 11.

111. Heb. 5:7.

112. Cf. 1 Tim. 3:16: "Justified in the Spirit." On Jesus and his "trust" or faith see Pannenberg, *Jesus—God and Man,* p. 159, especially note 100. Hebrews 5:7 would seem to provide a necessary exegetical link. For a recent extended argument that the Pauline "faith of Jesus" is to be understood as Jesus' own faith, rather than Jesus as the object of faith, see Richard B. Hays, *The Faith of Jesus Christ: An Investigation of the Narrative Substructure of Galatians 3:1—4:11* (Baltimore: Scholars Press, 1983).

113. Gal. 5:6.

114. Thüsing and Rahner, *A New Christology,* p. 92.

115. 2 Cor. 5:19.

116. Pannenberg, *Jesus—God and Man.* We accept his approach as the most helpful.

117. Thus Pannenberg, ibid., p. 66.

118. 1 Cor. 15:17.

119. Cf. Pannenberg, *Jesus—God and Man,* pp. 119f.
120. Thüsing and Rahner, *A New Christology,* p. 94; see all of chap. 4, especially pp. 80f., 92f., 111.
121. Ibid., p. 111; cf. E. Schweizer, *"Pneuma," Theological Dictionary of the New Testament,* ed. G. Kittel (Grand Rapids: Eerdmans, 1968): 421, 428.
122. Cf. the idea of *hypotaxis* (putting in subjection), as in 1 Cor. 15:27-28.
123. 1 Cor. 3:17.
124. 1 John 4:8.
125. 1 Cor. 8:5-6.
126. For a helpful discussion of the Amida (Amitabha) Buddha, or the Buddha of the Western Paradise or Pure Land, see the article "Amita," in *Encyclopaedia of Buddhism,* ed. G. P. Malalasekera (Colombo: Government of Ceylon, 1961—), 1:434-463. For a description of some Chinese expressions and techniques of faith in Amitabha see the chapter "Self-Cultivation according to the Pure Land School," in Lu K'uan Yu, *The Secrets of Chinese Meditation* (London: Rider, 1964), pp. 81-108. For a discussion of its Japanese development, particularly in Shin Buddhism, with a good discussion of the basic sutras involved, see Alfred Bloom, *Shinran's Gospel of Pure Grace,* Association for Asian Studies, Monographs and Papers 20 (Tucson: University of Arizona Press, 1965).
127. Lecture by Priest Bando in Tokyo, December 1984.
128. See John B. Cobb Jr., *Beyond Dialogue: Toward a Mutual Transformation of Christianity and Buddhism* (Philadelphia: Fortress, 1982). Here he calls for a "mutual transformation" of both the Buddhist and the Christian. For an intriguing discussion of how Buddhist thought might help to reshape a Christian understanding of love, see the relevant section on love in *Christ in a Pluralistic Age* (Philadelphia: Westminster, 1975).
129. See especially Mahmoud Ayoub, *Redemptive Suffering in Islam: A Study of the Devotional Aspects of "Ashura" in Twelver Shi'ism* (The Hague: Mouton, 1978). Even here the participation of the faithful in the sufferings of the martyr and of the prophet and the intercessory role of those who so suffer remains as a human, even cosmic, drama but without moving in the direction of divine condescension.
130. That is to say, to affirm that there is no God but God and to affirm, as in some forms of Sufism, that there is no reality but God is simply to state the *tauhid* doctrine in personal (will) and metaphysical (reality) terms. To be sure, orthodox Islam forbids the latter as inappropriate.
131. Genesis 8–9.
132. See especially Abraham Heschel, *The Prophets: An Introduction* (New York: Harper, 1962) and Terence E. Fretheim, *The Suffering of God: An Old Testament Perspective* (Philadelphia: Fortress, 1984).
133. Hsün-tzu, chap. 17; quoted from *Hsün-tzu: Basic Writings,* trans. Burton Watson (New York: Columbia University Press, 1963), p. 85.
134. *Hsün-tzu,* chap. 19; see H. H. Dubs, *The Works of Hsün Tzu* (London: Probsthain, 1928), p. 223.
135. *Meng-tzu,* 2a.6; cited from *Mensius,* trans. W. A. C. H. Dobson (Toronto: University of Toronto Press, 1963), p. 132.

Chapter 4: The Transforming Presence
1. A helpful attempt to begin giving some order to the diversity is Arthur F. Wright, "A Historian's Reflections on the Taoist Tradition," *History of Religions* 9 (1969-1970): 248-255.

NOTES

2. Quoted from Max Kaltenmark, *Lao Tzu and Taoism* (Stanford: Stanford University Press, 1969), pp. 9f.
3. Ibid., p. 14. For further discussion of historical and textual critical matters see *The Way of Lao Tzu*, trans. Wing-tsit Chan (New York: Bobbs-Merrill, 1963), as well as items listed by N. J. Girardo, *Myth and Meaning in Early Taoism: The Theme of Chaos (hun-tun)* (Berkeley: University of California Press, 1983), p. 337, n. 3.
4. Though, to be precise, making inquiry of the host concerning local practice is part of what is proper in the rites. In *Lun-yü* 10.15, Confucius does this when visiting the ancestral temple, even though he was well versed on ritual matters.
5. Cited in Kaltenmark, *Lao Tzu*, p. 8.
6. Cited in Girardo, *Myth and Meaning*, p. 309.
7. On this see Herrlee G. Creel, *What is Taoism?* (Chicago: University of Chicago Press, 1970), "The Great Clod," pp. 25-36.
8. *Tao-te-ching*, chap. 4 (6). The first chapter numberings follow that in Wei-yüan Ch'ing, *Lao-tzu pen-yi* (Taipei: Shih-chieh shu-chü, 1963) and the second (in parentheses) that of *The Way of Lao Tzu*, trans. Wing-tsit Chan.
9. *Tao-te-ching*, chap. 35 (42).
10. Ibid., chap. 62 (76) (my translation).
11. Ibid., chap. 43 (51).
12. Quoted, with modifications, from Girardo, *Myth and Meaning*, pp. 51-52.
13. Chapter 35 (42) of the *Tao-te-ching*, cited from ibid., pp. 56f.
14. *Tao-te-ching*, chap. 17 (21). I have combined the translations of Girardo, p. 65, and Chan, p. 137. The former's heavy reliance upon "chaos" to translate a variety of terms seems a bit overdrawn. Obscurity and elusiveness, the unmanifest character of this higher order of reality, seem to be closer to the sense of things.
15. *Tao-te-ching*, chap. 33 (40).
16. *Tao-te-ching*, chap. 48 (56); cf. Girardo, p. 53.
17. *Tao-te-ching*, chap. 17 (21). This is partially a paraphrasing of Girardo, p. 55, which attempts to use function language rather than substance language. One wonders how many of the translations would look if, like the Chinese original, the substance words such as "it" and "something" were not used.
18. Girardo, p. 277.
19. For a fairly comprehensive bibliography of writings on Taoism in Western languages see Laurence G. Thompson, *Studies of Chinese Religion: A Comprehensive and Classified Bibliography of Publications in English, French, and German through 1970* (Encino, California: Dickenson, 1976), sections 13-21. For a helpful, more recent collection of essays see Holmes Welch and Anna Seidel, *Facets of Taoism* (New Haven: Yale University Press, 1979).
20. On the early yin-yang school see Fung Yu-lan, *A History of Chinese Philosophy* (Princeton: Princeton University Press, 1952), 1:159-169, "Tsou Yen and the School of Yin and Yang and the Five Elements."
21. On the cosmogram see ibid., vol. 2, chap. 11, "Chou Tun-yi and Shao Yung."
22. This is of course to oversimplify, but there is some truth to it. Cf. Girardo, *Myth and Meaning*, p. 175, as well as Joseph Needham, *Science and Civilization in China* (Cambridge: Cambridge University Press, 1962), pp. 33f.
23. See Wolfgang Bauer, *China and the Search for Happiness* (New York: Seabury, 1976), p. 7 and note 10.

24. *The Chinese Classics,* trans. James Legge (reprint Hong Kong, 1960), 5:671 (Chao-kung, 18th year).
25. Donald J. Munro, *The Concept of Man in Early China* (Stanford: Stanford University Press, 1969), pp. 29ff., 131f. See the whole book for details on how this works out.
26. *Tao-te-ching* 66 (80), quoted from Chan, *The Way of Lao Tzu,* p. 238.
27. On the *Tao-te-ching* as a political document see, e.g., Joseph Needham, *Science and Civilization in China,* pp. 34f., 47.
28. *Lun-yü* 18.6; quoted from Waley, *The Analects of Confucius* (London: George Allen and Unwin, 1956), p. 220.
29. Bauer, *China,* p. 32.
30. Quoted from Girardo, *Myth and Meaning,* p. 81.
31. Bauer, *China,* is the most detailed and comprehensive study of Chinese utopian thought.
32. It seems more adequate to distinguish Lao-tzu and Chuang-tzu by oscillation and transformation rather than production and transformation, as in Munro, *The Concept of Mau in Early China,* p. 120.
33. For a helpful discussion see Bauer, *China,* pp. 44-49.
34. *Lieh-tzu* 7. In Chang-shen Chin, *Lieh-tzu chu* (Taipei: Shih-chieh shu-chü, 1958), p. 83.
35. For a celebration of this truth as Taoist materialism, see Creel, *What Is Taoism?*
36. *Chuang-tzu* 18; see Burton Watson, *The Complete Works of Chuang-tzu* (New York: Columbia University Press, 1968), pp 193-194.
37. Note Creel's comments on the contradiction between "purposive" and "contemplative" aspects of early Taoism (Creel, *What Is Taoism?* pp. 37-47, "On Two Aspects in Early Taoism").
38. On their basic ideas see, e.g., Fung, *A History,* vol. 1, chap. 13.
39. For a survey of this period see, e.g., Edwin O. Reischauer and John K. Fairbank, *East Asia: The Great Tradition* (Boston: Houghton Mifflin, 1958, 1960), chaps. 2-4.
40. Cf. the discussion of "immanental theocracy" in Joseph M. Kitagawa, *Religion in Japanese History* (New York: Columbia University Press, 1966), p. 154.
41. Li Zehou expounds this effectively in "Wei-jin fengdu" (The Spirit of the Wei and Jin Times), in *Zhongguo Kexüe* 2 (Beijing: Sanlian Shudian, 1980): 101-119.
42. For a helpful treatment of Islam in China see Israeli Raphael, *Chinese versus Muslims: A Study of Cultural Confrontation* (Ann Arbor: University Microfilms International, 1974).
43. Karl Jaspers, above all, has made this notion of an anthropocentric shift popular with his discussion of the "Axial Age." See *The Origin of History* (New Haven: Yale University Press, 1953).
44. Wang Yang-ming certainly showed this naivete. Thomas A. Metzger, *Escape from Predicament* (New York: Columbia University Press, 1977), pp. 33ff., attributes this easy identification of fact and value to the lack of the Humean kind of doubt concerning the objectivity of values.
45. See, e.g., the *ta-t'ung* and *t'ai-p'ing* citations below (nn. 57 and 59.)
46. Bauer, *China,* p. 14. On time see also especially Joseph Needham, *Time and*

Eastern Man (London: Royal Anthropological Institute of Great Britain and Ireland, 1965), and Bauer, pp. 57-84.

47. Bauer, *China*, p. 14.

48. *The Book of Chao*, trans. Walter Liebenthal (Peking, 1948), pp. 46-54; quoted from Bauer, *China*, pp. 171f.

49. Daisetz Suzuki and S. Ueda, "The Sayings of Rinzai," *Eastern Buddhist* 6.1 (1973): 93. For further discussion of this see "Emptiness and the Appreciation of World, History and Man," in Hans Waldenfels, *Absolute Nothingness: Foundations for a Buddhist-Christian Dialogue* (New York: Paulist Press, 1980), pp. 93-117.

50. Waldenfels, *Absolute Nothingness*, p. 112.

51. Keiji Nishitani, *Religion and Nothingness* (Berkeley: University of California Press, 1982), p. 161.

52. John Cobb, *Beyond Dialogue: Toward a Mutual Transformation of Christianity and Buddhism* (Philadelphia: Fortress, 1982), p. 91, puts it this way: "How one perceives one's historical past and future determines the most general and also the most fundamental grounds for the meaning of each fleeting moment. Hence the meaning and context of the moment derive precisely from our transcendence of that moment in that moment" (see also 90-94). For a further discussion of how the ideas of emptiness, time, and personhood relate see also *Christ in a Pluralist Age* (Philadelphia: Westminster, 1975), pp. 203-220.

53. Needham, *Science and Civilization*, p. ix.

54. Derk Bodde, "Dominant Ideas [in Chinese Culture]," in *China*, ed. H. F. McNair (Berkeley: University of California Press, 1946), p. 23; cited in Needham, *Science and Civilization*, p. 51.

55. Needham, *Science and Civilization;* note his conclusion (p. 50).

56. Ibid., p. 44.

57. The Li Lun chapter of the *Li Chi*, probably of the first century c.e.; quoted from ibid., p. 24, with minor changes.

58. For a useful introduction to Mohist thought see Fung Yu-lan, *A History*, vol. 1, chaps. 5 and 11.

59. The commentary of Ho Hsiu (129–182 c.e.) on the *Kungyang Chuan*, quoted from Needham, *Science and Civilization*, p. 28, with slight changes.

60. Needham, *Science and Civilization*, pp. 45f.

61. Robert W. Jenson, "The Holy Spirit," in *Christian Dogmatics*, ed. Carl E. Braaten and Robert W. Jenson, 2 vols. (Philadelphia: Fortress, 1984), 2:105.

62. Gen. 2:7.

63. 1 Cor. 2:10f.

64. 1 Cor. 2:13.

65. Cf. Jensen, in *Christian Dogmatics*, vol. 2, pp. 110, 112-114, 166f., 174f.

66. Ibid., p. 107.

67. Isa. 40:6-7, RSV alt.

68. Isa. 4:4; cf. 27:8; 30:27-28.

69. On personal transformation see, e.g., John 3:3. On the others see, e.g., Rom. 1:3; 8:23.

70. For example, in the case of China one thinks of the popular theory that the human

soul fragments upon death into seven earthbound elements (*p'o*) and three heavenly elements (*hun*). For a massive documentation of this kind of spirit eschatology see Jakob Maria Jan de Groot, *The Religious System of China*, 6 vols. (Leiden: E. J. Brill, 1982–1910). Halloween ghosts are a classic example of the end result of this sort of eschatological deterioration.

71. Jenson, in *Christian Dogmatics*, 2:171f. and note 16.

72. Cf. ibid., 2:171-172. One thinks also of Robert C. Neville's term "existential spontaneity" used of the Spirit. Among other things, he writes: "Inquiring into the ontology of events we may say that the Holy Spirit is their existential spontaneity." See *The Tao and the Daimon* (Albany: State University of New York Press, 1982), p. 44.

73. Gen. 1:2; cf. the exegesis of this passage by Claus Westermann, *Genesis 1–11* (Minneapolis: Augsburg, 1984), pp. 102-110.

74. For the detailing of this argument see Needham, *Science and Civilization*, vol. 2, especially pp. 33-164.

75. Robert C. Neville, *The Tao and the Daimon*, p. 144, rightly identifies the twin Taoist and Confucian naivetes and their complementarity.

76. The complex layers of meaning in the word *heaven (t'ien)* indicate something of the quality of this immanental transcendence. Fung, *A History*, 1:31, outlines five of the more common and important meanings: a physical heaven, a sovereign heaven, heaven as destiny, heaven as nature, a moral heaven; cf. §2, n. 42.

77. This optimism includes the Hsün-tzian pessimism (human nature as evil), which assumes the human possibility after all, as we have seen.

78. Munro, *The Concept of Man in Early China*, pp. 69f.

79. The best treatment on this complex process of appropriation is that of E. Zürcher, *The Buddhist Conquest of China* (Leiden: E. J. Brill, 1959), See also Kenneth K. S. Ch'en, *Buddhism in China: A Historical Survey* (Princeton: Princeton University Press, 1964), and especially Kenneth K. S. Ch'en, *The Chinese Transformation of Buddhism* (Princeton: Princeton University Press, 1973).

80. Representative of treatments that do take this seriously are Jürgen Moltmann, *The Crucified God* (New York: Harper and Row, 1974) and Robert W. Jenson, "The Triune God," in *Christian Dogmatics*, 1:83-191. Moltmann recounts his move in this direction thus: "For me, the work on this theology of the cross meant a surprising turning-point. Having asked in many different ways what the cross of Christ means for the church, for theology, for discipleship, for culture and society, I now found myself faced with the reverse question: what does Christ's cross really mean for God himself? Is God so absolute and sovereign that he reigns in heavenly glory, incapable of suffering and untouched by the death of his Son? And if God is essentially incapable of suffering, does this not mean that he is incapable of love as well?" (*Experiences of God* [Philadelphia: Fortress, 1980]).

81. Moltmann's title, *Experiences of God*, is intentionally ambiguous, including both the objective (our experiences of God) and subjective (God's experiences of us) genitives.

82. Rom. 8:18-27.

83. Rom. 8:15.

84. Matt. 27:46.

85. Showing a Western bias, to be sure, but nonetheless largely true for the West,

Ernst Bloch writes: "Even Christians, either with amazement or with a sleeping conscience, have spotted that all the Utopian aspirations of the great movements of human liberation derive from the Exodus and the messianic parts of the Bible" (*Das Prinzip Hoffnung*, 1959, 1.17; cited from James Bentley, *Between Marx and Christ* [London, 1982], p. 80). Speaking of this, Tillich notes that "providence still triumphs for both Hegel and Marx. For Hegel it triumphs in his own era; for Marx it will triumph in an indefinite future" (*Systematic Theology* [Chicago: University of Chicago Press, 1951]), 1:266. Ernst Bloch, a major figure introducing hope as an explicit category into Marxist thought, observes that "What man expressed in the hypostases of the gods was altogether nothing but *longed-for-future*" (*Das Prinzip Hoffnung*, 3.1402, cited from Bentley, *Between Marx and Christ*, p. 94). Habermas, of the Frankfurt school of Marxist thought, commenting on Bloch, writes that "God is dead, but his locus has survived him. The place in which mankind has hitherto imagined God and the gods, after the decay of these hypotheses, remains a hollow space, whose 'measurements in depth,' i.e., atheism, finally understood, reveal the blueprint of a future kingdom of freedom." The removal of God leaves an open space, an open future of hope, to be humanly filled.

86. For Marxist and Christian reflections on the significance of Prometheus for human self-understanding, see, e.g., James Bentley, *Between Marx and Christ* (London: Verso, 1982), chap. 6 and pp. 141-143.

87. Thus also Neville in *The Tao and the Daimon* in his interpretation of Spirit. On p. 99 he writes: "Many philosophical problems are involved in interpreting the extent to which the evidence of creation reveals God to have the character of what might be called a 'personality'; but at least the *structure* of creating is there, and it is that structure that lies at the heart of being a person."

88. Jenson, "The Holy Spirit," in *Christian Dogmatics*, 2:168.

89. On the potential theological significance of this kind of emphasis on the subject see Johannes Metz, *Faith in History and Society* (New York: Seabury, 1980).

90. Jenson, in *Christian Dogmatics*, 2:168.

91. For a Chinese Marxist philosopher's brief and cryptic comment on the tragedies of history see Li Zehou, "Kongzi zai pingjit" (A Reassessment of Confucius), *Zhongguo Shehui Kexüe* 2 (1980): 5-6. For contemporary literary expressions of the experience of tragedy see Helen F. Siu and Zella Stern, *Mao's Harvest* (New York: Oxford, 1983), and Perry Link, ed., *Roses and Thorns: The Second Blooming of the Hundred Flowers in Chinese Fiction 1979–1980* (Berkeley: University of California Press, 1984).

92. Rom. 8:37-39.

Chapter 5: Speaking the Truth

1. Max Scheler, *Selected Philosophical Essays* (Evanston: Northwestern University Press, 1973), p. 98.

2. See Paul V. Martinson, "Issue: Other Religions in the World," in *Call to Global Mission*, ed. John M. Mangam (New York: Lutheran Church in America, Division for World Mission and Ecumenism, 1982), p. 331.

3. George A. Lindbeck, *The Nature of Doctrine: Religion and Theology in a Postliberal Age* (Philadelphia: Westminster, 1984), p. 16.

4. Ernst Troeltsch, *The Absoluteness of Christianity and the History of Religions,* trans. David Reid (Richmond: John Knox, 1971), pp. 51f.

5. Islam, especially in its orthodox Asharite synthesis, represents perhaps the most systematic effort to protect revelation from compromise by means of a theology of occasionalism, asserting immediate divine agency for all that happens. See, e.g., Duncan B. MacDonald, *Development of Muslim Theology, Jurisprudence and Constitutional Theory* (New York: Scribner, 1903), pp. 201ff.

6. Lindbeck, *The Nature of Doctrine,* p. 16.

7. Cited from Paul F. Knitter, "Roman Catholic Approaches to Other Religions: Developments and Tensions," in *International Bulletin of Missionary Research* 8.2 (April 1984), p. 50.

8. Arthur Glasser, "Response," in *Christ's Lordship and Religious Pluralism,* ed. G. H. Anderson and T. F. Stransky (Maryknoll: Orbis, 1981), p. 37 (emphasis in the original).

9. Quoted from Gordon Rupp, *Christologies and Cultures* (The Hague: Mouton, 1974), p. 223. He modifies the English version of Troeltsch, *The Absoluteness of Christianity,* p. 85.

10. This is a modern adaptation of the text by Rupp, *Christologies and Cultures,* p. 226. For the original English version see Ernst Troeltsch, *Christian Thought: Its History and Application,* ed. F. von Hügel (New York: Living Age Books, 1957), p. 63. It should be made clear here that there is an unbridgeable gap between the historicist and ontologist pluralism, even though Troeltsch finally tried to wed the two. Troeltsch's historical studies led to his "wretched historicism," in which there was a collapse of human value since no content beyond the data was made available. Not even a complete survey of world culture would be able to solve this problem of the poverty of content. The clutch after God himself "where alone the ultimate unity and the final objective validity can lie" (ibid., p. 89) is made by appeal no longer to history ("brute fact") but to "a profound inner experience" which itself "is undoubtedly the criterion of its validity" (ibid., p. 86). The pluralism of Hick is based on this ontological grasp, and simply uses history to illustrate the ontology. Allen Race, commenting on this in *Christians and Religious Pluralism: Patterns in the Christian Theology of Religions* (Maryknoll: Orbis, 1982), pp. 81f., does not seem fully to see the fundamental discontinuity between the historicist assumptions and the ontologist assumptions which contradict them. Apart from this last grasp, Troeltsch's view was truly pluralist, so pluralist that no unity was discernable; the supposed pluralism of Hick is really a reflex of an ontological absolutism, a nonhistorical stance, which makes culture decidedly secondary.

11. Several recent publications in this area may be cited as indications of this trend: Wilfred Cantwell Smith, *Religious Diversity,* ed. Willard G. Oxtoby (New York: Crossroad, 1982), Harold Coward, *Pluralism: Challenge to World Religions* (1985), Paul F. Knitter, *No Other Name? A Critical Survey of Christian Attitudes toward the World Religions* (1985), Alan Race, *Christians and Religious Pluralism* (1982), the last three published by Orbis. Race states the assumption informing this trend quite boldly: "The starting-point for the pluralist theory is the validity of the notion of religious experience, which is embodied in various ways in the religious traditions of the world" (p. 139).

12. Paul Tillich, *Theology of Culture* (New York: Oxford University Press, 1964), p. 42.
13. See Knitter, *No Other Name?* p. 151. For the first citation see John Hick, *The Center of Christianity* (San Francisco: Harper and Row, 1968), p. 32.
14. See "Jesus and the World Religions," in *The Myth of God Incarnate,* ed. John Hick (Philadelphia: Westminster, 1977), p. 172.
15. See ibid., p. 172.
16. Adapted from Huston Smith's Introduction to Frithjof Schuon, *The Transcendent Unity of Religions* (Wheaton, Ill.: Theosophical Publishing House, 1984).
17. S. Radhakrishnan, *Eastern Religions and Western Thought,* 2nd ed. (London: Oxford University Press, 1940), p. 308.
18. On these categories see Hendrik Kraemer, *The Communication of the Christian Faith* (Philadelphia: Westminster, 1956).
19. See Lindbeck, *The Nature of Doctrine,* pp. 34, 36.
20. Ibid., p. 35.
21. Ibid., p. 34.
22. Acts 11:26.
23. Lindbeck, *The Nature of Doctrine,* p. 94.
24. One need only call to mind the discussion that has surrounded *The Myth of God Incarnate,* ed. John Hick.
25. Cited in Alan Watts, *The Way of Zen* (New York: Vintage, 1957), p. 22. For a more complete account see Daisetz Suzuki, *The Training of the Zen Buddhist-Monk* (New York: University Books, 1965), pp. xviii-xxii, especially pp. xxif.
26. Daisetz Suzuki, *Essays in Zen Buddhism,* First Series (London: Rider, 1958), p. 263. Leonard Hall Bridges, in *American Mysticism from William James to Zen* (New York: Harper and Row, 1970), brings these comments together (see pp. 104ff.).
27. On this matter of testing, we agree with the general lines of the chapter on "Accountability in Theology" in Neville, *The Tao and the Daimon,* pp. 11-25.
28. For Paul Tillich, missionary action, the church's function of "expansion," is seen under the "polarity of verity and adaptation" (see *Systematic Theology,* vol. 3 [Digswell Place: James Nisbet, 1964], pp. 195f., 198).
29. John B. Cobb Jr., *Beyond Dialogue: Toward a Mutual Transformation of Christianity and Buddhism* (Philadelphia: Fortress, 1982), p. 128. For the fuller discussion that introduces important qualifications, see pp. 123-128.

BIBLIOGRAPHY

Ali, Abdullah Yusuf. *The Meaning of the Glorious Qur'an.* 2 volumes. Cairo: Dar Al-Kitab Al-Masri, ca. 1934.

Anderson, G. H., and Stransky, T. F., editors. *Christ's Lordship and Religious Pluralism.* Maryknoll: Orbis, 1981.

Arapura, J. G. *Religion as Anxiety and Tranquillity: An Essay in Comparative Phenomenology of the Spirit.* The Hague: Mouton, 1972.

Arberry, A. J. *The Koran Interpreted.* 2 volumes. New York: Macmillan, 1964.

Aronson, Harvey B. *Love and Sympathy in Theravada Buddhism.* Delhi: Motilal Banarsidass, 1980.

Ayoub, Mahmoud. *Redemptive Suffering in Islam: A Study of the Devotional Aspects of Ashura in Twelver Shi'ism.* The Hague: Mouton, 1978.

Bakker, Dirk. *Man in the Qur'an.* Amsterdam: Drukkerij Holland, 1965.

Bary, William Theodore de. "Neo-Confucian Cultivation and the Seventeenth-Century 'Enlightenment,' " In *The Unfolding of Neo-Confucianism,* edited by de Bary. New York: Columbia University Press, 1975.

Bauer, Wolfgang. *China and the Search for Happiness: Recurring Themes in Four Thousand Years of Chinese Cultural History.* Translated by Michael Shaw. New York: Seabury, 1976.

Bentley, James. *Between Marx and Christ: The Dialogue in German-Speaking Europe 1870–1970.* London: Verso Editions and NLB, 1982.

Berger, Peter L. *The Heretical Imperative: Contemporary Possibilities of Religious Affirmation.* Garden City: Doubleday, 1979.

Bonino, Jose Miguez. *Christians and Marxists: The Mutual Challenge to Revolution.* Grand Rapids: Eerdmans, 1976.

Bowker, John Westerdale. *The Sense of God: Sociological, Anthropological and Psychological Approaches to the Origin of the Sense of God.* Oxford: Clarendon, 1973.

_____ . *The Religious Imagination and the Sense of God.* Oxford: Clarendon, 1978.

_____ . *Problems of Suffering in Religions of the World.* Cambridge: Cambridge University Press, 1970.

Boyd, James W. *Satan and Mara: Christian and Buddhist Symbols of Evil.* Leiden: E. J. Brill, 1975.

Braaten, Carl E., and Jenson, Robert W., editors. *Christian Dogmatics*. 2 vols. Philadelphia: Fortress, 1984.

Bridges, Leonard Hall. *American Mysticism from William James to Zen*. New York: Harper and Row, 1970.

Carmody, Denise Lardner. *What Are They Saying about Non-Christian Faith?* New York: Paulist, 1982.

Chan, Wing-tsit, translator. *Instructions for Practical Living and Other Neo-Confucian Writings*. New York: Columbia University Press, 1963.

—————— , compiler and translator. *Reflections on Things at Hand*. New York: Columbia University Press, 1967.

—————— , translator and editor. *The Way of Lao Tzu*. New York: Bobbs-Merril, 1963.

Chang, Chung-yuan. *Creativity and Taoism: A Study of Chinese Philosophy, Art, and Poetry*. New York: Harper, 1963.

Chang, Garma C. C. *The Buddhist Teaching of Totality: The Philosophy of Hwa Yen Buddhism*. University Park, Pa.: Pennsylvania State University Press, 1971.

Ch'en, Kenneth K. S. *Buddhism in China: A Historical Survey*. Princeton: Princeton University Press, 1964.

Cheng, Chung-ying. "Conscience, Mind and Individual in Chinese Philosophy." *Journal of Chinese Philosophy* 2 (1974): 16-25.

—————— . *The Chinese Transformation of Buddhism*. Princeton: Princeton University Press, 1973.

Ch'ien, Mu. *Lun-yü hsin-chieh* (A New Explanation of the Analects). 2 volumes. Kowloon, Hong Kong: Hsin-ya yen-chiu suo, 1963.

Chin, Chang-shen. *Lieh-tzu chu*. Taipei: Shih-chieh shu-chü, 1958.

Ching, Julia. *To Acquire Wisdom: The Way of Wang Yang-ming*. New York: Columbia University Press, 1976.

—————— . *Confucianism and Christianity: A Comparative Study*. Tokyo: Kodansha International, 1977.

Ch'ing, Wei-yuan. *Lao-tzu pen-yi*. Taipei: Shih-chieh shu-chü, 1963.

Chung-wen ta-ts'u-tien (The Encyclopedic Dictionary of the Chinese Language). 40 volumes. Taipei: Chung-guo wen-hua yen-chiu-suo, 1963.

Creel, Herrlee G. *What Is Taoism and Other Studies in Chinese Cultural History*. Chicago: University of Chicago Press, 1970.

Cobb, John B., Jr. *Christ in a Pluralistic Age*. Philadelphia: Westminster, 1975.

Dayal, Har. *The Bodhisattva Doctrine in Buddhist Sanskrit Literature*. Delhi: Motilal Banarsidass, 1970 (originally published in 1932).

Dobson, W. A. C. H., translator. *Mencius*. Toronto: University of Toronto Press, 1963.

Dubs, H. H. *The Works of Hsun Tzu*. London: Probsthain, 1928.

Dumoulin, Heinrich. *Christianity Meets Buddhism*. Translated by John C. Maraldo. Lasalle: Open Court, 1974.

Eliade, Mircea. *Cosmos and History*. Translated by W. R. Trask. New York: Harper and Row, 1959.

Feuerback, Ludwig. *The Essence of Christianity*. Translated by George Eliot. New York: Harper, 1957.

Foucher, A. *The Life of the Buddha: According to the Ancient Texts and Monuments of India*. Abridged translation by Simone Brangier Boas. Middletown: Wesleyan University Press, 1963.

BIBLIOGRAPHY

Frederick Franck, editor *The Buddha Eye: An Anthology of the Kyoto School.* New York: Crossroad, 1982.

Fretheim, Terence E. *The Suffering of God: An Old Testament Perspective.* Philadelphia: Fortress, 1984.

Fromm, Erich, editor. *Zen Buddhism and Psychoanalysis.* New York: Grove, 1963.

Fukaura, Seibun. "Alaya-Vijnana." *Encyclopaedia of Buddhism,* 1:382-388. Edited by G. P. Malalasekera. Colombo: Government of Ceylon, 1961—.

Fung, Yu-lan. *A History of Chinese Philosophy.* 2 volumes. Translated by Derk Bodde. Princeton: Princeton University Press, 1952.

Gardavsky, Vitezslav. *God Is Not Yet Dead.* Translated by Vivienne Menkes. Harmondsworth: Penguin, 1973.

Gardet, L. *Cultures and Time.* New York: Unipub, 1973.

Gibb, H. A. R. et al., editors. *The Encyclopaedia of Islam.* New Edition. Multivolume. Leiden: E. J. Brill, 1960—.

Girardot, N. J. *Myth and Meaning in Early Taoism: The Theme of Chaos (hun-tun).* Berkeley: University of California Press, 1983.

Glasser, Arthur. "Response." In *Mission Trends No. 2: Evangelism,* edited by G. H. Anderson and T. F. Stransky. Grand Rapids: Eerdmans, 1981.

Gould, Carol C. *Marx's Social Ontology: Individuality and Community in Marx's Theory of Social Reality.* Cambridge, Mass.: MIT Press, 1978.

Graham, A. C. *The Book of Lieh-tzu.* London, 1960.

Griffin, David, editor. *Philosophy of Religions and Theology, 1973 Proceedings.* Tallahassee: AAR/Florida State University, 1973.

Groot, Jan Jakob Maria de. *The Religious System of China.* 6 volumes. Leiden: E. J. Brill, 1892–1910.

Guddat, Kurt H., and Easton, Loyd D., editors. *Writings of the Young Marx on Philosophy and Society.* New York: Doubleday, 1967.

Guenther, Herbert V. *Philosophy and Psychology in the Abhidharma.* Berkeley: Shambala Publications, 1976.

Hacker, Paul. *Theological Foundations of Evangelization.* St. Augustin: Steyler Verlag, 1980.

Hallencreutz, Carl F. *Dialogue and Community: Ecumenical Issues in Inter-religious Relationships.* Studia Missionalia Upsaliensia 31. Uppsala: Swedish Institute of Missionary Research, 1977.

Hays, Richard B. *The Faith of Jesus Christ: An Investigation of the Narrative Substructure of Galatians 3:1—4:11.* Baltimore: Scholars Press, 1983.

Hebblethwaite, Brian. *Evil, Suffering and Religion.* New York: Hawthorn, 1976.

Hegel, G. W. F. *On Art, Religion, Philosophy.* Edited by J. Glenn Gray. New York: Harper, 1970.

Heschel, Abraham J. *The Prophets: An Introduction.* 2 volumes. New York: Harper, 1962.

Hick, John. *The Center of Christianity.* San Francisco: Harper and Row, 1968.

————. *God and the Universe of Faiths.* New York: St. Martin's Press, 1973.

————. "Jesus and the World Religions." In *The Myth of God Incarnate,* edited by John Hick. Philadelphia: Westminster, 1977, pp. 167-185.

Hirai, Tomio. *Psychophysiology of Zen.* Tokyo: Igaku Shoin, 1974.

Ishaq, Ibn. *The Life of Muhammad (Sirat Rasul Allah).* Translated by A. Guillaume. Lahore: Oxford University Press, Pakistan Branch, 1974 (1955).

Jaspers, Karl. *The Origin and Goal of History.* Translated by Michael Bullock. New Haven: Yale University Press, 1953.

Jenson, Robert W. *The Triune Identity.* Philadelphia: Fortress, 1982.

————. "The Holy Spirit." In *Christian Dogmatics,* edited by Carl E. Braaten and Robert W. Jenson. Philadelphia: Fortress, 1984, 2:105-178.

————. "The Triune God." In *Christian Dogmatics,* edited by Braaten and Jenson. Philadelphia: Fortress, 1984, 1:83-191.

Johansson, Rune E. A. *The Psychology of Nirvana.* London: Allen and Unwin, 1969.

Johnston, William. *Silent Music: The Science of Meditation.* New York: Harper and Row, 1974.

Kaltenmark, Max. *Lao Tzu and Taoism.* Translated by Roger Greaves. Stanford: Stanford University Press, 1969.

Kalupahana, David J. *Causality: The Central Philosophy of Buddhism.* Honolulu: University Press of Hawaii, 1975.

————. *Buddhist Philosophy: A Historical Analysis.* Honolulu: University Press of Hawaii, 1976.

Kamenka, Eugene. *The Ethical Foundations of Marxism.* New York: Frederick A. Praeger, 1962.

————. *Marxism and Ethics.* London: Macmillan, 1969.

Katz, Steven T., editor. *Mysticism and Philosophical Analysis.* New York: Oxford University Press, 1978.

Kautsky, Karl. *Foundations of Christianity.* Translated by Henry F. Mins. New York: Russell and Russell, 1953.

Kerr, David. "The Problem of Christianity in Muslim Perspective: Implications for Christian Mission." *International Bulletin* 5/4 (October 1981):152-162.

King, Winston L. *Buddhism and Christianity: Some Bridges of Understanding.* Philadelphia: Westminster, 1962.

————. *In the Hope of Nibbana: An Essay on Theravada Buddhist Ethics.* Lasalle: Open Court, 1964.

Kitagawa, Joseph M. *Religion in Japanese History.* New York: Columbia University Press, 1966.

Knitter, Paul F. *Towards a Protestant Theology of Religions: A Case Study of Paul Althaus and Contemporary Attitudes.* Marburger Theologische Studien 2. Marburg: N. G. Elwert Verlag, 1974.

————. "Roman Catholic Approaches to Other Religions: Developments and Tensions." *International Bulletin of Missionary Research* 8/2 (April 1984):50-54.

————. *No Other Name? A Critical Survey of Christian Attitudes toward the World Religions.* Maryknoll: Orbis, 1985.

Kolakowski, Leszek. *Main Currents of Marxism: Its Origins, Growth and Dissolution,* I: *The Founders.* Translated by P. S. Falla. Oxford: Oxford University Press, 1981.

————. *Religion.* New York: Oxford University Press, 1982.

Kraemer, Hendrik. *The Communication of the Christian Faith.* Philadelphia: Westminster, 1956.

La Vallee Poussin, Louis de. "Bodhisattvas." In *Encyclopedia of Religion and Ethics.*

Lai, Whalen. "The Search for the Historical Sakyamuni in Light of the Historical Jesus." *Buddhist-Christian Studies* 2 (1982): 77-91.

Lash, Nicholas. *A Matter of Hope: A Theologian's Reflections on the Thought of Karl Marx.* Notre Dame: University of Notre Dame Press, 1982 (1981).

BIBLIOGRAPHY

Legge, James, translator. *The Chinese Classics.* 5 volumes. Reprint, Hong Kong, 1960.

Li, Zehou. "Kongzi zai pingjia" (A Reassessment of Confucius). *Zhongguo shehui kexue* 2 (1980):77-96.

Liebenthal, Walter, translator. *The Book of Chao.* Peking, 1948.

Lindbeck, George A. *The Nature of Doctrine: Religion and Theology in a Postliberal Age.* Philadelphia: Westminster, 1984.

Ling, Trevor O. *Buddhism and the Mythology of Evil: A Study in Theravada Buddhism.* London: George Allen and Unwin, 1962.

Long, Charles H. *Alpha: The Myths of Creation.* New York: George Braziller, 1963.

MacDonald, Duncan B. *Development of Muslim Theology: Jurisprudence and Constitutional Theory.* New York: Scribner, 1903.

Machovec, Milan. *A Marxist Looks at Jesus.* Philadelphia: Fortress, 1976.

Macquarrie, John. *Principles of Christian Theology.* New York: Scribner, 1966.

Mahaparinibbana-suttanta. Translated by T. W. Rhys-Davids. Edited by F. Max Muller. Sacred Books of the East, volume 11. Oxford: Clarendon, 1881, p. xxxi-xlviii, 1-136.

Martinson, Paul V. "From Reciprocity to Contradiction: Aspects of the Confucian-Maoist Transformation." In *Transitions and Transformations in the History of Religions,* edited by F. E. Reynolds and T. M. Ludwig. Leiden: E. J. Brill, 1980, pp. 185-218.

————. "Issue: Other Religions in the World." In *Call to Global Mission,* edited by John M. Mangam. New York: Lutheran Church in America, Division for World Mission and Ecumenism, pp. 327-345.

————. "Evangelism and People of Other Faiths." In *The Continuing Frontier: Evangelism,* edited by Arthur O. F. Bauer. New York: Lutheran Church in America, 1984, pp. 58-72.

Marx, Karl. *Early Writings.* The Marx Library. Translated by Rodney Livingstone and Gregor Benton with introduction by Lucio Colletti. New York: Vintage Books, 1975.

Matsunaga, Alicia. *The Buddhist Philosophy of Assimilation: The Historical Development of the Honji-Suijaku Theory.* Tokyo: Charles E. Tuttle, 1969.

Matsunaga, Alicia, and Matsunaga, Daigan. "The Concept of Upaya *fang-pien* in Mahayana Buddhist Philosophy." *Japanese Journal of Religious Studies* 1/1 (1974): 51-72.

Maupin, Edward W. "Zen Buddhism: A Psychological Review." *Journal of Consulting Psychology* 26 (1962):362-378.

McGill, Arthur C. *Suffering: A Test of Theological Method.* Philadelphia: Geneva Press, 1968.

McKown, Delos B. *The Classical Marxist Critiques of Religion: Marx, Engels, Lenin, Kautsky.* The Hague: Martinus Nijhoff, 1975.

McLellan, David. *Marx before Marxism.* New York: Harper and Row, 1970.

McGovern, Arthur F. *Marxism: An American Christian Perspective.* Maryknoll: Orbis, 1981.

Metz, Johannes. *Faith in History and Society: Toward a Practical Fundamental Theology.* Translated by David Smith. New York: Seabury, 1980.

Metzger, Thomas A. *Escape from Predicament: Neo-Confucianism and China's Evolving Political Culture.* New York: Columbia University Press, 1977.

Miranda, Jose Porfirio. *Marx and the Bible: A Critique of the Philosophy of Oppression.* Translated by John Eagleson. Maryknoll: Orbis, 1974.

———. *Marx against the Marxists: The Christian Humanism of Karl Marx.* Translated by John Drury. Maryknoll: Orbis, 1980.

Mojzes, Paul, editor. *Varieties of Christian-Marxist Dialogue.* Philadelphia: Ecumenical Press, 1978.

———. *Christian-Marxist Dialogue in Eastern Europe.* Minneapolis: Augsburg, 1981.

Moltmann, Jürgen. *The Crucified God.* New York: Harper and Row, 1974.

———. *Experiences of God.* Translated by Margaret Kohl. Philadelphia: Fortress, 1980.

———. *The Trinity and the Kingdom: The Doctrine of God.* San Francisco: Harper and Row, 1981.

Mou, Tsung-san. *Chung-kuo che-hsüeh-ti t'e-chih* (The Uniqueness of Chinese Philosophy). Taipei: Taiwan hsüeh-sheng shu-chü, 1963.

———. *Hsin-t'i yü hsing-t'i* (The Moral Consciousness and Moral Nature of Man). Volume 1. Taipei: Cheng-chung shu-chü, 1968.

Munro, Donald J. *The Concept of Man in Early China.* Stanford: Stanford University Press, 1969.

———. *The Concept of Man in Contemporary China.* Ann Arbor: University of Michigan Press, 1977.

Murti, T. R. V. *The Central Philosophy of Buddhism: A Study of the Madhyamika System.* London: George Allen and Unwin, 1960 (1955).

Nakamura, Hajime. *Ways of Thinking of Eastern Peoples: India, China, Tibet, Japan.* Honolulu: East-West Center Press, 1964.

Needham, Joseph. *Science and Civilization in China.* Volume 2. Cambridge: Cambridge University Press, 1962.

Neville, Robert C. *The Tao and the Daimon: Segments of a Religious Inquiry.* Albany: State University of New York Press, 1982.

Nishitani, Keiji. *Religion and Nothingness.* Translated by Jan Van Bragt. Berkeley: University of California Press, 1982.

———. "Science and Zen." Translated by Richard de Martino. *Eastern Buddhist* 1/1 (1965): 79-108. See also Franck, 1982: 111-137.

———. "The Awakening of Self in Buddhism." Translated by Bando Shojun. *Eastern Buddhist* 1/2 (1966): 1-11. See also Franck 1982: 22-30.

———. "The I-thou Relation in Zen Buddhism." Translated by N. A. Waddell. *Eastern Buddhist* 2/2 (1969): 71-87. Also see Franck 1982: 45-60.

Padover, Saul K. *The Letters of Karl Marx.* Englewood Cliffs, N. J.: Prentice-Hall, 1979.

Pang, Pu. " 'Zhong-yong' ping-yi." *Zhongguo shehui kexue* 1 (1980): 94-97.

Pannenberg, Wolfhart. *Jesus—God and Man.* Translated by Lewis L. Wilkins and Duane A. Priebe. Revised edition. Philadelphia: Westminster, 1977.

———. *Basic Questions in Theology.* 2 vols. Translated by George H. Kehm. Philadelphia: Fortress, 1970 (vol. I), 1971 (vol. II).

———. *Theology and the Philosophy of Science.* Translated by Francis McDonagh. Philadelphia: Westminster, 1976.

Pannikkar, Raimundo. *"Sunyata and Pleroma:* The Buddhist and Christian Response to the Human Predicament." In *Religion and the Humanizing of Man,* edited by James M. Robinson. Council of the Study of Religion, 1972, pp. 67-86.

Perez-Remon, Joaquin. *Self and Non-Self in Early Buddhism.* Religion and Reason 22. The Hague: Mouton, 1980.

Pickthall, M. M. *The Meaning of the Glorious Koran.* New York: New American Library, n.d.

Popper, Karl R., editor. *The Open Society and Its Enemies.* 2 volumes. 5th edition. Princeton: Princeton University Press, 1966.

Prebish, Charles S., editor. *Buddhism: A Modern Perspective.* University Park: Pennsylvania State University Press, 1975.

Pye, Michael. *Skilful Means: A Concept in Mahayana Buddhism.* London: Gerald Duckworth, 1978.

Race, Alan. *Christians and Religious Pluralism: Patterns in the Christian Theology of Religions.* Maryknoll: Orbis, 1982.

Rad, Gerhard von. *Genesis: A Commentary.* Translated by John H. Marks. London: SCM, 1963.

Radhakrishnan, S. *Eastern Religions and Western Thought.* 2nd edition. London: Oxford University Press, 1940.

Rahner, Karl. *Hearers of the Word.* Translated by Michael Richards. New York: Herder and Herder, 1969.

Raphael, Israeli. *Chinese versus Muslims: A Study of Cultural Confrontation.* Ann Arbor: University Microfilms International, 1974.

Reischauer, Edwin O., and Fairbank, John K. *East Asia: The Great Tradition.* Boston: Houghton Mifflin, 1958 and 1960.

Reynolds, Frank E., and Ludwig, Theodore M., editors. *Transitions and Transformations in the History of Religions: Essays in Honor of Joseph M. Kitagawa.* Leiden: E. J. Brill, 1980.

Rhys, Davids, and William, Thomas, translators. *Buddhist Birth Stories or Jataka Tales.* New York: Arno, 1977 (reprint of 1880 edition).

Ricoeur, Paul. *Fallible Man: A Philosophy of the Will.* Translated by Charles Kelbley. Chicago: Henry Regnery, 1965.

————. *The Symbolism of Evil.* Boston: Beacon, 1969 (1967).

Robinson, Richard. *The Buddhist Religion: A Historical Introduction.* Belmont, Calif.: Dickenson, 1970.

Roest Crollius, Ary A. *The Word in the Experience of Revelation in Quran and Hindu Scriptures.* Rome: Universita Gregoriana, 1974.

Rupp, Gordon. *Christologies and Cultures: Toward a Typology of Religious World-views.* Religion and Reason 10. The Hague: Mouton, 1974.

Saddhatissa, H. *Buddhist Ethics.* New York: George Braziller, 1970.

Sarathchandra, E. R. *Buddhist Psychology of Perception.* Colombo: Ceylon University Press, 1958.

Scheler, Max. *Selected Philosophical Essays.* Translated by David R. Lachterman. Evanston: Northwestern University Press, 1973.

————. *The Nature of Sympathy.* Translated by Peter Heath. Hamden: Shoe String Press, 1973 (1954).

Schillebeeckx, Edward. *Interim Report on the Books Jesus and Christ.* Translated by John Bowden. New York: Crossroad, 1982.

Schlink, Edmund. *Theology of the Lutheran Confessions.* Translated by Paul F. Koehneke and Herbert J. A. Bouman. Philadelphia: Muhlenberg, 1961.

Schuon, Fritjhof. *The Transcendent Unity of Religions.* Translated by Peter Townsend. Revised edition. New York: Harper, 1975.

Schweizer, Eduard. *"Pneuma." Theological Dictionary of the New Testament,* volume 6. Grand Rapids: Eerdmans, 1968, pp. 389-455.

Shyrock, J. K. *The Origin and Development of the State Cult of Confucianism.* New York: Century, 1932 (reprinted 1966).

Silva, Lynn de. *The Problem of the Self in Buddhism and Christianity.* New York: Harper and Row.

Smart, Ninian. *The Philosophy of Religion.* New York: Oxford University Press, 1979 (1970).

Smith, D. Howard. *Confucius.* New York: Scribner, 1973.

Smith, Huston. "Introduction to the Revised Edition." In Fritjhof Schuon, *The Transcendent Unity of Religions.* Revised edition. New York: Harper, 1975, pp. ix-xxvi.

Smith, Wilfred Cantwell. *Religious Diversity.* Edited by Willard G. Oxtoby. New York: Crossroad, 1982.

Soothill, William Edward, and Hodous, Lewis. *A Dictionary of Chinese Buddhist Terms.* London, 1937 (reprinted Taipei, 1962).

Spiro, Melford E. *Buddhism and Society: A Great Tradition and Its Burmese Vicissitudes.* New York: Harper, 1970.

Sponheim, Paul R. *Faith and Process.* Minneapolis: Augsburg, 1979.

————. "Sin and Evil." In *Christian Dogmatics,* edited by Carl E. Braaten and Robert W. Jenson. Philadelphia: Fortress, 1984, pp. 359-464.

Stcherbatsky, Th. *The Central Conception of Buddhism and the Meaning of the Word "Dharma."* Calcutta: Susil Gupta (India), 1961 (1923).

Streng, Frederick J. *Emptiness: A Study in Religious Meaning.* Nashville: Abingdon, 1967.

Suchting, W. A. *Marx: An Introduction.* New York: New York University Press, 1983.

Suzuki, Daisetz Teitaro. *Outlines of Mahayana Buddhism.* New York: Schocken, 1963 (1907).

————. *The Training of the Zen Buddhist-Monk.* New York: University Books, 1965.

————. *Essays in Zen Buddhism.* First series. London: Rider, 1958 (1949).

Tachibana, S. *The Ethics of Buddhism.* London: Curzon, 1975 (reprint of 1926 edition).

Takeda, Ryusei, and Cobb, John B. *"Mosa-dharma* and Prehensions: A Comparison of Nagarjuna and Whitehead." *In Philosophy of Religions and Theology, 1973 Proceedings,* edited by David Griffin. Tallahassee: AAR/Florida State University, 1973, pp. 179-192.

T'ang, Chun-yi. *Chung-kuo wen-hua chih ching-shen chia-chih.* Taipei: Cheng-chung shu-chu, 1979, rev. ed.

————. *Chung-kuo che-hsueh yuan-lun.* Yuan-tao 2. Taipei: Hsin-ya yan-chiu suo, 1976.

————. *Sheng-ming ts'un-tsai yü hsin-ling ching-chieh.* 2 volumes. Taipei: Hsueh-shen shu-chü, 1978 (1977).

Thompson, Laurence G., compiler. *Studies of Chinese Religion: A Comprehensive and Classified Bibliography of Publications in English, French, and German through 1970.* Encino, Calif.: Dickenson, 1976.

BIBLIOGRAPHY

Thüsing, Wilhelm, and Rahner, Karl. *A New Christology.* New York: Seabury, 1980.

Tillich, Paul. *Theology of Culture.* New York: Oxford University Press, 1964.

————. *Systematic Theology.* Volume 1. Chicago: University of Chicago Press, 1951.

————. *Systematic Theology.* Volume 3. Digswell Place: James Nisbet, 1964.

Troeltsch, Ernst. *The Absoluteness of Christianity and the History of Religions.* Translated by David Reid. Richmond: John Knox, 1971.

Tu, Wei-ming. *Neo-Confucian Thought in Action: Wang Yang-ming's Youth (1472–1509).* Berkeley: University of California Press, 1976.

Tucker, Robert C. *Philosophy and Myth in Karl Marx.* Cambridge: Cambridge University Press, 1961.

————. *The Marxian Revolutionary Idea.* New York: W. W. Norton, 1970 (1969).

————, editor. *The Marx-Engels Reader.* 2nd edition. New York: W. W. Norton, 1978 (1972).

Waldenfels, Hans. *Absolute Nothingness: Foundations for a Buddhist-Christian Dialogue.* Translated by J. W. Heisig. New York: Paulist, 1980.

Waley, Arthur, translator. *The Analects of Confucius.* London: George Allen and Unwin, 1956 (1938).

Wang, Yang-ming. *Wang Wen-ch'eng kung ch'uan-shu* (Complete Works of Wang Yang-ming). Compiled by Hsieh T'ing-chieh. *Ssu-pu ts'ung-k'an.* Shanghai: Shangwu-yin-shu-kuan, 1922–1929, double leaves, photoreproduction.

Wansbrough, John. *Quranic Studies: Sources and Methods of Scriptural Interpretation.* Oxford: Oxford University Press, 1977.

Warren, Henry Clarke. *Buddhism: In Translations.* New York: Atheneum, 1963.

Watson, Burton, translator. *The Complete Works of Chuang-tzu.* New York: Columbia University Press, 1968.

————, translator. *Hsün-tzu: Basic Writings.* New York: Columbia University Press, 1963.

Watt, W. Montgomery. *Muhammad: Prophet and Statesman.* London: Oxford University Press, 1961.

————. *Bell's Introduction to the Kuran.* Edinburgh: Edinburgh University Press, 1970.

Watts, Alan Wilson. *The Way of Zen.* New York: Vintage Books, 1957.

Welbon, Guy Richard. *The Buddhist Nirvana and Its Western Interpreters.* Chicago: University of Chicago Press, 1968.

Welch, Holmes, and Seidel, Anna. *Facets of Taoism.* New Haven: Yale University Press, 1979.

Westermann, Claus. *Genesis 1–11.* Translated by John J. Scullion, s.j. Minneapolis: Augsburg, 1984.

Wingren, Gustaf. *Creation and Law.* Edinburgh: Oliver and Boyd, 1961.

Wolterstorff, Nicholas. *Until Justice and Peace Embrace.* Grand Rapids: Eerdmans, 1983.

Wright, Arthur F. "A Historian's Reflections on the Taoist Tradition." *History of Religions* 9 (1969–1970): 248–255.

Yu, Chai-Shin. *Early Buddhism and Christianity: A Comparative Study of the Founders' Authority, the Community, and the Discipline.* Delhi: Motilal Banarsidass, 1981.

Yang, C. K. *Religion in Chinese Society.* Berkeley: University of California Press, 1967.

Zurcher, E. *The Buddhist Conquest of China.* 2 volumes. Leiden: E. J. Brill, 1959.

Index of Names, Terms, and Concepts